Football Legends of Pennsylvania is Evan Burian's fourth volume on sports history in our great state. Pennsylvania has always been noted nationally for the production of coal, steel and tough football players, and Burian's encyclopedic presentation brings to life the Keystone State's most famous players, legendary coaches, and championship teams that were all stamped, "Made in Pennsylvania."

The author's research covers over 1,000 of the game's greatest names such as Herb Adderley of Philadelphia, Chuck Bednarik of Bethlehem, Fred Biletnikoff of Erie, Mike Ditka of Aliquippa, Jack Ham of Johnstown, Joe Montana of Monongahela, Lenny Moore of Reading, Mike Munchak of Scranton, Joe Namath of Beaver Falls, Mike Reid of Altoona and Johnny Unitas of Pittsburgh. Also featured are the top coaches such as Duffy Daugherty of Barnsboro, Frank Kush of Windber and George Welsh of Coaldale as well as all the championship teams from the University of Pennsylvania, Carlisle Institute, Lafayette, Lehigh, Penn State University and the University of Pittsburgh on the collegiate level, to the professional world of the Pottsville Maroons and Frankford Yellow Jackets of the 1920's, to the Philadelphia Eagles and Pittsburgh Steelers of today.

Football Legends of Pennsylvania is a magnificent history and a treat to read for all pigskin fans. So, relax and enjoy the journey through timeless autumns.

Allentown, Pennsylvania
Past Chairman
Pennsylvania Historical and Museum Commission

D1604556

FOOTBALL LEGENDS OF PENNSYLVANIA

was researched, written, and published
by Evan Burian in July, 2001

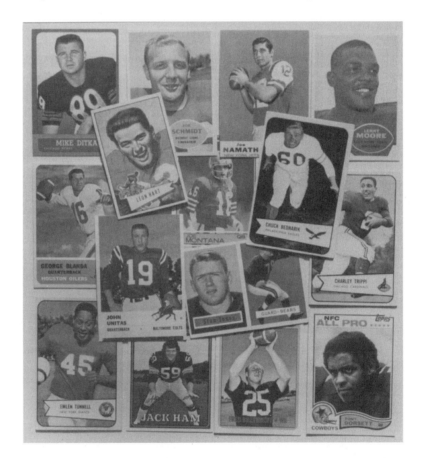

Send comments, corrections or additional information to:
Evan Burian
234 Seem Street
Emmaus, Pennsylvania 18049

ISBN 0-9713425-0-4

Printed in Canada

ACKNOWLEDGEMENT

Football Legends of Pennsylvania is an expanded state-wide extension covering the sport of football that originated in my previous book, ***Sports Legends of the Lehigh Valley***, which was published in 1998. Both of these "Legends" books were made possible because of a lot of very nice people who I contacted since February of 1998. I want to thank the hundreds of great football people - players, coaches, writers and fans from Pennsylvania who provided me with nuggets of information that adds up to a lot of knowledge.

A number of Pennsylvania sports writers and editors went out of their way to provide me with names and information. A big thank you goes to Jim Buss, Keith Groller, John Kunda, Terry Larimer, Ted Meixell, Mike Miorelli, Rich Petro, Paul Reinhard, Jeff Schuler and Mark Wogenrich of Allentown's *Morning Call*, Ed Rose of Beaver *County Times*, Ed Kracz and Brad Wilson of Doylestown's *The Intelligencer-Record*, Corky Blake and Ed Laubach of Easton's *Express-Times*, Jim Camp of Erie's *Times-News*, Ron Christ and Rod Frisco of Harrisburg's *Patriot News*, Ray Saul of Hazleton's *Standard-Speaker*, Mike Mastovich of Johnstown's *Tribune-Democrat*, Bob Parfitt and Bob Urban of Lehighton's *Times-News*, Norm Vargo of McKeesport's *The Daily News*, Todd H. Jones of Nazareth, Dennis Way of Norristown's *Times-Herald*, Ted Silary of Philadalphia's *Daily News*, Terry Shields of Pittsburgh's *Post Gazette*, Bob Vosburg of New Castle's *The News*; Mike Drago of Reading's *Eagle-Times*; Guy Valvano of Scranton's *Tribune-Scrantonian*, Tom DeSchriver and Kevin Grey of Stroudsburg's *Pocono Record*, George Guido of Tarentum's *Valley News Dispatch*, and Todd Trent of Uniontown's *Herald-Standard*.

Always at the ready were media and public relations directors of the professional football teams including Ron Howard, Derek Boyko and Jim Gallagher of the Philadelphia Eagles, David Lockett of the Pittsburgh Steelers plus the sports information directors from colleges and universities around the nation and throughout Pennsylvania including Keystone Staters Will Adair, John Alosi, E. J. Borghetti, Matt Daskivich, Tom DiCamillo, Mike Falk, Mike Ferlazzo, Mark Fleming, Susan Fumagalli, Marty Galosi, Jessica Hajek, Ed Hass, Mike Hoffman, Barry Jones, Dean Kenefick, Brian Kirschner, Joe Klimchak, Kevin Lorincz, Mark Lukens, George Matalas, Shaun May, Steve McCloskey, Tom McGuire, Jeff Michaels, Scott Morse, Jeff Nelson, Pete Nevins, Todd Newcomb, Joe Onderko, Bub Parker, Dave Saba, Matt Santos, Jeff Schaefer, John Seitzinger, Rich Schepis, Bill Stiles, Frank Thompson, Jay C. Whipple, Greg Wright and Mickey Minnich of the Big 33.

Also helping out with information were Barry Baumgardner of Steelton, A. J. Firestone of Mercersburg, Dick Flannery of Reading, Phil Gergen of Mt. Carmel, Robert Grube of Easton, David "Duke" Helm of Northampton, Chuck Hixson of Emmaus and Jay Langhammer of Ft. Worth , Texas.

And, a huge thank you goes to Steve Zarnas and the staff at G.C. Zarnas and Co., in Bethlehem for their assistance while I tracked down Pennsylvania football people around the state and throughout the country.

Photo credits start with all those people who shared their personal photographs. Images also came from the Allentown *Morning Call*, Boston College, University of California, Columbia University, Duke University, Florida State University, Fordham University, University of Georgia, University of Kentucky, Lafayette College, Lehigh University, University of Maryland, University of Notre Dame, Penn State University, University of Pennsylvania, University of Pittsburgh, Rutgers University, University of Southern California, Syracuse University, Temple University, University of Tennessee, U.S.Military Academy, U.S.Naval Academy, Widener University, Yale University, Buffalo Bills, Chicago Bears, Cleveland Browns, Dallas Cowboys, Denver Broncos, Detroit Lions, Green Bay Packers, Jacksonville Jaguars, Miami Dolphins, Minnesota Vikings, New York Jets, Oakland Raiders, Philadelphia Eagles, San Diego Chargers, San Francisco 49ers, Tennessee Titans, Washington Redskins and from the private collection of Corkey Blake, Frank Thierer, Henry Barr Collection / DIAMOND IMAGES.

The cover photo was taken of trading cards from the collection of Joe Piccerillo of Allentown with permission from The Topps Company, Inc. Back cover photo: Unknown Allentown Team.

Reference sources used for statistics include: Newspaper articles; Big 33 souvenir football game programs; college, high school and pro football team press guides; CFL Record Book, A Canadian Football League Book by Elan Press, 2000; Gridfax, by Clarence W. Funk and Associates 1967; NCAA Football Record Book, by the National Collegiate Athletic Association, 1993; NFL Football Encyclopedia, by Total Sports and NFL Properties, Inc., 1997; Philadelphia's The Daily News' Tribute to Philadelphia Scholastic Football, by Ted Silary, 2000.

Dedicated to all Pennsylvania football fans.

Photo by Frank Marsteller, Allentown Morning Call

Muhlenberg College under coach Ben Schwartzwalder hosts Lafayette College on a Saturday night in 1948 in the new Allentown High School Stadium which became the largest high school owned stadium in Pennsylvania with a seating capacity of 23,500. AHS Stadium was renamed, J. Birney Crum Stadium, in 1982 in honor of the legendary Allentown High School coach.

INTRODUCTION

The word that comes to mind when you think about Pennsylvania sports is "steel." I say that objectively and not just because I live in the steel town (well, the one-time steel town) of Bethlehem. The word speaks to the core toughness of the athletes themselves, men of strength and raw power, men whose football careers were forged on rock-hard turf and fields built near the mills. Bednarik (a Bethlehemite). Ditka. Hart. Modzelewski. Schmidt.

Even the quarterbacks are tough, steel-type guys: Blanda. Kelly. Marino. Montana. Unitas. And, there's Namath, you think he wasn't tough? To stand back there in the pocket with those bad knees and throw those kind of frozen ropes? Heck, even the names sound like steel: Andrulewicz. Babartsky. Conjar. Drazenovich. Eshmont. Jarmoluk. Katcavage. Maczuzak. Rechichar. Skrepenak. Yakavonis. That ain't no law firm, bubba. Pack a couple of bologna sandwiches - better yet make it a couple of Jack Ham sandwiches; he's a Pennsylvanian - and send those guys off to work.

Evan Burian has collected page after page of these tough guys - and much more - in his *Football Legends of Pennsylvania*, a must-have for any sports fan in the Keystone State. As usual, the research by author-historian Burian is exhaustive. Besides individual listings, Burian has a section on great Pennsylvania teams, which allows him to mention fascinating non-natives such as the Philadelphia Eagles' Tommy McDonald, my all-time favorite player. (To copy McDonald, I wore rolled-up sleeves during Pop Warner football practice; alas' I could not replicate Tommy Mac's abilities as a receiver.) And trivia nuts will find much stump-the-neighbor material in sections on, say, the Pottsville Maroons, the Pottstown Firebirds or the Philadelphia Stars who played in ...Well, find out for yourself.

The tough guys are waiting, so you had better quick pull out your wallet. They know where you live.

Jack McCallum

Jack McCallum
Bethlehem, Pennsylvania
Senior Writer
Sports Illustrated

NOTE TO THE READER

Football Legends of Pennsylvania salutes the great players, coaches and teams that have come from Pennsylvania since the birth of American football in 1869 when Princeton and Rutgers met in the first intercollegiate game in New Brunswick, New Jersey. From the beginning of this uniquely American sport, there have been thousands of outstanding Pennsylvania football players and hundreds of legendary coaches who have contributed to the state's historic reputation of gridiron greatness in the national consciousness. Most of the players profiled in this book are natives of Pennsylvania, however, there are a few biographies of players who were born in other states, but they played their high school football in the Keystone State, which was the key factor to having a bio appear in this project.

Football Legends of Pennsylvania identifies Pennsylvania high school football players who went on to college football careers and achieved "national recognition" from one of the following: being named to at least one of the numerous Division I All-American teams, won the Heisman Trophy or the Maxwell Award, was inducted into the College Football Hall of Fame, served at least four years in professional football, was named All-Pro or was inducted into the Professional Football Hall of Fame. The book also covers coaches at all levels of the game, from high school head coaches with over 200 victories to successful college and professional coaches. The research also salutes all championship teams from the scholastic ranks to the collegiate national champions of the Associated Press plus the NCAA and NAIA play-off championship teams. Also included are champions of the various professional leagues and the National Football League's Super Bowl teams.

Football Legends of Pennsylvania has over 900 biographies and it is easy to miss a name in the initial publicaton of this one-of-a-kind book. Therefore, if a player, coach, or team that should be included from one of the aforementioned catagories, but was not, please know that the oversight was strictly unintentional. For those players and coaches who do not fit into one of the above lists and yet were included in this book, it was done at the discretion of the author from available information.

FOOTBALL LEGENDS OF PENNSYLVANIA
Players, Coaches, and Teams
Collegiate, Professional and Scholastic

RAY ABRUZZESE was a halfback for the Philadelphia Southern High School Rams under **Joe Pitt** and at Alabama from 1959-61. He helped lead **Paul "Bear" Bryant's** 1961 Crimson Tide to a 11-0 record and the national title. Abruzzese was a defensive back in the AFL from 1962-66 with Buffalo and NY Jets. **Lou Saban's** Bills beat San Diego for the 1964 AFL title. Abruzzese had 10 career interceptions.

ED ADAMCHICK was a lineman for Johnstown High School as **Dave Hart's** Trojans won the 1958 WPIAL championship. He played at Pitt from 1961-63 as **John Michelosen's** 1963 Panthers went 9-1 for the #3 ranking in the nation. Adamchick was a New York Giant and Pittsburgh Steeler in 1964-65.

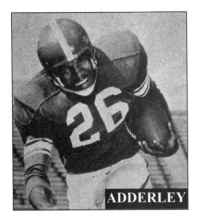

ADDERLEY

HERB ADDERLEY played for Philadelphia's Northeast High School Archives under **Charlie Martin**. He was a halfback at Michigan State from 1958-60 for **Duffy Daugherty's** Spartans. Adderley was the first round draft choice of Green Bay and spent 11 years with the Packers 1961-69 and Dallas 1970-71. As a top defensive back, Adderley helped lead **Vince Lombardi's** Packers to five NFL titles in 1961, 1962, 1965, 1966, 1967 and two Super Bowl wins over Kansas City in SB I in 1967 and Oakland in SB II in 1968. Adderley went to Dallas in 1970 and earned his third Super Bowl ring as **Tom Landry's** Cowboys defeated Miami in SB VI in 1972. The durable Adderley, who only missed three games, had 48 interceptions and scored 11 TD's. The six-time All-Pro went in the Pro Football Hall of Fame in 1980.

HERB AGOCS was an end for the Bethlehem High School Red Hurricanes under **John Butler** and at Pennsylvania for coach **George Munger** 1947-49. He was head coach at Montana State 1958-62 with a 30-13-2 record and developed three future coaching greats in **Dennis Erickson, Jim Sweeney, Joe Tiller**.

ALL THE RIGHT MOVES was name of the 1983 hit movie by 20th Century Fox about a fictional Pennsylvania steel town and the "coming of age" lives of it's high school football team, the Ampipe Bulldogs. Appearing in leading roles were screen stars **Tom Cruise** as Stef Djordjevic, **Lea Thompson** as his girlfriend Lisa, and **Craig T. Nelson** as coach Nickerson. **Michael Chapman** directed the movie, which was shot on location in Johnstown, Pennsylvania, with the screenplay by **Michael Kane**. Aliquippa High School coach, **Don Yannessa**, was the technical advisor for the movie.

ALLEGHENY COLLEGE GATORS in Meadville, Pennsylvania started football in 1893 and have appeared in seven NCAA Division III play-offs since 1987. **Peter Vaas** was the coach of Allegheny when the Gators lost to Washington & Jefferson in the first round of the 1987 playoffs. The Blue and Gold have gone to six NCAA play-offs for coach **Ken O'Keefe** and won the 1990 Division III national championship when they beat Lycoming College of Pennsylvania. The Allegheny offense was led by ends **Kurt Relser, Jim Carrol**, tackles **Craig Kuhn, T. J. McCarthy**, guards **Steve Menosky, Delmar Becker**, center **John Marzka**, quarterback **Jeff Filkovski**, and backs **Jordan Gest, Jerry O'Brien** and **Julio Lacayo**. The defensive line had **John Ploeger, John Yack, Ron Saunders, Jeff Gamble**, and **Jeff Pearson**, linebackers **Darren Hadlock** and **Wayne Mack** and defensive backs **Tony Biluco, Brian Kane, Dale Shaw** and **David LaCarte**. O'Keefe went 79-10-1 in eight years at Allegheny from 1990-97.

BARRY ALVAREZ played for the Burgettstown High School Blue Devils under **Pat McGraw**. He was a guard and linebacker at Nebraska for coach **Bob Devaney** from 1965-1967. As head coach at Wisconsin he went 60-42-4 from 1990-99. The American Football Coaches Association named Alvarez Coach of the Year in 1993 as his Badgers went 10-1-1, beat UCLA in the Rose Bowl and ranked #6 in the nation. He developed **Ron Dayne** who won the 1999 Heisman Trophy as the all-time NCAA career rusher.

CHUCK AMATO was a halfback for the Easton High School Red Rovers under **Bob Rute**. He was a three-year starting linebacker at North Carolina State 1965-67 for **Earle Edwards'** powerful Wolfpack. Amato became the head coach of North Carolina State in 2000 and has a 7-4 record.

RUDY ANABAKER played for the Donora High School Dragons under **Jimmie Rusell**. He was a guard at Pitt from 1949-51 and then spent three years with the Pittsburgh Steelers from 1952-54.

JOHN ANDERSON played for Carlisle High School and Ursinus College 1951-53. He was head coach of the Middlebury College Panthers 1969-72 and went 21-11-0. Anderson went to Brown University where he was considered the greatest coach in the Bears modern grid history with a 60-39-3 record from 1973-83 and the school's only Ivy League championship in 1976. His over-all college record was 81-50-3.

"ANTHRACITE HARD" was the term sportswriters used to describe the hard-nosed players who came out of the hard coal towns of northeastern Pennsylvania. Anthracite pros from the rough-tough days of the 1930's and 1940's include: Ashland's **Bill Kellagher**; Carbondale's **Ed Stacco**; Coaldale's **John Gildea, John Kuzman**; Dickson City's **"Big John" Koniszeweski**; Dunmore's **Patsy Martinelli, Lou Palazzi**; Duryea's **John Rogalla**; Glen Lyon's **Joe Tereshinski**; Hanover's **Andy Dudish, Ed Halicki, John Mellus**; Hazleton's **George Cherverko, Joe Dudeck, Mike Katrishen, George Kracum, John Yackanich**; Kingston's **Bill Kern, Ed Shedlosky, Len Supulski**; Kulpmont's **Bernie Barkouskie**; Lansford's **Mike Holovak, Mike Lukak, Joe Repko**; Larksville's **John "Bull" Lipski, John Siegal, Joe and Leo Skladany**; Mahanoy City's **John Durko, Tommy Myers, Joe Setcavage**; Mauch Chunk's **Fritz Ferko**; Mt. Carmel's **Ted Anrulewicz, Len Eshmont, Tony Kostos, Steve Filipowicz**; Nanticoke's **Doug Turley**; Nesquehoning's **John Kusko**; Old Forge's **Chuck Cherundolo, Lou "Babe" Tomasetti**; Pittston's **Al Kaporch, Vinnie Sites, Pete Stevens, Charlie Trippi**; Plymouth's **Vince Ragunas**; Pottsville's **Thomas "Potsy" Jones, George Somers**; Scranton's **Carl Butkus, Ed "Beef" Eiden, Edgar "Special Delivery" Jones, Hank Reese**; Shenandoah's **Al Babartsky, Al Matuza, Joe Pilconis, Larry Sartori**; Tunkhannock's **Glenn Frey**; West Hazleton's **George Platukis**; Wilkes'Barre's **Al Bednar, Chet Pudloski, Izzy Weinstock**, and **George Young**.

AL ANGELO played for Philadelphia's Frankford High School on **Worthington "Odie" Surrick's** teams that played for the 1947 and 1948 Philadelphia City League championship. He went to Mississippi State and graduated from West Chester State. Angelo coached the Frankford High School Pioneers from 1965-84, 1987 with a 184-39-5 record, the 1978 Philadelphia City championship and 10 Philadelphia Public League titles. Frankford was Philly's "Team of the Decade" for the 1970's with a 99-15-2 record. He developed pro **Blair Thomas**.

PETE ANTIMARINO played for Pitcairn High School from 1941-43 and after a service stint was a 1951 All-Skyline QB at New Mexico State. He coached Pitcairn High School from 1954-57 and then Gateway High School (a jointure of Pitcairn and Monroeville) from 1958-89 with an over-all record of 255-93-13. Antimarino's Gators won five WPIAL championships in 1969, 1972, 1974(co-champs with Upper St. Clair), 1985(co-champs with North Hills), and 1986. He developed pros **Bob Buczkowski** and **Joel Williams**.

MIKE ARCHER played for the State College High School Little Lions and was a defensive back at Miami of Florida from 1973-75 for coaches **Pete Elliott** and then **Carl Selmer**. Archer was head coach at LSU for four years from 1987-90, went 27-18-1 and to two bowl games.

MIKE ARCHIE rushed for 5,137 career yards and 75 TD's from 1989-91 for the Sharon High School Tigers under **Jim Wildman**. He played at Penn State from 1992-95 as **Joe Paterno's** 1994 Nittany Lions went 12-0 and the #2 ranking in the nation. Archie was with Tennessee 1995-99 as **Jeff Fisher's** Titans lost Super Bowl XXXIV to St. Louis in 2000.

THE ARMY-NAVY GAME started in 1890 with a Navy victory at West Point and in 1999 the two service academies met for the 100th game in their historic series. Seventy five of those contests have been played in Philadelphia as the "City of Brotherly Love" has become synonymous with college football's greatest rivalry. The first Army-Navy game in Philadelphia was played at Franklin Field on December 2, 1899 and continued off-and-on in Philly until 1936 when it found a home at Municipal Stadium with its 102,000 seating capacity. Municipal Stadium was renamed John F. Kennedy Stadium in 1964 in honor of the late President of the United States. In 1980 the Cadets and Midshipmen changed their Philadelphia venue to Veterans Stadium which opened in 1970 with a seating capacity of 65,352.

D. ARRINGTON

DICK ARRINGTON was a guard for the Erie East High School Warriors under **Duke Detzel**. He played at Notre Dame from 1963-65 and was a 1965 consensus All-American for **Ara Parseghian's** 7-2-1 Fighting Irish. Arrington, drafted by NFL Cleveland and AFL Boston, was a Patriot in 1966.

LAVAR ARRINGTON accounted for 4,357 career yards and 72 TD's from 1993-96 for Pittsburgh's North Hills High School under **Jack McCurry**. He led the Indians to the 1993 PIAA 4A state title and was Parade's 1996 Player of the Year. Arrington was a linebacker at Penn State from 1997-99 for **Joe Paterno**. He was a two-time All-American in 1998 and 1999 and won the 1999 Butkus Award as the nation's best linebacker. Arrington skipped his senior year at Penn State to play for Washington in 2000.

CARL ASCHMAN played for Charleroi High School and at Washington and Jefferson College. He coached California, Brownsville and Aliquippa High Schools from 1929-64. "King Carl" went 189-88-10 at AHS 1941-64, won three WPIAL titles 1952, 1955, 1964 and developed **Mike Ditka** and **Bob Liggett**.

ASSOCIATED PRESS HIGH SCHOOL ALL-STATE TEAM has appeared in newspapers throughout Pennsylvania every year since its inception in 1939. The first team eleven selected by the AP in 1939 were ends **George Wilkins** of Kingston and **Walter Griffith** of Pottsville; tackles **Mike Jarmoluk** of Philadelphia Frankford and **George Gagliardi** of Jeannette; guards **George Pavalko** of Blythe Township and **Larry Fellicetti** of Pittsburgh Garrick; center **Bob Orlando** of Erie St. Vincent; backs **Joe Andrejco** and **George Cheverko** of Hazleton, **Joe Pascarella** of Bradford, and **Bill Miller** of Clearfield.

AL ATKINSON played for the Monsignor Bonner High School Friars in Upper Darby, Pennsylvania under **Jack Ferrante**. At Villanova, he was a two-time All-East tackle in 1963 and 1964 for **Alex Bell's** Wildcats. Atkinson was a 10 year linebacker for the NY Jets 1965-74 and was All-AFL in 1968 as **Weeb Ewbank's** Jets won the AFL title and beat Baltimore in Super Bowl III in 1969. He had 21 interceptions.

GEORGE ATIYEH played for Allentown's Dieruff High School Huskies for **Bruce Trotter**. He was a two-time All-SEC nose guard at LSU in 1979-80. Atiyeh was with the Eagles 1981 and USFL 1983-85.

STEVE AUGUST was a tackle for the Jeanette High School Jayhawks and at Tulsa where he helped lead **F. A. Dry's** Hurricanes to three straight Missouri Valley Conference titles in 1974, 1975 and 1976. August was a 1976 All-American offensive tackle and the number one draft choice of Seattle. He spent eight years in the NFL trenches from 1977-84 with the Seahawks and Pittsburgh.

AL BABARTSKY was a tackle for the Shenandoah High School Blue Devils under **Bob Nork**. He was an All-American at Fordham where he was one of the immovable "Seven Blocks of Granite," along with **Vince Lombardi**, in 1936 and 1937 for **"Sleepy" Jim Crowley's** 15-1-2 Rams. Babartsky spent eight years with the Chicago Cards 1938-42 and Chicago Bears 1943-45. The Bears won the 1943 NFL title.

JOHN BABINECZ played for Pittsburgh Central Catholic High School and was a linebacker at Villanova from 1969-71 for **Lou Ferry**. He spent four years in the NFL with Dallas 1972-74 and Chicago 1975.

JOHN BADACZEWSKI was a guard for Windber High School Ramblers and at Case Reserve Tech in Cleveland, Ohio. "Baddie" was with Boston, Chicago Cardinals, Washington and the Bears from 1946-53.

BAGNELL

FRANCIS "REDS" BAGNELL was the ace runner for Philadelphia's West Catholic High School as he led **Bill McCoy's** Burrs to the Philadelphia City League title game in 1944 and 1945. He was at Germantown Academy 1946 and Pennsylvania 1948-50 for **George Munger's** powerful Quakers. In 1950 against Dartmouth, "Reds" set two NCAA single-game records with 490 yards of total offense and 14 straight completed passes. Bagnell, who accounted for 1,903 total yards and 16 TD's in 1950, won the Maxwell Award as the nation's most outstanding player and was third in the Heisman Trophy vote which was won by **Vic Janowicz** of Ohio State. Bagnell went into the College Football Hall of Fame in 1977.

CHRIS BAHR from Feasterville was a kicking specialist and All-American soccer player for the Neshaminy High School Redskins in Langhorne, Pennsylvania under **Jack Swartz**. He was the field goal kicker and punter at Penn State from 1973-75, was a 1975 All-American for **Joe Paterno's** 9-3 Nittany Lions and set an NCAA record by making 78.3 percent of his field goal attempts. Bahr was the second round draft choice of Cincinnati and spent 13 years in the NFL with the Bengals, Oakland/LA Raiders, and San Diego from 1976-89. He earned a Super Bowl ring as **Tom Flores'** Oakland Raiders defeated Philadelphia in Super Bowl XV in 1981. Bahr kicked 241 FG's, 490 PAT's for 1,213 points.

MATT BAHR from Feasterville was a kicking specialist and All-American soccer player in 1973 for the Neshaminy High School Redskins in Langhorne, Pennsylvania under **Jack Swartz**. He was the field goal kicker at Penn State from 1977-78 as **Joe Paterno's** Nittany Lions went 22-2. He broke his older brother's NCAA record when he made 81.5 percent of his kicks as a senior in 1978. Bahr was the sixth round draft choice of Pittsburgh and spent 17 years in the NFL from 1979-95 with the Steelers, San Francisco, Cleveland, New York Giants, Philadelphia, and New England. He earned two Super Bowl rings as **Chuck Noll's** Steelers defeated Los Angeles in SB XIV in 1980 and when **Bill Parcells'** Giants beat Buffalo in SB XXV in 1991. Bahr kicked 300 FG's, 522 PAT's for 1,422 points.

A. BAKER

ART BAKER was a fullback for the Erie Academy Lions under coaches **Jack Komora** and **Lou Tullio**. He played at Syracuse from 1958-60 and was a member of the talented 1959 backfield, with **Ernie Davis**, **Dave Sarette** and **Gerhard Schwedes**, who led **Ben Schwartzwalder's** Orangemen to the national crown. Baker, a two-time NCAA 191 pound wrestling champion, was the #1 draft choice of Philly, but was with Buffalo 1961-62 and in Canada with Hamilton 1963-65 and Calgary 1966. Hamilton appeared in three straight Grey Cups 1963-65 and **Ralph Sazio's** Tiger-Cats beat BC Lions in 1963 and Winnipeg in 1965.

RALPH BAKER played for the Lewistown High School Panthers under **Alex Ufema**. He was a linebacker at Penn State from 1961-63 for **Rip Engle** and captain of the 1963 Nittany Lions. Baker spent 11 years with the New York Jets from 1964-74. **Weeb Ewbank's** Jets won the 1968 AFL title and defeated Baltimore in Super Bowl III in 1969.

STEW BARBER played for the Bradford High School Owls and at Penn State from 1958-60 as a tackle and linebacker for **Rip Engle**. He spent nine years as an offensive tackle with Buffalo in the AFL from 1961-69. **Lou Saban's** Bills appeared in three straight AFL championship games 1964-66 and beat San Diego in 1964 and 1965. Barber was All-AFL in 1963 and 1964.

BOB BARBIERI played at Old Forge High School for **Elio Ghigiarelli** and at George Washington University. He coached Pittston High School in 1964-65 and went 11-9 and at Pittston Area High School from 1966-88 and went 146-91-5. His over-all record was 157-100-5 and developed pro **Jimmy Cefalo**.

GEORGE BARCLAY played for Har-Brack Union High School Tigers in Brackenridge, Pennsylvania under **Dick Williams**. Barclay was a guard at North Carolina 1932-34 and was a 1934 All-American for **Carl Snavely's** 7-1-1 Tar Heels. Barclay was North Carolina's coach from 1953-55 and went 11-18-1.

BERNIE BARKOUSKIE played for the Kulpmont High School Wildcats under **Mike Terry**. He was the starting left guard at Pitt all four years from 1946-49 for **Walt Milligan** and was a 1949 All-American. Barkouskie started with the Pittsburgh Steelers in 1950, but was then drafted into the military service.

MIKE BARNES played for Pittsburgh's Peabody High School Highlanders and at Miami of Florida from 1970-72 for **Fran Curci's** Hurricanes. The defensive tackle spent nine years in Baltimore from 1973-81.

BRIAN BASCHNAGEL rushed for 3,371 career yards and 36 TD's in 1970-71 for the North Allegheny High School Tigers in Wexford, Pennsylvania under **Frank Walton**. He played at Ohio State 1972-75 and was a 1975 co-captain for **Woody Hayes'** 11-1 Buckeyes ranked #4 in the nation. Baschnagel spent nine years with the Chicago Bears as a wide receiver and defensive back from 1976-84 and scored 10 TD's.

CHARLIE BATCH quarterbacked the Steel Valley High School Ironmen in Munhall, Pennsylvania under coach **Jack Giran** in 1990-91. He played for Eastern Michigan University from 1994-97 for **Rick Rasnick's** Eagles. Batch set or tied 19 EMU career offensive records including 579 completions for 7,592 yards and 53 TD's. He was the second round draft choice of Detroit and has been a Lion since 1998.

AARON BEASLEY played for the Pottstown High School Trojans under **Jim Tsakonas** and then at Valley Forge Military Academy. He was a defensive back at West Virginia from 1992-95 for **Don Nehlen** and had a career record 19 interceptions. Beasley was a co-captain and a 1995 All-American for the Mountaineers. He has been in the NFL since 1996 with the Jacksonville Jaguars.

DICK BEDESEM played for Philadelphia's North Catholic High School Falcons under **Jack Gillespie** and at Villanova from 1950-52 for **Jim Leonard** and **Art Raimo**. He was coach of Philadelphia's Bishop Egan High School 1963-70, a 46-8-2 record, four Philadelphia City League titles in 1963 (co-champs with Roxborough), 1966, 1967, 1969, and lost the 1970 title game. Bedesem coached Archbishop Wood 1971-72 and had an over-all scholastic record of 85-30-5. He coached Villanova 1975-80 and went 30-35-1.

BEDNARIK

Photo by Ed Mahan

JOE BEDENK from Williamsport was a 1923 All-American guard and captain at Penn State for **Hugo Bezdek's** 6-2-1 Nittany Lions. Bedenk was head football coach of Penn State in 1949 and went 5-4. He was also the Lion's baseball coach 1931-62 and went in the College Baseball Hall of Fame in 1966.

CHARLES "CHUCK" BEDNARIK played for the Bethlehem High School Red Hurricanes under **John Butler**. At Pennsylvania, Bednarik was a star center and linebacker from 1945-48 and a two-time All-American in 1947 and 1948 for **George Munger's** Quakers. Bednarik won the 1948 Maxwell Award as the nation's most outstanding player and placed third in the Heisman Trophy vote which was won by **Doak Walker** of SMU. He was the first draft choice of Philadelphia in 1949 and played for the Eagles for 14 years through 1962. "Concrete Charlie" earned two NFL championship rings as **Earle "Greasy" Neale's** Eagles beat Los Angeles in 1949 and in 1960, when as the last of the "Sixty Minute Men," he helped **Lawrence "Buck" Shaw's** Eagles beat Green Bay. Bednarik had 20 interceptions and was an eight-time All-Pro. He went in the Pro Football Hall of Fame in 1967 and the College Football Hall of Fame in 1970.

JIM BEIRNE caught 69 passes for 1,075 yards and 7 TD's in 1963 for the McKeesport High School Tigers under **Duke Weigle**. He was a record-setting receiver at Purdue 1965-67 for **Jack Mollenkopf** and was a 1966 All-American with 8 TD's. Beirne was a 1967 Academic All-American. He spent nine years with Houston 1968-73, 1975-76 and San Diego 1974. He caught 142 passes for 2,011 yards and 11 TD's.

BEIRNE

BERT BELL from Philadelphia was a quarterback at Pennsylvania from 1915-19. He was a sophomore on **Bob Folwell's** 1916 Quakers that went 7-3-1, but lost the 1917 Rose Bowl to Oregon. Bell, who was captain of the 1919 Quakers, was a founder and co-owner of the Philadelphia Eagles from 1933-40. He went 10-44-2 as the coach of the team from 1936-40. After selling the Eagles to **Lex Thompson**, Bell was a co-owner of **Art Rooney's** Pittsburgh Steelers from 1941-45. Bell was commissioner of the NFL from 1946-59. He died unexpectedly during his term in office in 1959 while watching an Eagles-Steelers game at Franklin Field. Bell was a charter inductee of the Pro Football Hall of Fame in 1963.

EDDIE BELL was an end for the West Philadelphia High School Speedboys under **Wesley Hackman**. He played at Pennsylvania 1950-52 for **George Munger** and was a two-time All-American in 1951 and 1952. Bell was with Philadelphia 1955-58 and was All-CFL with Hamilton in 1959 as **Jim Trimble's** Tiger-Cats lost the Grey Cup. He was with the NY Titans in 1960. Bell had 11 interceptions and one TD.

BOB BELL played for the West Philadelphia High School Speedboys under coach **Tom Jacoby** and was a defensive end at the University of Cincinnati from 1970-72. Bell, a first round draft pick, spent six years in the NFL from 1973-78 with Detroit and St. Louis. He scored one TD.

AL BEMILLER played for the Hanover High School Hawkeyes near Wilkes-Barre under **Ed Halicki**. He was a center at Syracuse 1958-60 and a member of the impenetrable "Sizable Seven" line, along with Reading's **Fred Mautino**, that helped lead **Ben Schwartzwalder's** Orangemen to a 11-0 record and the 1959 national championship. Bemiller spent nine years with Buffalo from 1961-69. **Lou Saban's** Bills appeared in three straight AFL title games 1964-1966 and beat San Diego in 1964 and 1965.

TONY BENJAMIN played for the Monessen High School Greyhounds under **Joe Gladys** and was fullback at Duke 1973-76 for **Mike McGee**. The 1976 Blue Devil co-captain gained 2,251 career yards and scored 15 TD's. The sixth round pick of Seattle spent four years with the Seahawks from 1977-80.

WOODY BENNETT was an end for York's William Penn High School Bearcats under **Don Young**. He went Arizona Western College and then Miami of Florida in 1976-77. Bennett was a ten year veteran running back with the NY Jets and Miami from 1978-87. He scored 13 TD's.

BRAD BENSON from Lakemont played for the Altoona High School Mountain Lions under **Earl Strohm**. The offensive lineman played at Penn State from 1973-76 for **Joe Paterno**. Benson was the eighth round pick of New England and spent 12 years in the NFL from 1977-87 with the Patriots and the NY Giants. Benson earned a Super Bowl ring when **Bill Parcells'** Giants beat Denver in SB XXI in 1987.

TROY BENSON played for the Altoona High School Mountain Lions under **Ron Rickens** and was a linebacker at Pitt from 1981-84. Benson, who had 351 career tackles and led the Panthers in interceptions in 1983-84, was the fifth round pick of the NY Jets and spent four years in the "Big Apple" from 1985-89.

ART BERNARDI played for Thiel College and coached the Butler High School Golden Tornadoes from 1955-85 and went 179-64-7. He developed four pros in **Bill, Rich** and **Ron Saul**, and **Terry Hanratty**.

HANK BERNAT played for Phoenixville High School and graduated from Tampa U. 1953. He coached Owen J. Roberts High School in Bucktown, Pennsylvania from 1960-90, went 195-133-17 and developed two pros in **Dan Strock** and **Jerry Ostroski**.

ANDY BERSHAK was a two-way end for Clairton High School and at North Carolina from 1935-37 for **Carl Snavely** and **Ray Wolf**. He was an honor student and a two-time All-American in 1936 and 1937.

ED BERRANG was an end for Blythe Township High School and at Villanova from 1942, 1946-48 under **Jordan Oliver**. He was a four-year NFL veteran with Washington 1949-51 and Green Bay 1952.

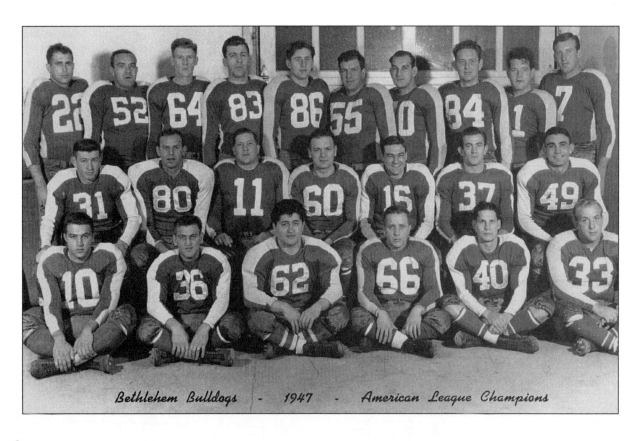

Bethlehem Bulldogs - 1947 - American League Champions

BETHLEHEM BULLDOGS were champions of the American Football League in 1947. The Bulldogs were owned by **Bob Sell**, a construction magnet, and were members of the AFL from when the league formed in 1946 until the loop disbanded in 1950. **J. Birney Crum**, Allentown High School grid mentor, was head coach and was assisted by **Leo Prendergast**, former Easton and Lafayette star and ex-coach of Bethlehem High School and Lehigh. Other noted AFL franchises were the Newark Bears, Norfolk Neptunes, Patterson Giants, Richmond Rebels, Scranton Miners, and Wilmington Blue Bombers. The Bulldogs, who played pre-season games against the Chicago Bears, NY Giants, and Philadelphia Eagles, beat Patterson 23-7 for the 1947 AFL title. The Bulldogs were led by ends **Perry Scott**, Muhlenberg, Lions, **Pete Schneider** from Northampton, Muhlenberg, **Bert Kuczynski** from Philadelphia, Penn, Eagles, tackles **Pete Sukeena** from Allentown, **Joe Wardenski** from Bethlehem, guards **Ray Stengel** from Catasauqua, Penn, **John Durko** from Mahanoy City, Albright, Eagles, center **John Sweatlock** from Mt. Union, Muhlenberg, quarterbacks **Ray Dini** from Allentown, **Warren Harris** future Bethlehem High School coach, backs **John Baranchok** from Allentown, **Billy Kline** from Allentown, **Bobby Kurtz** from Allentown, **Hal Nerino** from Bangor, **Walt Zirinsky** from Northampton, Lafayette, Cleveland Rams, **Pete Gorgone** from Windber, Muhlenberg, NY Giants. The Bulldogs had ties with the Philadelphia Eagles.

BIG 15 FOOTBALL CONFERENCE was considered the premier schoolboy football league in the history of the state when 15 of the largest eastern Pennsylvania high schools battled on the gridiron from 1938-45. The Big 15, which was officially called the East Central Pennsylvania Football Conference, started in 1935 with 12 schools, which were referred to as the, "Dirty Dozen," before it expanded into the 15 team league in 1938. The Big 15 scholastic powerhouses were: Allentown, Bethlehem, Easton, Harrisburg John Harris, Harrisburg William Penn, Hazleton, Lancaster, Lebanon, Pottsville, Reading, Shamokin, Steelton, Sunbury, Williamsport and York. The Big 15 champions were: 1938-Pottsville; 1939-Hazleton; 1940-Bethlehem; 1941-Allentown; 1942-Bethlehem; 1943-Allentown; 1944-Harrisburg John Harris; 1945-Allentown. The end of these hard fought and sometimes bitter scholastic grid wars came in 1946 when league members split into two groups - the Central Penn League and the Eastern League.

BIG 33 FOOTBALL CLASSIC is the "Super Bowl of Prep Football" as the country's foremost high school all-star contest. **Al Clark**, the executive sports editor of the Harrisburg Patriot-News, and his assistants, **John Travers** and **Ron Christ**, named the first Pennsylvania Big 33 team in 1957 as they compiled the first star-studded list with a panel of sportswriters and coaches from around the state. The first Big 33 summer-time grid classic was played the following year in 1958 when the Pennsylvania Big 33 team defeated a national high school All-American team 6-0 before 20,000 fans in Hershey Park Stadium. Since that time, the Big 33 teams have played all-star squads from Maryland and Ohio as well as intra-state East-West games. However, the most "famous" games in the Big 33 series were the Pennsylvania vs. Texas battles from 1964-67. Legendary Football Hall of Famers, **Bobby Layne** and **Doak Walker** coached the Texas All-Star team. Sports Illustrated covered those shootouts as the Coal Carckers won the first game over the Cowpokes in 1964, but dropped the next three tilts to the Lone Star state in 1965, 1966, and 1967. Today, under the leadership of Executive Director, **Mickey Minnich**, former head coach of Harrisburg John Harris and Steelton, the Big 33 game against Ohio is a quality-of-life event for all players, band members, cheerleaders, parents and fans alike from both states. At least one Big 33 game alumnus has participated in every one of the NFL's Super Bowls since Super Bowl I in 1967.

FRED BILETNIKOFF scored 115 points in 1960 for the Erie Tech Memorial Centaurs under coach **Walt Strosser**. He was an end at Florida State 1962-64 and was a 1964 consensus All-American for **Bill Peterson's** 9-1-1 Seminoles. The glue-fingered Biletnikoff spent 15 years with Oakland 1965-79. **John Rauch's** Raiders won the 1967 AFL title, but lost Super Bowl II to Green Bay in 1968. Biletnikoff earned a Super Bowl ring when **John Madden's** Raiders beat Minnesota in SB XI in 1977 as he was the MVP. Biletnikoff, a four-time All-Pro, had 589 receptions for 8,974 yards and 76 TD's. He finished his career in Canada with Montreal in 1980. Biletnikoff went in the Pro Football Hall of Fame in 1988 and the College Football Hall of Fame in 1991.

BILETNIKOFF

GEORGE BLANDA played for the Youngwood High School Railroaders. He was at Kentucky from 1945-48 for **Paul "Bear" Bryant** and threw for over 1,400 yards and 12 TD's in 1947-48. Blanda spent 26 years in pro football. He was with Chicago from 1949-58 as **George Halas'** Bears lost the 1956 NFL championship to New York. Blanda then played for Houston in the new American Football League from 1960-66. The veteran QB led the Oilers to two straight AFL titles in 1960 for **Lou Rymkus** and again in 1961 for **Wally Lemm**. Blanda finished his career with Oakland from 1967-75. **John Rauch's** Raiders lost Super Bowl II in 1968 to Green Bay. In a NFL record of 340 games over 26 years, Blanda completed 1,911 of 4,007 passes for 26,920 yards and 236 TD's. He kicked 335 FG's and 943 PAT's for a NFL record of 2,002 points. Blanda, a six-time All-Pro, went in the Pro Football Hall of Fame in 1981.

BLANDA

PHIL BLAZER from Whitaker was a tackle/kicker for Munhall High School under **Nick Kliskey** and at North Carolina from 1956-58 for **Jim Tatum**. The 1958 All-American was a Buffalo Bill in 1960.

JEFF BLEAMER was a tackle for Allentown's Dieruff High School Huskies for **John "Jeep" Bednarik** and at Penn State 1971-74 for **Joe Paterno**. He was with Philadelphia and NY Jets 1975-77.

BLOOMSBURG UNIVERSITY HUSKIES in Bloomsburg, Pennsylvania started football in 1892 and had unbeaten seasons in 1948 at 9-0 and in 1951 at 8-0 under **Robert Redman**. The Maroon and Gold have been a power since 1993 when **Danny Hale** arrived from West Chester University where he played and also was head coach. Hale went 40-13 in five years as coach of the Golden Rams. Bloomsburg's greatest year was in 2000 as Hale's Huskies went 12-3, but lost the NCAA Division II national championship game to Delta State of Mississippi. Heroic Huskies on offense were ends **Brian Sullivan, Tierell Johnson** and **Mike Lelko**, tackles **Sean Fluseo, Jeff Smith**, guards **Chris Mullin, Manny Henrie**, center **Matt Russel**, quarterback **Eric Miller** and backs **Marques Glaze** and **Doug Werner**. On defense were linemen **Jim Lannigan, Dwayne Davis, Brian Sims, Aaron Bordas**, linebackers **Greg Roskas, Jeremiah Dyer, Matt Keys,** and d-backs **Trent Flick, Toyae Berry, Rudy Garcia** and **Luke Murray**.

MATT BLUNDIN quarterbacked the Ridley Township High School Green Raiders in Folsom, Pennsylvania under **Joe McNicholas**. He played at Virginia from 1988-91 and threw for 2,554 career yards and 23 TD's. Blundin was the 1991 captain, All-ACC, Academic All-ACC and the ACC's Player-of-the-Year for **George Welsh's** 8-3-1 Cavaliers. He was drafted in the second round by Kansas City and spent three years with the Chiefs from 1992-94 behind **Joe Montana**.

STEVE BONO quarterbacked the Norristown High School Eagles under **Roger Grove**. He played for UCLA from 1980-84 for **Terry Donahue**. As a senior in 1984, Bono threw for 1,576 yards and 9 TD's as he led the Bruins to a 9-3 record and the #9 ranking in the nation. He was a 15 year veteran with Minnesota 1985-86, Pittsburgh 1987-88, San Francisco 1989-93, Kansas City 1994-96, Green Bay 1997, St. Louis Rams 1998 and Carolina 1999. Bono has thrown for over 3,788 yards and 57 TD's. As a back-up to **Joe Montana** at San Francisco from 1989-93, Bono earned a Super Bowl ring as **George Seifert's** 49ers beat Denver in SB XXIV in 1990.

DENNIS BOOKER scored 25 TD's and had 1,331 yards of total offense for the Kiski Area High School Cavaliers in 1968 under **Dick Dilts**. He played at Millersville State for **Gene Carpenter** and rushed for 900 yards and scored 14 TD's in 1974. Booker was the #10 draft pick of Dallas and was a 1975 Cowboy.

R. J. BOWERS played at West Middlesex High School under **Tom Trimmer**. After a five year stint in the Houston Astros minor league baseball chain, Bowers went back to the gridiron as a fullback for the Grove City College Wolverines in Grove City, Pennsylvania for coach **Chris Smith**. In four years from 1997-2000, Bowers broke 11 Division III records and set the all-time NCAA all-division records of 7,353 career rushing yards and 562 career points. He was a two-time Divison III All-American in 1999 and 2000.

BILL BOWES from Blanchard was a quarterback for the Lock Haven High School Bobcats in 1959-60 under coach **Don Malinak**. He was an end at Penn State from 1962-64 for **Rip Engle**. Bowes was head coach at New Hampshire University from 1972-98 and posted a 175-106-5 record in 27 years. His Wildcats won four Yankee Conference titles and appeared in four NCAA post-season play-offs.

WALT BOWYER played for the Wilkinsburg High School Tigers under **Al Mauro**. He was a defensive end at Arizona State 1979-82. Bowyer spent six years in the NFL with Denver from 1983-88.

JERRY BOYARSKY played for the Lakeland High School Chiefs under coach **Jerry Wasilchak**. He was a four-year defensive tackle on **Jackie Sherrill's** powerful Pitt Panther teams that went 39-8-1 from 1977-80. Boyarsky spent seven years from 1981-87 with the Saints, Cincinnati, Buffalo, and Green Bay.

DAVE BRADLEY from Burnham caught 5 TD's and blocked 7 punts for the Chief Logan High School Mingos in 1964 under **Steve Prisuta**. He was a defensive back at Penn State from 1966-68 for **Joe Paterno**. Bradley spent four years with Green Bay 1969-71 and St. Louis 1972.

KYLE BRADY from New Cumberland caught 35 passes for 844 yards and 11 TD's in 1989 as the Gatorade's Pennsylvania Player of the Year for the Cedar Cliff High School Colts under **Bob Craig**. He was a tight end at Penn State from 1990-94 for **Joe Paterno**. Brady, who caught 76 career passes (second only to **Ted Kwalick**) was a two-time All-American in 1993 and 1994 for the 22-2 Nittany Lions. The first round draft choice of the New York Jets has been in the NFL since 1995 with NY and Jacksonville.

JIM BRAXTON had a total offense of 1,435 yards and scored 78 points in 1966 for the Connellsville High School Falcons under **Stan McLaughlin**. He played at West Virginia from 1968-70 and was a co-captain and 1970 All-American tight end for **Bobby Bowden's** 8-3 Mountaineers. Braxton spent eight years as a fullback with Buffalo 1971-78. Braxton, who was mainly a blocker for **O. J. Simpson**, rushed for 2,890 yards and 25 TD's, caught 144 passes for 1,473 yards and 6 TD's. He had a total of 31 TD's.

GENE BREEN was a lineman for the Mt. Lebanon High School Blue Devils under **Ralph Fife** and at Virginia Tech where he was 1963 All-Southern. He was with Green Bay, Pittsburgh and LA in 1964-68.

PHIL BRIDENBAUGH went to Martinsburg Central High School and Franklin and Marshall College. He coached New Castle High School for 34 years from 1922-55 with a 265-64-25 record. His Red Hurricanes won seven WPIAL titles in 1922, 1932, 1933, 1934, 1942, 1948, 1949, went undefeated nine times and won more games than any other school in the state. Only four high schools in the nation - **Paul Brown**-led Massillon, Ohio, Canton McKinley, Ohio, Louisville Male, Kentucky, Little Rock Central, Arkansas - won more games during the Bridenbaugh-led New Castle era. He developed seven pros in **Ben Ciccone, Alec Shellogg, Mike Roussos, Bill McPeak, Lindy Lauro, Paul Cuba** and **Nick DeCarbo**.

MARTY BRILL from Philadelphia was a halfback at Pennsylvania in 1927 before he transferred to Notre Dame where he helped pace **Knute Rockne's** Fighting Irish to a 19-0 record and two straight national championships in 1929 and 1930. The 1930 All-American played in the NFL with Staten Island in 1931.

BRODHEAD

BOB BRODHEAD quarterbacked the Kittaning High School Wildcats under **Jim Rearic**. He played at Duke from 1956-58 for **Bill Murray** and directed the Blue Devils to the 1958 Orange Bowl. Brodhead was drafted by Cleveland in 1959 and was with Buffalo in 1960 before he led the Philadelphia Bulldogs to the 1966 Continental Football League championship over the **Don Jonas**-led Orlando Panthers.

GEORGE BROOKE from Philadelphia was a 1895 All-American halfback at Pennsylvania. He was coach of the Quakers from 1913-15 and went 13-12-4. Brooke is in the College Football Hall of Fame.

GARY BROWN rushed for 4,135 career yards, scored 74 TD's from 1984-86 and was the AP's 1986 Player of the Year for the Williamsport High School Millionaires under **Tim Montgomery**. He played at Penn State for **Joe Paterno** from 1987-90. Brown spend nine years with Houston, San Diego, and NY Giants from 1991-99.

JAMES BROWN played for Philadelphia's Jules E. Mastbaum Vo-Tech Panthers under **John Murphy** and at Virginia State. The offensive tackle has been with Dallas 1992, NY Jets 1993-95 and Miami since 1996. **Jimmy Johnson's** Cowboys beat Buffalo in Super Bowl XXVII in 1993.

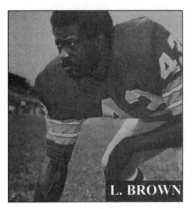
L. BROWN

LARRY BROWN played for Pittsburgh's Schenley High School Spartans, Dodge City JC in Kansas and then for Kansas State in 1967-68. He became one of the NFL's most explosive, durable and versatile running backs in eight years with Washington from 1969-76. Brown was the NFL's 1972 Player of the Year as he led **George Allen's** Redskins to Super Bowl VII in 1973 against Miami. He rushed for 5,875 yards and 35 TD's, caught 238 passes for 2,485 yards and 20 TD's. The three-time All-Pro had 55 TD's.

OMAR BROWN was a halfback for York's William Penn High School under **Jeff Julius**. He was a cornerback at North Carolina 1993-97 for **Mack Brown** and was All-ACC in 1997 for the 11-1 Tar Heels. Brown went to Atlanta in 1998, but was "inactive" as the Falcons lost Super Bowl XXXIII in 1999.

TOM BROWN was a running back for Lower Burrell High School and at Pitt from 1983-86 for **Foge Fazio** and **Mike Gottfried**. He spent three years with Miami from 1987-89.

GORDON BROWNE was a tackle for the Chambersburg High School Trojans and at Boston College from 1971-73 for **Joe Yukica**. He was with the New York Jets in 1974-75.

TOM BROZA played for the Neshannock High School Lancers near New Castle under **Bob Bleggi**. He was a four-year starting center at Pitt from 1974-77 as **Johnny Majors'** 1976 Panthers went 12-0 and won the national championship. Broza was a consensus 1977 All-American and was drafted by Pittsburgh.

CHARLIE BRUECKMAN from McKees Rocks was a center and linebacker for Sto-Rox High School and at Pitt from 1955-57 for **John Michelosen**. He was with San Francisco, Washington and LA Chargers 1958-60. **Sid Gillman's** Chargers lost the 1960 AFL title game to Houston.

SCOTT BRUNNER led the West Chester Henderson High School Warriors under coach **Mike Hancock**. At Delaware, Brunner took over at quarterback as a senior in 1979 and led **Harold "Tubby" Raymond's** Blue Hens to their second straight NCAA Division II national championship game. Delaware lost to Eastern Illinois in 1978, but beat Youngstown State behind Brunner for the 1979 national crown. Brunner, who was a 1979 All-American with 24 TD passes, spent six years in the NFL from 1980-85 with the New York Giants and St. Louis. He threw for 6,457 yards and 29 TD's.

LARRY BRUNO played for Geneva College and coached 34 years, first at Monaca High School from 1947-58 and then Beaver Falls High School from 1959-79. He had an over-all record of 197-82-18 and five undefeated teams. Beaver Falls won the 1960 WPIAL title with a 23 game win streak 1960-62. He developed four Tiger pros in **Joe Namath, Dwight Collins, Glenn Dennison** and **Steve Hathaway**.

HUBIE BRYANT was an end for Penn Hills High School Indians and at Minnesota from 1965-67 for **Murray Warmath**. He was with Pittsburgh and New England in 1970-72.

BUCKNELL UNIVERSITY in Lewistown, Pennsylvania started football in 1883 and had her first All-American in **Christy Mathewson** who was from Factoryville. "Matty," who was one of five original inductees in the Baseball Hall of Fame as a star pitcher for the New York Giants, scored 13 TD's and kicked eight field goals from 1898-1900 for the Bison and was a 1900 Walter Camp All-American. **Carl**

Snavely (Hall of Fame), who was from Nebraska and Lebanon Valley College, put Bucknell in the gridiron spotlight with a 42-16-8 record from 1927-33. **Clarke Hinkle**, his prize fullback in 1929-31, starred for the Green Bay Packers and was inducted into both the College and Pro Football Hall of Fame. In 1934 **Edward "Hooks" Mylin** (Hall of Fame), a former Franklin & Marshall quarterback, took over the Bucknell helm from the legendary Snavely and directed the Orange and Blue to a 7-2-2 record and then blanked Miami of Florida in the first-ever Orange Bowl of January 1, 1935. Bruiser Bisons were ends **John Filer, Bill Wilkinson**, tackles **George Boiston, Joe Rosati, Marty Pocius**, guards **Ralph Furiell, Ralph Green, Walt Dobie**, center **Joe Fazio**, backs **John Sitarsky**, who will be head coach of Bucknell in 1943, **Paul Miller, Ed Raymaley, Harold Whipkey** and **Joe Reznihac**. In 1950, Bucknell went 9-0 under coach Harry Lawrence and were ranked #20 in the nation by the AP for November 20. The Bison boasted such stars as Little All-Americans tackle **George Young**, a long time executive with the Colts and Giants, halfback **Bob Albert** and end **Joe Gallagher**, as well as **Ton Dean, Martin McKibbin, Brad Myers, Jim Ostendarp** and **Herb Stiefel**. Bucknell twice won the Lambert Cup under **Bob Odell**, a former Penn All-American, as both his 1960 and 1964 teams went 7-2 to win the award. The 1960 team was led by four Little All-Americans in quarterback **Paul Terhes**, tackle **Kirk Foulke**, halfback **Mickey Melberger**, end **Dick Tyrrell**, while the 1964 Bison had Little All-Americans in quarterback **Bill Lerro** and end **Tom Mitchell**. Other Bucknell All-Americans include: **Paul Maczuzak** OT 1966-67, **Sam Havrilak** QB 1968, **Randy Ruger** DB 1969, **Mitch Farbstein** FB 1971-72, **Stan Durtan** OT 1972, **Larry Schoeneberger** LB 1973-74, **Mike Axe** OT 1974, **Irv Renneisen** TE 1974, **Kerry Snow** QB 1975, **Dave Ogden** DE 1975, **Mike McDonald** OT 1980, **Ken Jenkins** HB 1980, **McKinley Norris** DB 1980, **Brad Henneman** DT 1983, **Bob Gibbon** QB 1983, **Dave Kucera** WR 1983, **Earl Beecham** HB 1985, **Mark Wisniewski** DT 1985, **Jim Given** QB 1986, **Mike Guerrini** WR 1988, **Dan Meenan** OG 1988, **Jay Butler** OT 1990, **Ed Burman** DE 1995, **Brandon Little** LB 1996, and **Willie Hall** LB 1997. In 1989, Bucknell renamed their 13,000 seat stadium Christy Mathewson-Memorial Stadium.

BOB BUCZKOWSKI played for the Gateway High School Gators under **Pete Antimarino** and was a star defensive end at Pitt from 1983-85 for **Foge Fazio**. He was the #1 draft choice of the Los Angeles Raiders and spent five years in the NFL with the Raiders, San Diego, Cleveland, and Seattle from 1986-90.

DOUG BUFFONE played for the Shannock Valley High School Spartans in Rural Valley, Pennsylvania. He was a record-setting linebacker at the University of Louisville 1963-65 for **Frank Camp**. Buffone spent 13 years in the NFL with Chicago from 1966-79 and had 24 interceptions and one fumble recovery.

MARC BULGER threw for 1,673 yards and 12 TD's in 1994 for Pittsburgh's Central Catholic High School Vikings under **John Fischetti**. A National Honor Society student, Bulger starred at West Virginia from 1996-99 for **Don Nehlen** as he set 25 Mountaineer passing and offensive records including 8,153 career passing yards and 59 TD's. Bulger was drafted by New Orleans in 2000.

BUNDRA

MIKE BUNDRA played for the Catasauqua High School Rough Riders under coach **Bert Kuczynski**. He was a star tackle at USC from 1959-61 for the "Fight On" Trojans under **Don Clark** and **John McKay**. Bundra spent four years in the NFL defensive trenches from 1962-65 with Detroit, Cleveland and the NY Giants. "Big Mike" earned a 1964 NFL title ring as **Blanton Collier's** Browns defeated Baltimore.

ED BURKE was a guard for Larksville High School and at the US Naval Academy from 1926-28 for **Bill Ingram** as the Midshipmen went 20-6-2. He was the 1928 captain and All-American for the Middies.

JOHN BUTLER played for Charleroi High School and Washington and

Jefferson College. He coached at Shamokin High School and then Bethlehem High School from 1936-51 where he was the winningest coach in Red Hurricane history at 117-36-9. At Bethlehem, he developed 23 All-Staters, four pro stars **Chuck Bednarik, John "Bull" Schweder, Steve Meilinger, Joe Wardenski** plus other greats like **Herb Agocs, Rocco Calvo, Ed Hudak, George Marinkovich** and **Art Statum**. In the 1960's, Bethlehem (now Liberty High School) coach **Bob Buffman** produced five pros in **Dan Yochum, Tom Donchez, Mike Hartenstine, Rich Garza** and **Jim Villani**.

HARRY BUTSKO was a fullback for the Pottsville High School Crimson Tide under **Bill Flynn** and at Maryland from 1960-62 for **Tom Nugent**. He was a Washington Redskin in 1963.

ROCCO CALVO played for the Bethlehem High School Red Hurricanes under **John Butler**. He was a star quarterback at Cornell 1949-51 for **George "Lefty" James'** Red Raiders. Calvo was head coach at Moravian College for 25 years in two different stints 1955-76, 1982-85 and had a 122-102-9 record.

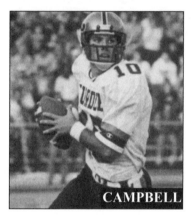

CAMPBELL

SCOTT CAMPBELL threw for over 2,000 career yards and 20 TD's from 1977-79 for Hershey High School under coach **Bob May**. He was the field general of the Purdue Boilermakers 1980-83 and threw for 7,636 career yards and 45 TD's. Campbell spent seven years in the NFL with Pittsburgh and Atlanta from 1984-90 and threw for 2,983 yards and 19 TD's. He ended his career with Ottawa in Canada.

JOHN CAPPELLETTI gained 1,336 yards in total offense in 1969 for the Monsignor Bonner High School Friars in Upper Darby, Pennsylvania under **Jack Gottshalk**. The Upper Darby "Iceman" was a durable running back at Penn State from 1971-73 for **Joe Paterno**. As a senior in 1973, Cappelletti rushed for 1,522 yards and 17 TD's (29 career TD's) as Penn State went 12-0 for the #5 ranking in the nation. He was a 1973 consensus All-American and won both the Heisman Trophy and Maxwell Award as the nation's most outstanding player. "Cappy," the #1 draft choice of Los Angeles, spent 10 years with the Rams 1974-79 and San Diego 1980-83. **Ray Malavasi's** Rams lost Super Bowl XIV to Pittsburgh in 1980. He rushed for 2,951 yards, 24 TD's, had 135 receptions for 1,233 yards, 4 TD's, for 28 total TD's.

CARLISLE INSTITUTE was a trade school for Native Americans in Carlisle, Pennsylvania and started football in 1890. **Vance McCormick**, who was from Harrisburg and a 1892 All-American quarterback at Yale, was one of the first volunteer coaches of the Carlisle Indians. In 1899, **Glenn Scobey "Pop" Warner** (Hall of Fame), a former Cornell star, was signed as the first paid coach of Carlisle at $1,200. Warner put the small central Pennsylvania school on the national football map

CAPPELLETTI

from 1899 to 1914. Although Warner's "football boys" played home games on Wednesday afternoons against small local Pennsylvania colleges such as Albright, Dickinson, and Lebanon Valley, his Red and Gold clad Indians travelled to lucrative Saturday away games against such collegiate gridiron titans as Pennsylvania, Pittsburgh, Washington and Jefferson, plus California, the University of Chicago, Harvard, Michigan, Nebraska, Ohio State and West Point. Warner's most famous Carlisle clubs were the 1911 and 1912 teams that featured All-American halfback **Jim Thorpe** from Oklahoma. The 1912 Indians went 12-1-1 and scored 504 points to 114 as Thorpe led the nation in scoring with a new college record of 198 points. Other valiant Indians during the Warner era were **Pete Calac, William "Lone Star" Dietz**, who would coach Washington State to their first-ever Rose Bowl in 1917 and later coach at Albright, **Joe Gunyon** (Pro Hall of Fame) who would also become an All-American at Ga. Tech and be called "the greatest running back in the South" by the Atlanta Constitution, **Gus Welch** (College Hall of Fame), **Joel Wheelock, Bemus Pierce, Jimmie Johnson, Pete Hauser** and **Frank Hudson**. A number of the Carlisle Indians then played pro ball for Thorpe's Canton Bulldogs. Warner, who later coached at Pitt, Stanford and Temple, had 313 career victories and went into the College Football Hall of Fame in 1951. Thorpe, who starred for the Canton Bulldogs, football Cleveland Indians, Oorang Indians, Toledo Maroons, Rock Island Independents, New York Giants and Chicago Cardinals from 1915-28, went into both the College and Pro Football Hall of Fame. He was also the first president of the National Football League in 1920.

HAROLD "DOC" CARLSON was an end for Pittsburgh's Westinghouse High School and at Pitt from 1914-17 as the Panthers went 34-1. He was the 1917 captain and All-American for **"Pop" Warner's** undefeated Panthers. Carlson was the basketball coach at Pitt for 31 years with a 369-247 record and two national championships in 1928 and 1930. He is in the Basketball Hall of Fame.

CARNEGIE TECH SKIBOS or TARTANS in Pittsburgh, Pennsylvania started football in 1906 and had an outstanding team in 1928 under coach **Wally Steffin** when the Skibos went 7-1 behind triple-threat tailback, **Howard Harpster** (Hall of Fame), and defeated the three national powerhouses on their schedule in Pitt, Notre Dame, Washington and Jefferson. In 1938, Carnegie Tech under **Bill Kern**, from Kingston and a Pitt tackle 1925-27, went 7-1 and was ranked #6 in the nation. However, Carnegie Tech lost the 1939 Sugar Bowl to #1 ranked TCU who was led by Heisman Trophy winner **Davey O'Brien**. Stellar Skibos were ends **Karl Striegel**, whose father managed the famed professional Pottsville Maroons, **Ted Fisher**; tackles **Pete Dobrus, Gumbert**; guards **Bill Reith, Musial**; center **John Schmidt**, and backs **Ray Carnelly, Merle Condit, George Muha, Paul Friedlander, Pete Moroz, Jack Lee,** and **Tony Laposki**. Today, Carnegie Tech is called Carnegie-Mellon University and plays NCAA Division III football. The Tartans were a national power again from 1976-85 under coach **Chuck Klausing** as the Cardinal, White and Gray went 77-15-2, won six league titles and made four trips to the NCAA Division III play-offs.

BILL CARPENTER was a halfback for the Springfield (DelCo) High School Cougars under coach **Evan Koons**. He was an end at

B. CARPENTER

West Point from 1957-59 for **Earl "Red" Blaik**. Army went 8-0-1 in 1958 for the #3 ranking in the nation behind three All-Americans in halfbacks **Bob Anderson, Pete Dawkins**, who also won the Heisman Trophy, and guard **Bob Novogratz**, but it was Carpenter who was college football's most unique player as Army's "Lonely End" because he stayed out to one side of the field and never joined the offensive huddle. Carpenter was a 1959 All-American. During Carpenter's military duty in Viet Nam, he received a Silver Star for his heroism in action and a Special Award from the National Football Foundation and Hall of Fame in 1966. He went in the College Football Hall of Fame in 1982 and received the "Distinguished American of the Year" Award from the Walter Camp Football Foundation in 1984.

GENE CARPENTER played for Cornwall High School and at Huron University in South Dakota. He coached at Adams State in Colorado in 1968 and the Indians won the Rocky Mountain Conference title. Dr. Carpenter has been the head coach of Millersville University since 1970 with a 220-90-6 record and his Marauders won the 1988 Lambert-Meadowlands Cup.

EDDIE CARR was a halfback for Philadelphia's Olney High School in 1943-44 under **Bert Barron**. He did not play college football, but was at San Francisco in the All-American Football Conference 1947-49. **Buck Shaw's** 49er's lost the 1949 AAFC title to Cleveland. Carr scored 9 TD's with 16 interceptions.

ELMER CARROLL played for Scottdale High School and Washington and Jefferson in 1919-20. He coached Greensburg High School in 1920, Wilkinsburg High School from 1927-34, Easton High School from 1935-46, and Abington High School from 1947-55 with an over-all scholastic record of 255-69-12.

BUD CARSON played for the Freeport High School Yellowjackets under **Henry Furrie** and at North Carolina from 1949-51 for **Carl Snavely's** Tar Heels. He was head coach at Georgia Tech from 1967-71 and went 27-27-0. As head man of the Cleveland Browns in 1989-90, Carson had a 12-14-1 record.

RUSSELL CARTER played for the Lower Merion High School Bulldogs in Ardmore, Pennsylvania under **Roger Frassnei**. He had a record of 18 interceptions as a defensive back at SMU 1980-83 for **Ron Meyer** and **Bobby Collins** as the high-powered Mustangs went 39-7-0. Carter was a 1983 All-American. He had 4 interceptions in six years in the NFL with the NY Jets 1984-87 and LA Raiders 1988-89.

CEFALO

FRANK CASE played for the Central Bucks West High School Bucks in Doylestown, Pennsylvania under **Mike Pettine**. He was a defensive end at Penn State 1978-80 and with Kansas City 1981 and the USFL.

CARMEN CAVALLI was lineman for Philadelphia's St. Thomas More High School under **Dave DiFilippo** and for the University of Richmond Spiders. He was an Oakland Raider in 1960.

JIMMY CEFALO rushed for 4,427 yards and 64 TD's plus had 5,150 all-purpose yards and 67 TD's and 386 points in his career from 1971-73 for the Pittston Area High School Patriots under **Bob Barbieri**. He was a running back and wide receiver at Penn State from 1974-77 for **Joe Paterno**. Cefalo spent seven years with Miami from 1978-84. **Don Shula's** Dolphins lost Super Bowl XVII to Washington in 1983 and Super Bowl XIX to San Francisco in 1985. Cefalo had 93 career receptions for 1,739 yards and 13 TD's.

KARL CHANDLER was a lineman for the Marple Newton High School Tigers in Newton Square, Pennsylvania and at Princeton 1971-73. He spent six years with the NY Giants and Detroit 1974-79.

GEORGE CHAUMP from West Pittston was a guard at Bloomsburg State from 1955-57. He was head coach of Harrisburg's John Harris High School from 1962-67 and went 58-4 with a 35 game win streak 1964-67 behind Pioneer stars such as **George Buchanan, Tom Buskey, Dennis Green, Jimmie Jones, Dale Palmer, Art "Death" Ray, Milan Vecanski** and **Jan White**. He was also head coach at Indiana University of Pennsylvania from 1982-85 and went 24-16-1, Marshall University from 1986-89 as his Thundering Herd lost the 1987 NCAA Division II national title to NE Louisiana, and the United States Naval Academy from 1990-94 with a 14-41-0 record. Chaump is now coaching high school ball in PA.

GEORGE CHEVERKO from Beaver Meadows, who along with **Joe Andrejco**, was one of the unstoppable "Touchdown Twins" that combined for 28 TD's for Hazleton High School in 1939 under coach **Stan Oleniczak**. He played at Fordham for **"Sleepy" Jim Crowley's** nationally ranked Rams in 1940-42. Cheverko caught 3 TD's and had 9 interceptions for the NY Giants and Washington in 1947-48.

CHUCK CHERUNDOLO was a center and linebacker for the Old Forge High School Blue Devils under coach **Danny Semenza**. He played at Penn State for **Bob Higgins** 1934-36 and was the 1936 captain and All-American honorable mention for the Nittany Lions. He spent 10 years in the NFL with Cleveland 1937, Philadelphia 1938-40, and Pittsburgh 1941-42, 1945-48. Cherundolo, a 1942 All-Pro, had five career interceptions.

NICK CHICKILLO was a lineman for West Scranton High School under **Sam Donato** and at Miami of Florida for **Andy Gustafson** 1950-52. The 1952 All-American played for the Chicago Cardinals in 1953.

LARRY CHRISTOFF played for the Northampton High School Konkrete Kids under **Al Erdosy**. At Rutgers, he was a 1972 All-American honorable mention tight end. He was a Baltimore Colt in 1973.

DICK CHRISTY rushed for 1,520 yards and 19 TD's, and also passed for 6 TD's in 1953 for Chester's St. James High School, as **Francis "Beans" Brennan's** Bulldogs were the Philadelphia City League co-champions with Northeast. He scored a school record 20 TD's at North Carolina State from 1955-57 for **Earle Edwards** and was a 1957 All-American. Christy spent five years in the pros with Pittsburgh, Boston Patriots, NY Titans from 1958-62 and scored 20 TD's.

D. CHRISTY

GREG CHRISTY played for the Freeport High School Yellowjackets for coach **Don Earley** and **Gary Kepple**. He was a tackle at Pitt from 1980-84 for coach **Foge Fazio**. Christy was a Buffalo Bill in 1985.

JEFF CHRISTY was the 1985 Pennsylvania scholastic scoring leader with 208 points as a junior fullback for the Freeport High School Yellowjackets under **Don Earley**. As a senior in 1986, Christy played for coach **Gary Kepple**. He was a center at Pitt from 1987, 1990-91. Christy, a three-time Pro Bowler, anchored NFL offensive lines with Arizona 1992, Minnesota 1993-99 and Tampa Bay 2000.

GUS CIFELLI was a tackle for Philadelphia's La Salle High School Explorers under **Jim Bodner** and the received the Purple Heart during World War II. He went to Notre Dame and was a member of **Frank**

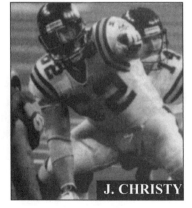

J. CHRISTY

Leahy's three national championship teams in 1946, 1947 and 1949. The Fighting Irish were #2 in 1948. Cifelli spent five years in the NFL from 1950-54 with Detroit, Green Bay, Philadelphia and Pittsburgh.

RALPH CINDRICH played for Avella High School under coach **Dick Novak**. He was a linebacker at Pitt from 1969-71 for **Carl DePasqua's** Panthers. Cindrich spent four years in the NFL with New England, Houston and Denver from 1972-75. He became one of the nation's top sports agents.

SAM CLANCY played for Pittsburgh's Bradshear High School Bulls. At Pitt, Clancy was a defensive lineman on **Jackie Sherrill's** nationally ranked Panther clubs that went 41-7 from 1978-81. He spent 12 years in the NFL trenches from 1982-93 with Seattle, Cleveland and Indianapolis and had 30 sacks.

B. CLARK

BRUCE CLARK played for New Castle High School as **Lindy Lauro's** Red Hurricanes won the 1973 and 1975 WPIAL titles. He was a defensive tackle at Penn State from 1976-79 for **Joe Paterno** and was a two-time All-American in 1978 and 1979. Clark won the 1978 Lombardi Award as a junior. He was the #1 draft choice of Green Bay, but played for Toronto in Canada 1980-82 and was All-CFL. Clark played in the NFL with New Orleans 1983-88, Kansas City 1989 before he finished in the WLAF.

JON CLARK was a tackle for Philadelphia's John Bartram High School Maroon Wave under coach **Tom Lodge**. He played at Temple from 1992-95 for **Ron Dickerson**. Clark has been with the Bears and Cardinals since 1996.

BOB CLEMENS was a halfback for the Munhall High School Indians under **Nick Kliskey**, a former Steeler. He played at Pitt from 1959-61 for **John Michelosen** and was one of the Panther's famous "C-boys" backfield along with halfback **Fred Cox** and fullback **Jim Cunningham**. He was a Baltimore Colt in 1962.

TOM CLEMENTS from McKees Rocks quarterbacked the Canevin Catholic High School Crusaders under coach **Raymond DiLallo**. He was the Notre Dame field general from 1972-74 and led **Ara Parseghian's** 1973 Fighting Irish to a 11-0 record and the national championship. The 1974 All-American spent 13 years in pro ball in Canada from 1975-87 with Ottawa, Saskatchewan, Hamilton and Winnipeg. Clements earned two Grey Cup rings with Ottawa in 1976 and Winnipeg in 1984. The two-time All-CFL QB, was the CFL's 1987 MVP. Clements, who went in the CFL Hall of Fame in 1994, had 2,807 completions in 4,657 attempts for 39,041 yards and 252 TD's. He was a Kansas City Chief in 1980.

DON CLUNE was an end for Philadelphia's Cardinal O'Hara High School Lions under **Leo Broadhurst**. He was an All-Ivy record-setting receiver at Pennsylvania from 1971-73 for **Harry Gamble** with 121 receptions for 2,419 yards and 21 TD's. Clune was with the NY Giants in 1974-75 and Seattle in 1976.

COALDALE BIG GREEN were champions of the Anthracite League in 1921, 1922, and 1923. The Big Green started organized football in 1913 and was one of the best independent teams that played in the early days of professional football. Big Green players came from the coal communities of Coaldale, Lansford, Nesquehoning, Summit Hill and Tamaqua. Other Anthracite League powers were Mahanoy City, Mt. Carmel, Pottsville Maroons (who joined the NFL from 1925-28), Shenandoah, and the Wilkes-Barre Panthers. These teams consisted of local players who worked in the coal mines six days a week and then knocked heads against "all comers" on the weekends. The heyday of rough-tough coal miner football was in the "Roaring Twenties," as championship games drew crowds of 15,000 with large pools of money bet on the contest. The 1921 Coaldale Big Green team photo hangs in the Pro Football Hall of Fame in Canton, Ohio. Managed by **James "Casey" Gildea**, Coaldale greats were: **James "Blue" Bonner, Bob "Dauber" Parfitt, Bill "Honeyboy" Evans, Jack "Honeyboy" Evans, Len Lithgow, Stan Giltner, Ben Herring, Vince Gildea, Metro Roadside, Ervin Nussbaum, James Melly, Simon Lewchick, Joe Garland, Mike Pavlick, Foger Giltner, Ed "Scoop" Boyle, Albert "Abby" Morgan, Henry Bouck** and **John Walters**.

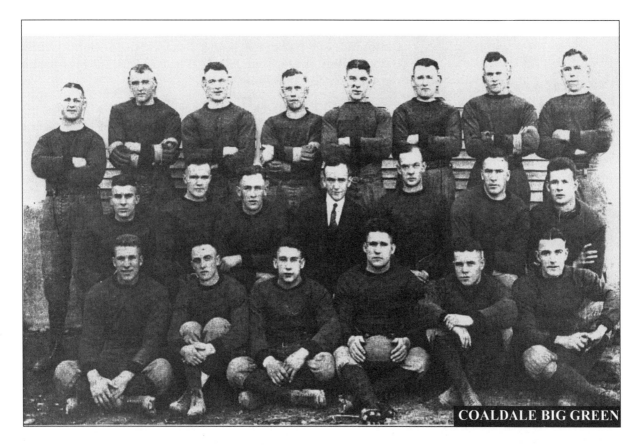

COALDALE BIG GREEN

ANGELO COIA was a big, fast halfback-track man for Philadelphia's Northeast High School Archives under **Charlie Martin**. He went to the Citadel and then starred at USC in 1958-59 for **Don Clark's** "Fight On" Trojans. Coia spent seven years with Chicago, Washington and Atlanta from 1960-66. He rushed for 2,037 career yards, scored 20 TD's and earned a 1963 NFL title ring as **George Halas'** Bears beat NY.

ANDRE COLEMAN rushed the Hickory High School Hornets in Hermitage, Pennsylvania to the 1989 2A state crown under **Guy Gibbs**. He played at Kansas State and was a 1993 All-American wide receiver for **Bill Snyder's** 9-2-1 Wildcats. Coleman scored 5 TD's with San Diego 1994-97, Pittsburgh 1997-98. He set four Super Bowl records, but **Bobby Ross'** Chargers lost SB XXIX in 1995 to San Francisco.

DWIGHT COLLINS played for the Beaver Falls High School Tigers under coach **Larry Bruno**. He was a wide receiver at Pitt from 1980-83 where he caught 133 passes for 2,264 yards and 24 TD's for the 39-8-1 Panthers under **Jackie Sherrill** and **Foge Fazio**. Collins played for the Minnesota Vikings in 1984.

G. COLLINS

GARY COLLINS played for Williamstown High School under **Frank Snyder**. He played at Maryland from 1959-61 for **Tom Nugent** and was called, "the greatest end in Terrapin history," with a career record 12 TD's. Collins was a 1961 All-American and was eighth in the Heisman Trophy vote, which was won by **Ernie Davis** of Syracuse. He was the first draft choice of Cleveland and spent 10 years with the Browns from 1962-71. **Blanton Collier's** Browns appeared in two straight NFL championship games and Collins earned a NFL title ring from the 1964 win over Baltimore. Cleveland lost the 1965 NFL crown to Green Bay. Collins, a two-time All-Pro, had 331 career receptions for 5,299 yards and 70 TD's.

KERRY COLLINS threw for 2,043 yards and 17 TD's in 1989 for Wilson High School of West Lawn, Pennsylvania as **Gerry Slemmer's** Bulldogs won the PIAA 4A state title. He was Penn State's signal caller from 1992-94 and guided **Joe Paterno's** 1994 Nittany Lions to a perfect 12-0 record, a Rose Bowl victory and the #2 ranking in the nation. Collins, who had 5,304 career passing yards and 39 TD's at PSU, was a 1994 All-American, won the Maxwell Award as the nation's most outstanding player, and finished fourth in the Heisman Trophy vote which was won by **Ron Dayne** of Wisconsin. He has been in the NFL since 1995 with Carolina, New Orleans, and the NY Giants. Collins threw for 3,610 yards and 22 TD's as he led **Jim Fassel's** Giants to Super Bowl XXXV in 2001.

LARRY CONJAR was a fullback for Harrisburg's Bishop McDevitt High School Crusaders under **Tony Cernugel**. He played at Notre Dame from 1964-66 and was a 1966 All-American as he helped lead **Ara Parseghian's** Fighting Irish to a 9-0-1 record and the national crown. "The Croatian Crusher" was the second round draft choice of Cleveland and spent four years with the Browns, Philly, and Baltimore 1967-70.

CHRIS CONLIN from Glenside played for the Bishop McDevitt High School Lancers under **Pat Manzi**. He was an offensive tackle at Penn State from 1983-86 and was a 1986 All-American for **Joe Paterno's** Nittany Lions who went 12-0 and won the national championship. Conlin, who was nominated for the Outland Trophy, spent five years in the NFL with Miami 1987-88 and Indianapolis 1989-91.

CONJAR

DAN CONNORS played for the St. Mary's High School Flying Dutchmen. He was a tackle at Miami of Florida from 1961-63 for **Andy Gustafson** and was a 1963 All-American for the Hurricanes. Connors spent 11 years with Oakland from 1964-74. **John Rauch's** Raiders defeated Houston for the 1967 AFL title, but lost Super Bowl II to Green Bay in 1968. Connors had 15 interceptions and scored 5 TD's.

BILL CONTZ was a tackle for the Belle Vernon High School Leopards and at Penn State 1980-82 as **Joe Paterno's** Nittany Lions were the 1982 national champs. He was with Cleveland, New Orleans from 1983-88.

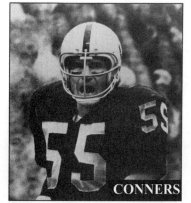

CONNERS

JOE CONWELL was a tackle for the Lower Merion High School Bulldogs in Ardmore, Pennsylvania. He was at North Carolina 1981-83, USFL champion Philly/Baltimore Stars in 1984-85, Eagles 1986-87.

BOB COOLBAUGH played for the Dallas High School Mountaineers and was an end for the University of Richmond Spiders from 1958-60. He was with the Oakland Raiders in 1961.

ED COOK was a guard for Philadelphia's South Catholic High School under **Paul Bartolomeo** and at Notre Dame in 1953-54. He was a 10 year NFL vet with the Chicago Cards and Atlanta from 1958-67.

JIM COOPER was a lineman for Philadelphia's Cardinal Dougherty High School Cardinals under **Jack Boyle** and at Temple for **Wayne Hardin's** high-flying Owls in 1973-75. Cooper spent 10 years with Dallas from 1977-86. **Tom Landry's** Cowboys defeated Denver in Super Bowl XII in 1978.

JIM CORBETT played for Erie's McDowell High School under **Joe Moore** and **Ted Dean**. He was a tight end at Pitt from 1973-76 and helped lead **Johnny Majors'** 1976 Panthers to a 12-0 season and the national championship. Corbett caught one TD in five years with Cincinnati from 1977-81.

MIKE CORVINO played for Pius X High School in Roseto, Pennsylvania under **Jack Ortelli** and **John Smith**. He was All-ACC nose guard with a record 24 sacks at Maryland from 1979-82. USFL 1983-85.

CHUCK CORREAL played for Laurel Highlands High School Mustangs in Uniontown, Pennsylvania under **Fred Botti** and **Bill Elias**. He was a center at Penn State 1977-78 as **Joe Paterno's** Nittany Lions went 22-2. Correal played for Atlanta in 1979-80, Cleveland 1981 and in the USFL.

WALT COREY played for Derry High School and at Miami of Florida from 1957-59 for **Andy Gustafson**. He was a seven year veteran linebacker with the Dallas Texans/Kansas City Chiefs in the AFL from 1960-66. **Hank Stram's** Texans defeated Houston for the 1962 AFL crown.

BILL COTTRELL played for the Chester High School Clippers and was an offensive tackle at Delaware Valley College from 1964-66. He was with Detroit from 1967-70 and Denver in 1972.

TED COTTRELL played for the Chester High School Clippers and was a linebacker at Delaware Valley College from 1966-68. He was with Atlanta 1969-70 and Canada's Winnipeg Blue Bombers in 1971.

STEVE COURSON played his senior year at Gettysburg High School under **Leo Ward** and at South Carolina 1973-76. He was an offensive guard with Pittsburgh and Tampa Bay 1977-85. Courson earned two Super Bowl rings as **Chuck Noll's** Steelers beat Dallas in SB XIII in 1979, LA in SB XIV in 1980.

COVERT

JIM "JIMBO" COVERT from Conway played at Freedom High School. "Jimbo" was an offensive tackle at Pitt 1979-82 as the Panthers went 41-5 and was a two-time All-American in 1981 and 1982. He spent nine years with Chicago from 1983-91 and earned a Super Bowl ring as **Mike Ditka's** Bears defeated New England in SB XX in 1986. The three-time All-Pro was the NFL's 1986 Lineman of the Year.

BILL COWHER played for the Carlynton High School Cougars in Crafton, Pennsylvania and was a linebacker at North Carolina State from 1975-78 for **Lou Holtz** and **Bo Rein**. Cowher spent five years in the NFL with Cleveland 1980-82 and Philadelphia 1983-84. He has been the head coach of Pittsburgh since 1992 with a 91-65 record. Cowher's Steelers lost Super Bowl XXX in 1996 to Dallas. He was the NFL's Coach of the Year in 1992.

COX

FRED COX played for the Monongahela High School Wildcats under **Al Cree**. He was a leading scorer halfback at Pitt from 1959-61 for **John Michelosen** as one of the "C-boys" backfield along with **Bob Clemens** and **Jim Cunningham**. Cox spent 15 years in the NFL as a kicker with Cleveland 1961-62 and Minnesota 1963-77. Cox appeared in four Super Bowls with **Bud Grants's** Vikings and was All-Pro in 1969. He scored 1,365 points on 282 FG's and 519 PAT's.

ERIC CRABTREE scored 13 TD's and passed for 12 TD's in 1961 for Monessen High School as **Joe Glady's** Greyhounds won the WPIAL title. He was a halfback at Pitt from 1963-65 for **John Michelosen**. Crabtree spent six years as a wide receiver and defensive back with Denver, Cincinnati and New England from 1966-71. He had 164 receptions for 2,663 yards and 22 TD's.

BOB CRAIG went to Pottsville High School and played at Lock Haven State. He coached at Newport 1957-59 and at Cedar Cliff High School 1963-00 where he went 274-124-10 and won the 1989 PIAA 4A state title. Craig's over-all record was 282-144-11 in 40 seasons and he developed pro **Kyle Brady**.

DON CROFTCHEK from Allison played for the Redstone High School Blackhawks in Republic, Pennsylvania under **Joe Bosnic**. He was a two-way guard at Indiana University from 1962-64 and was a 1964 All-American for **Phil Dickens'** Hoosiers. Croftchek was in Washington 1965-66 and Chicago 1967.

RON CROSBY from Glassport played for the South Allegheny High School Gladiators under coach **Rich Zauauckas**. He was a linebacker and co-captain at Penn State 1974-76 for **Joe Paterno's** Nittany Lions. Crosby spent seven years with Detroit, New Orleans and NY Jets 1977-83. He finished in the USFL.

CROFTCHEK

CROUTHAMEL

JOHN "JAKE" CROUTHAMEL played for the Pennridge High School Rams in Perkasie, Pennsylvania under **Ray Whispell** and **Wayne Helman**. At Dartmouth, Crouthamel set the Big Green's career rushing record and was a 1958 All-American for **Bob Blackman's** Indians who won the Ivy League crown. "Jake" played for AFL's Boston in 1960. Crouthamel was head coach at Dartmouth 1971-77, went 41-20-2 and won three Ivy League titles in 1971, 1972, 1973. He became the Athletic Director at Syracuse in 1978.

CROWDER

RANDY CROWDER played for the Farrell High School Steelers under **Bill Garland** and was a defensive tackle at Penn State from 1971-73 for **Joe Paterno**. He helped lead the 1973 Nittany Lions to a 12-0 record, was an All-American and was also named Defensive Player-of-the-Year by the Washington D.C. Touchdown Club. Crowder spent nine years with the Dolphins 1974-76 and Tampa Bay 1977-82.

J. BIRNEY CRUM was a three sport star at Muhlenberg College and coached at Somerville, NJ 1923 and Carnegie High School 1924 before he became head coach in football, basketball, and baseball at Allentown High School for 25 years from 1925-50. Crum had 205 career football victories going 190-51-17 at AHS, 490 wins in basketball and 4 PIAA state titles as his Canaries were featured in Time magazine in 1947. Besides AHS, Crum was also the head coach of the professional Bethlehem Bulldogs who won the 1947 American Football League title. In 1948 the 23,500 AHS Stadium opened as the largest high school owned stadium in Pennsylvania. He developed six pros in **Bob "Buck" Friedman, Ray Dini, John Baranchok, Leo Crampsey, Billy Kline** and **Pete Sukeena**. Crum's handpicked successor, **Perry Scott**, who played for Muhlenberg, Detroit Lions, Bethlehem Bulldogs, went 93-49-11 from 1950-64 and developed two pros in **Larry Seiple** and **Bill Wood**, plus pro signees **Vel Heckman** and **Joe Petro**. AHS Stadium was renamed J. Birney Crum Stadium in 1982.

DOUG CRUSAN was a tackle for the Monessen High School Greyhounds under **Joe Gladys**. He played at Indiana University where he was captain and a 1967 All-American for **John Pont's** 9-2 Hoosiers. Crusan was with Miami from 1968-74. Miami appeared in three straight Super Bowls and Crusan earned two rings as **Don Shula's** Dolphins beat Washington in SB VII in 1973 and Minnesota in SB VIII in 1974.

JIM CUNNINGHAM was a fullback for Connellsville High School Cokers under coach **Dan Galbraith**. He played at Pitt for **John Michelosen** from 1958-60 and was one of the "C-boys" backfield along with halfbacks **Bob Clemens** and **Fred Cox**. Cunningham scored 5 TD's with the Redskins from 1961-63.

FRAN CURCI from Pittsburgh was a southpaw quarterback at Miami of Florida from 1957-59 for **Andy Gustafson**. He started the tradition of great quarterbacks at Miami when he was a 1959 All-American and Academic All-American. The "Little General" spent 1960 with the Dallas Texans and was head coach at Miami of Florida 1971-72 and Kentucky 1970-81 with an over-all record of 56-64-2.

JAMES "RAB" CURRIE coached Monessen High School for four years and Charleroi High School for 32 years. In 36 years, "Rab" produced a 212-106-10 record, the 1959 WPIAL title and **Myron Pottios**.

GEORGE CURRY was a lineman for Larksville High School in 1960-61 and at Temple from 1963-65. He has been the coach of Berwick High School since 1971 and is the winningest coach in Pennsylvania scholastic history with a 344-68-5 record. Curry's Bulldogs were the USA Today's #1 team three times in 1983, 1992, 1995, won six PIAA 3A state championships in 1988, 1989, 1992, 1995, 1996, 1997, had 11 undefeated regular seasons and posted a 47 game winning streak. Because of Curry's success, Berwick is the third winningest high school program in the state behind Mt. Carmel and Easton with a 657-275-43 record since 1888. He developed seven pros in **Bo Orlando, Troy Maneval, Tom Robsoch, George Schechterly, Kurt Kehl, Jake Kelchner,** and **Ron Powlus**.

RANDY CUTHBERT played for Central Bucks West High School in Doylestown, Pennsylvania under **Mike Pettine**. He rushed for 2,771 yards, scored 20 TD's at Duke 1989-92 and was a Steeler in 1993-94.

D'AGOSTINO

FRANK D'AGOSTINO was a tackle for Philadelphia's Northeast Catholic High School Falcons under **Jack Gillespie**. He went to Auburn 1953-55 and was a 1955 All-American for **Ralph "Shug" Jordan's** nationally ranked Tigers. D'Agostino, the #2 draft pick of Philly, was with the Eagles in 1956-57 and NY Titans in 1960.

BILL DADDIO from Meadville went to Pitt where he was a two-time All-American end in 1937 and 1938. As a junior in 1937, **"Jock" Sutherland's** Panthers went 9-0-1 and won the national championship. He was with the Chicago Cardinals in 1941-42 and Buffalo in the AAFL in 1946.

AVERELL DANIELL played for Mt. Lebanon High School and was a star tackle at Pitt from 1934-36. He was a 1936 All-American for **"Jock" Sutherland's** 8-1-1 Rose Bowl winning Panthers. Daniell, played for Green Bay in 1937 and went in the College Football Hall of Fame in 1975.

JIM DANIELL played for Mt. Lebanon High School and was a star tackle at Ohio State from 1939-41. He spent 1945 with the Chicago Bears and 1946 with **Paul Brown's** AAFC champion Cleveland Browns.

NORBERT "NORBIE" DANZ played for Lancaster Catholic and George Washington U. He had 222 victories in 37 years at Lebanon Catholic, Cedar Crest and Lancaster's J. P. McCaskey High School.

DAN DARRAGH from Pittsburgh quarterbacked William and Mary from 1965-67 for **Marv Levy** as the Indians were Southern Conference champs. He threw 4 TD's with the AFL's Buffalo Bills from 1968-70.

DREW DARRAH was a quarterback for Upper Moreland High School, at Florida State and Millersville State 1958-59. He coached the Souderton High School Indians for 34 years 1964-97 and went 223-140-6.

HUGH "DUFFY" DAUGHERTY from Barnesboro was a lineman at Syracuse from 1937-39 for coach **Ossie Solem**. He was the top assistant to **Clarence "Biggie" Munn** at Michigan State as the Spartans went undefeated in 1951 and 1952 and won the 1952 national championship. "Duffy" followed Munn as head coach at Michigan State for 19 years from 1954-72 and posted a 109-69-5 record. His 1955, 1965 and 1966 Spartans were ranked #2 in the nation. Daugherty's most famous team was the 1966 Spartans who played Notre Dame to a 10-10 tie in the "Game of the Century" at East Lansing. Although both clubs finished with identical 9-0-1 records, Notre Dame was named national champion and Michigan State #2. Daugherty, who appeared on the cover of Time magazine in 1956, was named Coach of the Year in 1955 and 1965. He developed 29 All-Americans and was inducted in the College Football Hall of Fame in 1984.

BOB DAVIE played for the Moon High School Tigers in Coraopolis, Pennsylvania under **Rip Scherer**. He was a three-year starter at tight end for powerful Youngstown State in Ohio from 1973-75. Davie has been the head coach of Notre Dame since 1997 and has a 30-19-0 record with the Fighting Irish.

TOM DAVIES from Pittsburgh was Pitt's greatest running back as a 150 pound tailback for **Glenn "Pop" Warner** from 1918-21. He was a two-time All-American in 1918 and 1920. Davies set a Panther record of 3,931 career yards and scored 181 points. He played in the NFL with Hammond and Frankford.

JULIUS DAWKINS played for the Monessen High School Greyhounds under **Joe Gladys**. At Pitt, he was a four-year letterman and record-setting receiver from 1979-82 as the powerful Panthers went 42-6. The 1981 All-American was with Buffalo in 1983-84 and caught 32 passes for 413 yards and 3 TD's.

TED DEAN was a big, fast halfback for the Radnor High School Red Raiders, near Philadelphia, under coach **Warren Lentz**. He was the whole offense at Wichita State in 1957-59 for **Woody Woodard**. Dean spent five years with

Philadelphia and Minnesota from 1960-64. He was a rookie sensation in 1960 and earned a NFL title ring when he scored the winning TD as **Buck Shaw's** Eagles defeated Green Bay 17-13 for the championship.

JEFF DELANEY played for the Upper St. Clair High School Panthers under **Joe Moore**. He was a defensive back at Pitt from 1975-79 and helped lead **Johnny Majors'** 1976 Panthers to a 12-0 record and the national championship. Delaney, a 1976 and 1978 Academic All-American, spent five years in the NFL from 1979-83 with LA, Detroit, Tampa Bay and Baltimore. He had 8 interceptions and 3 TD's.

GREG DELONG was the 1990 Gatorade Player of the Year as a tight end for the Parkland High School Trojans in Orefield, Pennsylvania under **Scott LeVan**. He was at North Carolina 1991-94 for **Mack Brown's** Tar Heels. DeLong has been in the NFL since 1995 with Minnesota, Baltimore and Jacksonville.

JACK DELUPLAINE was a halfback for the Pottstown High School Trojans under **John Schoenwolf** and at Salem College. He was in the NFL with Pittsburgh 1976-78, Washington 1978 and Chicago 1979.

AL DEMAO was a center for the Arnold High School Lions for **Brooks Kuhn** and at powerful Duquesne from 1937-40 for **Aldo "Buff" Donelli**. He was captain and a nine year vet with Washington 1945-53. The Redskins lost the 1945 NFL title. Demao was a 1952 Pro Bowler and had 8 career interceptions.

DENNISON

DOUG DENNISON was a halfback for Lancaster's J. P. McCaskey High School Red Tornadoe under **Boyd Sponaugle**. He starred at Kutztown State from 1971-73 for **George Baldwin's** Golden Bears. Dennison scored 19 TD's with Dallas from 1974 to 1978 for **Tom Landry**. He earned a Super Bowl ring as the **Tony Dorsett**-led Cowboys defeated Denver in SB XII in 1978. Dallas lost SB XIII in 1979.

DARRELL DESS was a lineman for the Union High School Scotties near New Castle for **Jack Schantz**. He played at North Carolina State for **Earle Edwards** from 1955-57. Dess spent 11 years with Pittsburgh 1958, NY Giants 1959-64, 1966-69 and Detroit 1965. At New York, Dess appeared in four NFL title games in five years in 1959, 1961, 1962, 1963, 1964. He was a 1963 All-Pro and in two Pro Bowls.

JOE DEVLIN played for the Great Valley High School Patriots in Malvern, Pennsylvania under coach **Bill Marion**. At Iowa, he was a 1975 All-American offensive guard for **Bob Commings'** Hawkeyes. Devlin was the second round draft choice of Buffalo and spent 14 years with the Bills from 1976-89.

RICHARD DILTS was a lineman for Butler High School and Slippery Rock. He was coach of Richland High School 1959-61and went 20-9 and at Kiski Area High School 1962-91 and went 214-109-7 with one WPIAL championship in 1971 and two undefeated seasons. His over-all record in 35 years was 234-90-7.

TONY DIMIDIO played for the Upper Darby High School Royals and was a tackle and center at West Chester State 1961-63. He was drafted by AFL's Kansas City and was a Chief from 1964-67. **Hank Stram's** Chiefs beat Buffalo for the 1966 AFL title, but lost Super Bowl I in 1967 to Green Bay.

DEVLIN

JOE "JAZZ" DIMINICK was a halfback for the Kulpmont High School Wildcats under **Mike Terry**. At Boston College, he was a two-time All-American honorable mention back in 1948 and 1949. Diminick coached Coal Township 1956-57 with a 15-4-1 record, Susquenita 1958-59 with a 4-11-1 record and the Mt. Carmel High School Red Tornadoes 1962-92 with a 267-81-7 record. His over-all record in 35 years was 286-96-9. "Jazz" developed pro back **Henry Hynoski**. Because of top coaches like Diminick and **Dave "Whitey" Williams**, from Tamaqua, who won three state crowns in 1994, 1996 and 1998, Mt. Carmel is the winningest high school football program in the state with a 704-255-57 record since 1893.

PETE DIMPERIO, SR. was a Little All-American lineman at Thiel College. He coached Pittsburgh's Westinghouse High School Bulldogs from 1946-66, went 118-5-1 in league games and won 17 Pittsburgh City League championships in 21 years. Dimperio's over-all record was 158-26-1 and he developed three pros in **Tony Liscio**, **Jon Henderson** and **Dave Kalina**.

MIKE DITKA played for Aliquippa High School as **Carl Aschman's** Quips won the 1955 WPIAL title. He played at Pitt for **John Michelosen** from 1958-60 and was considered the greatest Panther since the immortal **Marshall Goldberg**. Ditka was a consensus 1960 All-American end and sixth in the Heisman Trophy vote. He was the #1 draft choice of Chicago and played for the Bears 1961-66, Philadelphia 1967-68, and Dallas 1969-72. "Iron Mike" earned an NFL title ring as **George Halas'** Bears defeated the NY Giants in 1963 and received a Super Bowl ring as **Tom Landry's** Cowboys beat Miami in SB VI in 1972. In 12 seasons, Ditka caught 427 passes for 5,812 yards and 45 TD's and was a five-time All-Pro. Ditka was head coach of Chicago for 11 years from 1982-92 with a 106-60-0 record. He earned another Super Bowl ring as "Da Bears" defeated New England in SB XX in 1986. Ditka, who was the NFL's Coach of the Year in 1985 and 1988, was inducted into both the Pro Football Hall of Fame in 1988 and the College Football Hall of Fame. He came out of retirement to coach New Orleans from 1997-99 and went 15-33-0.

JACK DOLBIN had 1,846 yards of total offense and scored 24 TD's in 1965 for the Pottsville High School Crimson Tide under **Bill Ruddy**. He led the ground attack at Wake Forest 1967-69 and played for **Dave DiFilippo's** Pottstown Firebirds, 1970 ACFL champions. Dolbin was in

DOLEMAN

Denver 1975-79 as **"Red" Miller's** Broncos lost Super Bowl XII to Dallas in 1978. He had 94 receptions for 1,576 yards, 7 TD's.

CHRIS DOLEMAN played for York's William Penn High School Bearcats from 1980-82. Doleman was a defensive end/linebacker at Pitt from 1981-84. He was the #1 draft choice of Minnesota and spent 14 years in the NFL with the Vikings, Atlanta and San Francisco from 1985-98. The three-time All-Pro was the NFL's 1992 Defensive Player of the Year. Doleman had 8 career picks, 3 TD's, 2 safeties and 116 sacks.

SAM DONATO played for Dunmore High School and was captain of Penn State in 1937 for **Bob Higgins**. He coached the West Scranton High School Invaders from 1946-72, went 151-94-12 in 26 years and developed three pros in **Nick Chickillo**, **Don Jonas** and **Cosmo Iacavazzi**.

DITKA

TOM DONCHEZ rushed for 1,388 yards, 15 TD's and 99 points as a senior in 1969 for Bethlehem's Liberty High School Hurricanes under **Bob Buffman**. The Lehigh Valley's scholar-athlete played at Penn State for **Joe Paterno** in 1971, 1973-74 and was an excellent runner and blocker for 1973 Heisman Trophy winner **John Cappelletti**. He was the #4 draft choice of Buffalo, but played for Chiacgo in 1975.

ALDO "BUFF" DONELLI was the star running back for the South Fayette High School Lions and at Duquesne where in 1929 he helped lead **Elmer Layden's** Dukes to a 9-0-1 season. He was head coach of nationally ranked Duquesne from 1939-42 and went 29-4-2. "Buff" was head coach at Columbia for 11 years from 1957-67 with a 60-73 record and the 1961 Ivy League championship.

DORNEY

KEITH DORNEY from Macungie was an end for the Emmaus High School Green Hornets under **George "Fritz" Halfacre** and **Allen Fields**. He was an offensive tackle at Penn State 1975-78 and was a two-time All-American and Academic All-American in 1977 and 1978 as **Joe Paterno's** Nittany Lions went 22-2. Dorney, the first round draft pick of Detroit, started for the Lions for ten years 1979-88 and was All-Pro.

TONY DORSETT from Aliquippa rushed for 1,238 yards and 23 TD's in 1972 for the Hopewell High School Vikings under coach **Richard "Butch" Ross**. At Pitt from 1973-76, Dorsett's durable running led **Johnny Majors'** Panthers to a 12-0 record and the 1976 national championship as he set or tied 18 NCAA records including 6,082 yards rushing and 356 points. He was four-time All-American and won the Heisman Trophy in 1976. Dorsett, who was the #1 draft choice of Dallas and the first "millionaire" pro rookie, spent 12 years with the Cowboys 1977-87 and Denver 1988. He earned a Super Bowl ring as **Tom Landry's** Cowboys defeated Denver in SB XII in 1978. In 12 seasons, Dorsett rushed 2,936 times for 12,739 yards and 77 TD's, and caught 398 passes for 3,554 yards and 13 TD's. Dorsett, with a total of 90 TD's, went in both the Pro and College Football Hall of Fame in 1994.

DENNY DOUDS was a guard at Indiana High School under **Dick Farbaugh** and at Slippery Rock where he was a 1962 NAIA All-American. He has been the head coach of East Stroudsburg University since 1974 with a 155-117-3 record. Douds had two undefeated teams and developed 17 Little All-Americans.

WALT DOWNING played for the Coatesville High School Red Raiders. He was a center at Michigan 1974-77 and was a co-captain and 1977 All-American center for **"Bo" Schembechler's** 10-2 Wolverines. Dowling was the #2 draft choice of San Francisco and spent six years as a guard with the 49er's from 1978-83. He earned a Super Bowl ring when **Bill Walsh's** 49ers defeated Cincinnati in SB XVI in 1982.

DORSETT

NICK DRAHOS was a tackle for the Ford City High School Sabres and at Cornell where he was a two-time All-American in 1939-40 for **Carl Snavely's** nationally ranked Red Raiders who had a 18 game undefeated streak. He was with New York in the AFL in 1941 and is in the College Football Hall of Fame.

TROY DRAYTON caught 51 passes for 632 yards and 7 TD's in 1988 for the Steelton-Highspire High School Steamrollers under coach **Nick Govelovich**. He played at Penn State for **Joe Paterno's** Nittany Lions from 1989-92 and was a 1992 All-American. Drayton was the #2 draft choice of Los Angeles and has been a tight end in the NFL since 1993 with the Rams 1993-95 and the Miami Dolphins since 1996.

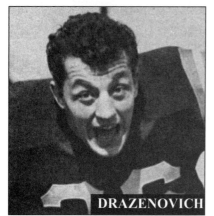

DRAZENOVICH

CHUCH DRAZENOVICH played for the Brownsville High School Brownies and at Penn State from 1945, 1947-49 for **Bob Higgins**. A tough fullback and linebacker, Drazenovich was a 10 year veteran with the Washington Redskins from 1950-59. Always popular with the "Capital City" fans, Drazenovich, who was a 1956 All-Pro, rushed for 8 TD's, intercepted 15 passes and recovered 7 fumbles.

JIM DRUCKENMILLER quarterbacked the Northampton High School Konkrete Kids under **Andy Melosky**. He was at Virginia Tech 1991-95 and as a starter in 1994-95 threw for 4,597 yards and 37 TD's. He was the #1 draft choice of San Francisco and was with the 49ers in 1996-98 and Miami in 1999.

AL DRULIS played at Girardsville High School and was a fullback and linebacker at Temple from 1940-42 for **Ray Morrison**. Drulis spent three years in the NFL with the Chicago Cardinals in 1945-46 and Pittsburgh Steelers in 1947. He was a two-time All-Pro with the Cardinals in 1945 and 1946.

CHUCK DRULIS played at Girardsville High School and at Temple where he was a two-time All-East guard for the Owls in 1939 and 1940. He spent seven years with the Chicago Bears in 1942, 1945-50 and was All-Pro in 1948. The Bears lost the 1942 title to Washington, but won the 1946 title over New York.

RICK DRUSCHEL was a tackle for Hempfied High School and North Carolina State 1972-73 for **Lou Holtz**. He was with Pittsburgh 1974 as **Chuck Noll's** Steelers beat Minnesota in Super Bowl IX in 1975.

MARK DUDA played for the Wyoming Valley West High School Spartans in Plymouth, Pennsylvania under **George Yaniger**. A four-year starter at Maryland from 1979-82, Duda was a 1982 All-American honorable mention defensive tackle for **Bobby Ross'** Terrapins. He had 10 sacks with the St. Louis Cardinals from 1983-87. Since 1992, Duda has been the head coach of the highly successful and nationally recognized Lackawanna Junior College Falcons in Scranton.

JOE DUDECK was a guard-linebacker for Hazleton High School and at powerful North Carolina from 1949-51 for the legendary **Carl Snavely**. He was captain and a 1951 All-American for the Tar Heels.

CRAIG DUNAWAY played for Upper St. Clair High School Panthers and was a tight end at Michigan from 1980-82 for **"Bo" Schembechler**. He was a Pittsburgh Steeler in 1983.

DUQUESNE DUKES in Pittsburgh, Pennsylvania startred football in 1891 and had its first undefeated season in 1929 with an 9-0-1 record for coach **Elmer Layden** (Hall of Fame) who was one of Notre Dame's legendary Four Horsemen. Layden guided Duquesne to a 10-1 record in 1933 and defeated Miami of Florida in the Festival of Palms Bowl in Miami which was the forerunner of the Orange Bowl. In 1936 the Dukes under **"Clipper" Smith** (Hall of Fame), went 8-2 and defeated Mississippi State in the Orange Bowl. Dangerous Dukes were ends **Ernie Hefferle, Kirsling**; tackles **Joe Maras, Laputka, Geneva**; guards **John Perko, Horn, Amann**; center **Mike Basrak**; and backs **Boyd Brumbaugh, George Matsik, John Karrs, Bill Bechtloff**. **Aldo "Buff" Donelli**, from McDonald and the legendary running back on the undefeated 1929 team, took over in 1939 and the Dukes immediately went 8-0-1 for the #10 ranking in the nation and followed that in 1941 with a 8-0 record and the #8 national ranking. Donelli's darlings included linemen **Al DeLucia, "Big Joe" Cibulas, John Matisi, Nopper, Sirochman, Squires** and **Maliczewski** and fleet-footed backs in **Alan Donelli, George Gonda, Joe Chadonic** and **"Smokey Hub" Ahwesh**. Since 1994, Red and Blue football has been one of the top NCAA Division III programs under coach **Greg Gattuso** who was a fullback under **Tom Donahoe** at Pittsburgh's Seton-LaSalle that won the 1979 and 1980 WPIAL crowns and then was an All-American honorable mention nose guard on **Joe Paterno's** 1982 national championship Penn State team. He was the 1995 Division I-AA Coach of the Year.

DURANKO

PETE DURANKO scored 301 career points from 1959-61 as the hard charging fullback for Johnstown's Bishop McCort High School Crushers under **Joe Shumock**. He was a fullback/defensive tackle at Notre Dame from 1963-66 for **Ara Parseghian** and was a 1966 All-American as the Fighting Irish went 9-0-1 for the national championship. "The Deisel" spent eight years with Denver from 1967-74.

JOHN EBERSOLE was a tackle for the Altoona High School Mountain Lions under **Earl Strohm**. He was a linebacker at Penn State 1967-69 for **Joe Paterno** as the 1968 and 1969 Nittany Lions went 22-0 and the #2 ranking in the nation. Ebersole was a NY Jet from 1970-79.

EARLE EDWARDS from Huntington played at Penn State from 1927-30 for coach **Hugo Bezdek**. A successful Pennsylvania prep school coach, Edwards was an assistant on the staff of Michigan State's 1952 national championship club before he became the father of modern football at North Carolina State. In 17 seasons from 1954-70, Edwards' Red and White clad Wolfpack went 77-88-8, won five ACC titles and went to two bowl games. He developed eight All-Americans including Chester's **Dick Christy** and was a four-time ACC Coach of the Year.

LEO ELTER was a fullback for Pittsburgh's Shaler High School Titans, at Duquesne and Villanova. He scored 13 TD's with Pittsburgh 1954-55, 1958-59 and in Washington 1955-57.

BOBBY EPPS was a fullback for Swissvale High School and at Pitt from 1951-53. He scored 2 TD's with NY Giants 1954-57 as **Jim Lee Howell's** Giants beat Chicago for the 1956 NFL title.

TONY EPPS played for the Uniontown High School Red Raiders and at Memphis State 1991-93. He was a six year veteran nose tackle with Atlanta, Chicago, New Orleans from 1990-95.

CHARLES A. "RIP" ENGLE from Salisbury played at Western Maryland from 1926-29 for coach **Dick Harlow**. He was coach at Waynesboro High School for 11 years with a 86-17-5 record. Engle was head coach at Brown University from 1944-49 and went 28-20-4. He then went to Penn State and coached the Nittany Lions for 16 years from 1950-65 with a 104-48-4 record, three bowl wins and three Lambert Trophies in 1961, 1962 and 1964. At Penn State, "Rip" developed seven All-Americans in **Lenny Moore, Sam Valentine, Richie Lucas, Bob Mitinger, Dave Robinson, Roger Kochman** and **Glenn Ressler**. Engle had an over-all college record of 132-68-8 and was inducted into the College Football Hall of Fame in 1974.

AL ERDOSY went to Northampton High School and Muhlenberg College. He was coach of the Northampton High School Konkrete Kids from 1939-67 and went 194-55-10 in 29 years. Erdosy had four undefeated teams in 1949, 1955, 1956, 1959 and his Orange and Black won 57 straight games in the prestigious Lehigh Valley League from 1954-62. He developed five pros in **Dennis Onkotz, Joe Novogratz, Larry Christoff, Richard Reimer** and **Jerry Rutledge**.

SCOTT ERNEY threw for 1,232 yards and 6 TD's in 1985 for Mechanicsburg High School under **Rich Lichtel**. At Rutgers from 1986-89 for **Dick Anderson**, he set Scarlet Knights' carreer records of 7,188 yards and 41 TD's and was a two-time All-American in 1988 and 1989. Erney led Barcelona to the 1991 WLAF championship game against **Stan Gelbaugh**-led London.

ESHMONT

LEN ESHMONT scored 137 points in 1936 for Mt. Carmel Township under **Al Masciantonio**. He starred at Fordham 1938-40 and was a two-time All-American halfback in 1939 and 1940 as the press called him, "another **Red Grange**." Eshmont led **"Sleepy" Jim Crowley's** Rams to a 15-4 record and two straight bowl games. "The Polish Lancer" played for the NY Giants in 1941 and San Francisco in the All-American Football Conference from 1946-49. **Buck Shaw's** 49ers played Cleveland for the 1949 AAFC title. Eshmont scored 15 TD's and had 10 interceptions.

MIKE EVANS played for Philadelphia's North Catholic High School Falcons for **Joe Lauletta**. He was a center at Boston College for **Jim Miller's** Golden Eagles from 1965-67. Evans spent seven years in the pivot with Philadelphia 1968-73 and WFL's Southern California Sun in 1974.

ED "SCRAPPER" FARRELL was a tailback for Catasauqua High School and at Muhlenberg in 1934-37 for **Al "Doggie" Julian**. He scored 3 TD's with Pittsburgh and Brooklyn in 1938-39.

BERNIE FALONEY played at Scott Township High School near Pittsburgh and for Maryland from 1951-53 for **Jim Tatum**. He was a 1953 All-American quarterback and paced the Terrapins to a 10-1-0 season and the national championship. Faloney, who was fourth in the 1953 Heisman Trophy vote, which was won by **Johnny Lattner** of Notre Dame, was the first round draft choice of San Francisco, but spent 14 years in the Canadian Football League from 1954-67 with Edmonton, Hamilton, Montreal and British Columbia. He earned a Grey Cup ring with **Frank Ivy's** Edmonton Eskimos in 1954 and then directed the Hamilton Tiger Cats to seven Grey Cup finals bewteen 1957-64 and earned two rings in 1957 and 1962. Faloney was the CFL's MVP in 1961 and was inducted into the CFL Hall of Fame in 1974.

LOU FALCONI played for Farrell High School in 1963-64 and for Edinboro State 1966-68. He is the present coach of the Farrell High School Steelers and has a record of 177-63-5 with four WPIAL crowns in 1986, 1990, 1995, 1996 plus two PIAA 1A state titles in 1995 and 1996.

MIKE FANUCCI was an end for the Dunmore High School Bucks under **Lou Costanzo**. He played at Arizona State 1968-70 for **Frank Kush**. Fanucci was a ten year pro in Washington 1971-72 as **George Allen's** Redskins played in Super Bowl VII in 1973, Houston 1973, Green Bay 1974. He finished his career in Canada with Montreal 1975-76, Calgary 1977, Ottawa 1978-80 and was All-CFL.

PAUL FARNAN quarterbacked Midland High School and St. Vincent's College. He coached Pius X, Warren Hills, NJ and Bangor High Schools from 1965-97 and had a 231-107-13 record.

RALPH FELTON was a fullback, linebacker and kicker at Midway High School near Pittsburgh. He played at Maryland from 1951-53 for **Jim Tatum** and was a 1953 All-American honorable mention as he helped lead the Terrapins to a 10-1 record and the national title. Felton spent nine years with Washington and Buffalo from 1954-62. He had 19 TD's, 16 FG's, and 7 interceptions.

JIM FENNELL coached at Kingston, Wyoming Valley West and Bishop Hoban High Schools from 1955-87 and posted a 204-106-11 record. He developed pro **Ed Rutkowski**.

JACK FERRANTE did not go to high school or college, but played sandlot football for the Seymore Club of Philadelphia. "Blackjack" caught 31 TD's as a 10 year end for the Philadelphia Eagles from 1941-50. **Greasy Neale's** Eagles appeared in three straight NFL title games 1947-49 and beat the Chicago Cards in 1948 and Los Angeles in 1949. Ferrante coached Monsignor Bonner High School from 1955-61, went 40-14-4 and won two Philadelphia City Championships in 1959 and 1961.

LOU FERRY played for Chester's St. James Catholic High School under **Francis "Beans" Brennan**. He was a tackle at Villanova 1945-48 and captain of **Jordan Olivar's** 8-2-1 Wildcats in 1948. Ferry spent seven years from 1949-55 with Green Bay, Chicago Cards, and Pittsburgh. He was the head coach of Villanova from 1970 into the 1974 season and had a 20-25-1 record.

FICCA

DAN FICCA from Atlas was a bruising fullback for the Mt. Carmel High School Red Tornadoes under **Mike Terry**. He went to USC where he was a star guard for the "Fight-On" Trojans from 1958-60 for **Don Clark** and **John McKay**. Ficca spent seven years in the pros with San Diego 1961, Oakland 1962 and the NY Jets 1963-66. He was a 1965 All-AFL guard with the Jets.

ROSS FICHTNER quarterbacked the McKeesport High School Tigers under **Duke Weigle**. He led Purdue from 1957-59 for **Jack Mollenkopf** and was a defensive back in the NFL with Cleveland 1960-68 and New Orleans 1969. Fichtner earned a 1964 NFL title ring as **Blanton Collier's** Browns defeated Baltimore, but lost the 1965 crown to Green Bay. The 1966 All-Pro had 27 picks and 3 TD's.

RALPH FIFE was a 1941 All-American guard at Pitt and played with the Cardinals and Steelers. He coached Mt. Lebanon High School, where he won the 1966 WPIAL title, and Chartiers Valley High Schools with an over-all record of 169-66-0.

FICHTNER

Photo by Henry Barr / DIAMOND IMAGES

FRANK FILCHOK from Grindstone was a tailback for the Redstone High School Blackhawks in Republic, Pennsylvania. He played at Indiana University 1935-37 and then spent 13 years in pro ball with Washington 1938-45, New York 1946 and in Canada with Hamilton and Montreal 1947-50. Filchok earned a 1942 NFL title ring when **Ray Flaherty's** Redskins beat Chicago. The three-time All-Pro, threw for 47 TD's and rushed for 8 TD's. In Canada, Filchock earned a 1949 Grey Cup ring with Montreal and was head coach at Edmonton 1952 and Saskatchewan 1953-57 with a 50-41-5 record. Filchock was the first head coach of the Denver Broncos in the new American Football League in 1960-61 and went 7-20-1.

SCOTT FITZKE was a sprint champion-halfback for the Red Lion High School Lions under **Don Dyke**. He was a wide receiver at Penn State for **Joe Paterno's** Nittany Lions from 1976-78. Fitzke caught 4 TD passes with Philadelphia 1979-80 and San Diego 1981-82. **Dick Vermeil's** Eagles lost Super Bowl XV to Oakland in 1981. He ended his career with **Jim Mora's** USFL champion Philadelphia/Baltimore Stars.

ED FLANAGAN played for the Altoona High School Mountain Lions under **Earl Strohm**. He was an outstanding center for **Jack Mollenkoft's** Purdue Boilermakers from 1962-64. Flanagan spent 12 years in the NFL trenches as the anchor in the lines of the Detroit Lions and San Diego Chargers from 1965-76.

JIM FLANIGAN played for the West Mifflin High School Titans under **Dick Scherbaum** and at Pitt from 1964-66 where he captained the 1966 Panthers. He spent four years as a linebacker with Green Bay and New Orleans from 1967-71. **Vince Lombardi's** Packers defeated Oakland in Super Bowl II in 1968.

FLANNERY

JOHN FLANNERY played for the Pottsville High School Crimson Tide under **Kevin Keating**. He was a center at Syracuse 1987-90 and was a consensus 1990 All-American for **Dick MacPherson's** Orangemen. Flannery was the #2 draft pick of Houston and anchored offensive lines with the Oilers 1991-94, Dallas 1996-97, and St. Louis 1998-99. He was named 1991 All-Rookie and earned a Super Bowl ring as **Dick Vermeil's** Rams defeated Tennessee in SB XXXIV in 2000.

BOB FLECK played for the Phoenixville High School Phantoms and was a two-time All-American guard at Syracuse in 1952 and 1953 for **Ben Schwartzwalder's** Orangemen. He was drafted by Green Bay.

JUDSON FLINT was a halfback for the Farrell High School Steelers. He played at Memphis State and California State, PA. Flint had 3 interceptions with Cleveland from 1980-82 and Buffalo in 1983.

BERNIE FLOWERS from Erie was an end at Purdue from 1950-52 and was a 1952 consensus All-American for **Stu Holcomb**. He was All-CFL with the Ottawa in 1953 and was a Baltimore Colt in 1956.

TOM FLYNN was a quarterback for Penn Hills High School as **Andy Urbanic's** Indians won the 1978 and 1979 WPIAL titles. He was a top defensive back on the great Pitt Panther teams that went 39-8-1 from 1980-83 for **Jackie Sherrill** and **Foge Fazio**. Flynn had 11 interceptions with Green Bay 1984-86 and New York 1986-88 as **Bill Parcells'** Giants beat Denver in Super Bowl XXI in 1987.

BOB FOLWELL from Philadelphia went to the University of Pennsylvania from 1904-07 and was captain of 1907 Quakers that went 11-1 for **Carl Williams**. He coached at Lafayette, Washington and Jefferson, Pennsylvania, and Navy from 1909-24 and went 106-29-7 in 16 years. Folwell's 1923 Navy team went 5-1-3 and tied Washington in the

Rose Bowl. Folwell also coached the professional Philadelphia Quakers to the 1926 American Football League championship.

FRALIC

BILL FRALIC played for Penn Hills High School as **Andy Urbanic's** Indians won the 1978 and 1979 WPIAL titles. As a senior in 1980, Fralic was chosen as Dial's Male Scholastic Athlete of the Year. He was an offensive tackle at Pitt 1981-84 and was a three-time All-American in 1982, 1983 and 1984 for **Serafino "Foge" Fazio's** powerful Panthers. Fralic became the first offensive lineman to finish twice in the top ten of the Heisman Trophy vote when he placed eighth in 1983 and sixth in 1984. Because of Fralic's awesome blocking ability, the Pitt Sports Information Office introduced the term "Pancake" into today's football language for an offensive lineman putting his opponent on his back. He was the first round draft choice of Atlanta and spent nine years with the Falcons from 1985-92 and Detroit in 1993. Fralic, who was a five-time All-Pro, was inducted into the College Football Hall of Fame in 1998.

JOHN FRANK played for the Mt. Lebanon High School Blue Devils under **Art Walker**. He was a tight end at Ohio State for **Earle Bruce** and was a a two-time Academic All-American in 1982 and 1983 for the Buckeyes. Frank caught 10 TD's with the San Francisco 49crs from

1984-88. He earned two Super Bowl rings as **Bill Walsh's** 49ers defeated Miami in SB XIX in 1985 and Cincinnati in SB XXIII in 1989.

FRANKFORD YELLOW JACKETS were champions of the National Football League in 1926. The Yellow Jackets, who were sponsored by the Frankford Athletic Association, played in the NFL from 1924 to 1931 and had a total record of 69-45-14. In 1926, Frankford, a section of Philadelphia, posted a 14-1-1 record for coach **Guy Chamberlain** to earn the NFL crown. Top Yellow Jackets over the years were ends **Heinie Miller** an All-American at Penn, **Whitey Thomas** an All-American at Penn State, **Milt O'Connell** an All-American at Lafayette and **Rae Crowther**; tackles **Al Bednar** an All-Ameican at Lafayette, **John Budd** from Lafayette and **Joe Spagna** from Lehigh; guards **Bill Hoffman** from Lehigh, **Russ "Bull" Behman** from Lebanon Valley and Dickinson and **Joe "Stonewall" Jackson**; center **"Big Bill" Springsteen** from Lehigh; quarterback **Charlie Rogers** of Penn; and backs **Jack Finn**, from Villanova, **Joe Lehecka** from Lafayette, **George Seasholz** from Lafayette, **Jack Storer** of Lehigh, **George Sullivan** of Penn, and **George "Mike" Wilson** from Philly's Northeast High School and Lafayette All-American.

JIM FRASER played for Philadelphia's Germantown High School under **Wilbert Augustin** and was a linebacker at Wisconsin 1956-58. He spent seven years with Denver, KC, Boston, New Orleans 1962-68

MIKE FREDERICK played for the Neshaminy High School Redskins in Langhorne, Pennsylvania under coach **John Chaump**. He was a star defensive end at Virginia 1991-94 and was co-captain and 1994 All-ACC for **George Welsh's** 9-3 Cavaliers. Frederick has been in the NFL since 1995 with Cleveland, Baltimore, NY Jets and Tennessee. **Jeff Fisher's** Titans lost Super Bowl XXXV in 2000 to St. Louis.

RUSS FREEMAN played for Pittsburgh's Allderdice High School Dragons under **Mark Wittgartner**. As a junior offensive tackle at Ga.Tech, he helped lead **Bobby Ross'** 11-0-1 Yellow Jackets to the 1990 national championship. Freeman spent four years in the NFL with Denver 1992-94 and Oakland 1995.

GUS FREROTTE quarterbacked the Ford City High School Sabres from 1986-88 for **Harry Beckwith**. In 1987, he led Ford City to it's only WPIAL play-off appearance in the school's history since 1908. Frerotte played at Tulsa for **Dave Rader's** Hurrricanes from 1990-93. Frerotte has thrown 30 TD passes in the NFL since 1994 with Washington 1994-98, Detroit 1999 and Denver in 2000.

MITCH FREROTTE played for the Kittaning High School Wildcats under **Harry Beckwith**. He was an offensive guard at Penn State 1983-86 for **Joe Paterno** and the 1986 Nittany Lions won the national championship. He has spent eight years in the NFL with Buffalo 1987-92 and Seattle 1993-94. **Marv Levy's** Bills appeared in three straight Super Bowls in 1991, 1992 and 1993.

FRANK FULLER was a tackle for the DuBois High School Beavers and at Kentucky from 1950-52 for **Paul "Bear" Bryant's** nationally ranked Wildcats. He spent 11 years with Los Angeles, St. Louis and Philadelphia from 1953-63. **Sid Gillman's** Rams lost the 1955 NFL title to Cleveland. Fuller was a 1960 All-Pro defensive tackle for the Cardinals.

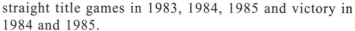
FUSINA

CHUCK FUSINA from McKees Rocks played for the Sto-Rox High School Vikings under **Steve Wargo**. At Penn State from 1976-78, he threw for a career record of 5,140 yards and 37 TD's. Fusina was a 1978 All-American and won the Maxwell Award as the nation's most outstanding player and was runner-up for the Heisman Trophy to Oklahoma's **Billy Sims**. He spent seven years in pro ball with Tampa Bay 1979-81, Philly/Baltimore Stars in the USFL 1983-85, and Green Bay 1986. Fusina, the USFL's 1984 MVP, led **Jim Mora's** Stars to three straight title games in 1983, 1984, 1985 and victory in 1984 and 1985.

ARNOLD GALIFFA played for Donora High School as **Jimmie Russell's** Dragons won the 1944 and 1945 WPIAL titles. He was a quarterback at West Point 1946-49 and led **Earl "Red" Blaik's** Cadets to undefeated seasons in 1948 and 1949. Galiffa, who had 1,947 career yards passing and 21 TD's, was a 1949 All-American and was fourth in the Heisman Trophy vote, won by Notre Dame's **Leon Hart** from Turtle Creek. After military service, Gallifa played for the NY Giants in 1953 and San Francisco in 1954. He went in the College Football Hall of Fame in 1983.

FRANK GALLAGHER played for Chester's St. James Catholic High School. He went to North Carolina where he was an offensive guard from 1961-63. **Jim Hickey's** Tar Heels went 9-2 in 1963. Gallagher was a seven year vet with Detroit 1967-72 plus Minnesota and Atlanta in 1973.

GALIFFA

RICH GANNON quarterbacked Philadelphia's St. Joseph Prep Hawklets under **Jack Branka**. He went to Delaware 1983-86 and was a 1986 All-American honorable mention QB as he paced **Tubby Raymond's** Blue Hens to the NCAA I-AA quarterfinals. Gannon has been in the NFL since 1987 with Minnesota, Washington, Kansas City and Oakland. The 14 year vet was a 2000 All-Pro as he passed for a career season high of 3,430 yards and 28 TD's and led **Jon Gruden's** Raiders to the AFC title game. Gannon has thrown for 18,428 yards and 118 TD's.

GANNON

BOB GAONA played for the Ambridge High School Bridgers under **Moe Rubenstein** and was a 1952 All-Southern guard at Wake Forest. He was with Pittsburgh 1953-56 and Philadelphia in 1957.

GARBISCH

EDGAR GARBISCH from Washington was a center and kicker at West Point from 1921-24. He starred as a sophomore on **Charles Daly's** 1922 Army team that went unbeaten at 8-0-2 and was captain of the 1924 Cadets as his four field goals beat Navy 12-0. Garbisch was a two-time All-American in 1922 and 1924 and went in the College Football Hall of Fame in 1954.

GREGG GARRITY played for the North Allegheny High School Tigers in Wexford, Pennsylvania under **Robert Miller**. He was a wide receiver at Penn State from 1980-82 for **Joe Paterno** as the 1982 Nittany Lions went 11-0 for the national championship. Garrity caught 6 TD's with Pittsburgh and Philadelphia from 1983-89.

JIM GARRY played for Monongahela High School and at Wake Forest from 1946-49. He was coach of McDonald High School in 1958 and Fort Cherry High School in 1959 when the McDonald, Hickory and Midway schools merged. In 40 years at "The Fort," Garry's Rangers went 232-151-14. He coached **Marty** and **Kurt Schottenhiemer**, **Marvin Lewis**, **Brad Tokar**, and **Perry Kemp**.

RICH GARZA was a guard/center for Bethlehem's Liberty High School for **Bob Buffman** and at Temple 1976-80. He was three-time All-USFL with Philadelphia and San Antonio 1983-85.

JOE GASPARELLA from Apollo played for the Vandergrift High School Blue Lancers under coach **Ted Rosenweig**. He was a quarterback at Notre Dame in 1944-45. Gasparella threw 10 TD passes with Pittsburgh 1948-50 and Chicago Cardinals 1951.

CHARLIE GAUER was an end for Upper Darby High School Royals and Colgate 1939-41 for the legendary **Andy Kerr**. He was with Philly 1943-45 and long-time Eagles assistant coach.

GENE GEDMAN was a halfback for the Duquesne High School Dukes and Indiana University 1950-52 for **Bernie Crimmins'** Hoosiers. "The Baron" spent six years with Detroit 1953-58. The Lions appeared in three NFL championship games against Cleveland and won two of them when **Buddy Parker's** Lions won in 1953 and as **George Wilson's** Lions won in 1957. Gedman rushed for 1,221 yards, 17 TD's, caught 53 passes for 504 yards, 4 TD's for a total of 21 TD's.

STAN GELBAUGH threw for over 2,000 yards and 21 TD's from 1978-80 for the Cumberland Valley High School Eagles in Mechanicsburg, Pennsylvania under **Harry Chapman III**. He went to Maryland where he helped lead **Bobby Ross'** Terrapins to ACC championships in 1984 and 1985. Gelbaugh threw 10 TD's with Buffalo 1986-89 and Seattle 1992-95. He directed the London Monarches to the 1991 WLAF championship over **Scott Erney**-led Barcelona.

BRIAN GELZHEISER was a quarterback for the Baldwin High School Highlanders under **Don Yannessa**. He was a linebacker at Penn State from 1991-94 for **Joe Paterno** and was the Nittany Lions #2 all-time tackler with 315 career tackles. He was with Indianapolis in 1995-96.

B. GEORGE

BILL GEORGE played for the Waynesburg High School Raiders. He was a tackle at Wake Forest 1948-51 for **D. C. "Peahead" Walker** and then **Tom Rogers**. As a sophomore in 1949, George was an All-American defensive tackle for the Demon Deacons. "The Friendly Greek" was the second round draft choice of Chicago and was a linebacker in the NFL with the Bears from 1951-65 and the Los Angeles Rams in 1966. During his 14 year career in "the Windy City," Chicago lost the 1956 NFL championship game to New York, but in 1963 the Bears under coach **George Halas** defeated the Giants to capture the NFL crown. George, who was an eight-time All-Pro, had 18 career interceptions. He went in the the Pro Football Hall of Fame in 1974.

E. GEORGE

EDDIE GEORGE went to Abington High School, but did not play football in high school. He went to Fork Union Military Academy in Virginia and then Ohio State from 1992-95 for **John Cooper** where he was the all-time leading ball carrier in Buckeye history with 3,889 yards. As a senior in 1995, George rushed for 1,927 yards and 24 TD's for the 11-2 Buckeyes. The Buckeye co-captain was All-American and won both the Heisman Trophy and Maxwell Award as the nation's most outstanding player. George was the NFL's 1996 Rookie of the Year with Houston and helped lead **Jeff Fisher's** Tennessee Titans to Super Bowl XXXIV in 2000. His career stats include 6,874 yards rushing for 42 TD's, 164 catches for 1,447 yards and 8 TD's for a total of 50 TD's.

JOE GERENCSER was a halfback for Northampton High School under coach Al Erdosy and at Moravian College 1954-55. He was coach at Parkland High School in Orefield, Pennsylvania from 1962-75 and went 97-36-7 and at Whitehall High School from 1976-86 and went 87-33-3. His over-all record was 184-69-10 in 25 years from 1962-86 with three undefeated teams.

JOE GERI was a halfback for Phoenixville High School and at Georgia for **Wally Butts** 1946-48. He scored 12 TD's, passed for 13 TD's at Pittsburgh 1949-51 and Chicago Cardinals 1952.

ELIO GHIGIARELLI went to Old Forge High School and the University of Scranton. He coached the Old Forge Blue Devils for 30 years from 1947-76 with a 202-89-27 record.

SEAN GILBERT was a lineman for Aliquippa High School as **Don Yannessa's** Quips won the the 1987 WPIAL title. He played at Pitt from 1988-91 for **Mike Gottfried** and **Paul Hackett**. The first round draft choice of Los Angeles has been in the NFL since 1992 with the Rams 1992-95, Washington 1996-97 and Carolina since 1998. Gilbert was a 1983 All-Pro.

GILCHRIST

CARLTON "COOKIE" GILCHRIST scored 122 points in 1953 for Har-Brack Union High School in Brackenridge, Pennsylvania as **Kenny Karl's** Tigers won the WPIAL co-championship with Donora. He did not go to college, but signed with Cleveland as an 18 year-old out of high school, however, because of NFL rules, Gilchrist had to play in Canada until his college class graduated. "Cookie" became a five-time CFL all-star fullback/linebacker 1956-60 with Hamilton, Saskatchewan and Toronto. **Jim Trimble's** Tiger-Cats won the 1957 Grey Cup. Gilchrist spent seven years in the AFL with Buffalo 1962-64, Denver 1965, 1967, Miami 1966. **Lou Saban's** Bills defeated San Diego for the 1964 AFL title. Gilchrist, three-time All-AFL, rushed for 4,293 yards, 37 TD's, caught 110 passes for 1,135 yards, 6 TD's. He had 43 total TD's.

JOHN GILDEA was a halfback for the Coaldale High School Tigers under **Tom Raymer** and at St. Bonaventure from 1932-34. The Little All-American was with Pittsburgh 1935-37 and New York 1938. He scored 6 TD's and was a 1937 All-Pro for **Johnny "Blood" McNally's** Steelers.

JOE GLADYS was a quarterback for Monessen High School in 1945-46 and at Fairmont State College in West Virginia from 1947-50. He coached the Monessen High School Greyhounds for 23 years from 1960-82, went 153-64-9 and won the 1961 WPIAL title. Monessen had early day pros in **Len Frketich, Jack Maskas, George Nickisch, Armand Niccolai** and **John Popovich**, but Gladys developed eight more pros at MHS in **Tony Benjamin, Eric Crabtree, Doug Crusan, Julius Dawkins,** his son **Eugene Gladys, Sam Havrilak, Jo Jo Heath,** and **Bill Malinchak.**

JOE GLAMP played for Mt. Pleasant High School and was a halfback at LSU in 1942 along with future Hall of Famer, **Steve Van Buren.** He scored one TD with Pittsburgh 1947-49.

BILL GLASSFORD from Pittsburgh was a 1936 All-American guard at Pitt for **Jock Sutherland** as the Panthers went 8-1-1, beat Washington in the Rose Bowl, and were ranked #3 in the nation. Glassford was head coach of Nebraska from 1949-55 and had a 31-35-3 record, produced three All-Americans and took the Cornhuskers to their first Orange Bowl.

LARRY GLUECK played for the Lansdale Catholic High School Crusaders and at Villanova for **Alex Bell** from 1960-62. He spent four years in the NFL as a defensive back for Chicago from 1963-66. **George Halas'** Bears defeated New York for the 1963 NFL championship. Glueck was head coach of Fordham from 1986-93 and went 30-51-0 in eight years.

ART GOB played for the Baldwin High School Highlanders and was an end at Pitt 1956-58 for **John Michelson.** He was with Washington 1959 and the LA Chargers in 1960 as **Sid Gilman's** Chargers lost the AFL title to Houston.

MICKEY GORHAM was All-State for Wilkes-Barre's GAR High School and graduated from Notre Dame in 1960. He coached St. Lawrence High School in Utica, Michigan, Bellflower, California and then Wilkes-Barre's Elmer L. Meyers High School for 24 years from 1966-80 and won 163 games. He developed such pros as **Raghib "Rocket"** and **Qadry "Missle" Ismail.**

PETE GOIMARAC was a center for the Charleroi High School Cougars under **James "Rab" Currie.** He went to Notre Dame and played at West Virginia 1961-63 and was captain and a 1963 All-American for **Gene Corum's** Mountaineers. He was drafted by Philly and San Diego.

PETE GORGONE was a fullback for the Windber High School Ramblers and a 1942 Little All-American at Muhlenberg. He spent 1946 with New York as **Steve Owen's** Giants lost the NFL title to Chicago. Gorgone ended his career with the 1947 AFL champion Bethlehem Bulldogs.

BRUCE GOSSETT played for Cecil Township High School and at Clarion State, Duquesne, and Richmond. An outstanding kicker, Gossett spent 11 years in the NFL from 1964-74 with LA and San Francisco. Gossett, a 1966 All-Pro, kicked 219 FG's and 374 PAT's for 1,031 points.

DON GRAHAM played for the Brentwood High School Spartans and was a linebacker at Penn State from 1983-86. As a senior in 1986 he helped lead **Joe Paterno's** Nittany Lions to 12-0 season and the national championship. Graham spent 1987-88 with Tampa Bay and Wahington.

HAROLD "RED" GRANGE considered by many as the greatest runner of all time was born in Forksville, Pennsylvania on June 13, 1903. When he was five years old, his mother died, and his father later moved the family to Wheaton, Illinois. Grange was a star halfback at Wheaton High School and was a three-time All-American in 1923, 1924 and 1925 at the University of Illinois. He was with the Chicago Bears in 1925, 1928-34 and the AFL's New York Yankees in 1926. Grange was a charter inductee in the Pro Football Hall of Fame in 1963.

PERCY "RED" GRIFFITHS played for the Taylor High School Trojans, Bloomsburg and then at Penn State where he was a 1920 All-American guard for **Hugo Bezdek's** 7-0-2 Nittany Lions. "Red" played for the Canton Bulldogs in 1921 and coached Dickinson in 1929-30.

BUCKY GREELEY was a center for Wilkes-Barre's James M. Coughlin High School Crusaders and at Penn State from 1991-94 for **Joe Paterno**. He was a co-captain of the 1994 Nittany Lions that went 12-0 and ranked #2 in the nation. Greeley was with the Carolina Panthers 1996-99.

D. GREEN

DENNIS GREEN played for Harrisburg's John Harris High School under **George Chaump** in 1965-66 and was a halfback at Iowa from 1968-70 for **Ray Nagel**. He was a defensive back for the British Columbia Lions in Canada in 1971. Green was head coach at Northwestern 1981-85 and went 10-45-0, Stanford 1989-91 and went 16-20-0, and has returned the Minnesota Vikings back into a NFL powerhouse since 1992 with a record of 95-59-0.

JOHN GREENE played for Pittsburgh's Westinghouse High School Bulldogs and at Michigan where he played on **Fritz Crisler's** 1943 8-1 Wolverine team. Greene was a seven year veteran end with the Detroit Lions from 1944-50. He had 175 receptions for 2,965 yards and 26 TD's.

BEN GREGORY was a halfback for the Uniontown High School Red Raiders under **Bill Power** and **Leon Kaltenbach**. He was an Academic All-Big 8 halfback at Nebraska 1965-67 for **Bob Devaney's** Cornhuskers. Gregory was with Buffalo 1968-69 and Canada's Hamilton Tiger-Cats.

RUSS GRIMM from Scottdale was a quarterback and lineman for Southmoreland High School Scotties under **John Bacha**. He was an offensive guard at Pitt for **Jackie Sherrill's** powerful Panthers that posted a 30-6 record from 1978-80. Grimm spent 11 years in Washington 1981-91. He was one of the "Hogs" in the mammoth Redskins offensive line that paved the way for three Super Bowl rings in the "Nation's Capitol." The five-time All-Pro helped lead **Joe Gibbs'** Skins' to defeat Miami in SB XVII in 1983, Denver in SB XXII in 1988, and Buffalo in SB XXVI in 1992. As the "Boss Hog" of the most celebrated offensive line in pro history, LG Grimm was linemates with RT **George Strake**, RG **Mark May**, C **Jeff Bostic** and LT **Joe Jacoby**.

GRIMM

BURT GROSSMAN played for Philadelphia's Archbishop Carroll High School Patriots under coach **Kevin Clancy**. He was a defensive end for **Mike Gottfried's** Pitt Panthers from 1985-88. Grossman was the #1 draft choice of San Diego in 1989 and spent six years in the NFL with the Chargers and Philadelphia from 1989-94. He recorded 3 safeties.

R. GROSSMAN

RANDY GROSSMAN was a receiver for record setting QB **Steve Joachim** at Haverford High School in 1968-69. He caught 10 TD's at Temple from 1971-73 for **Wayne Hardin** and was a 1973 All-American for the high-scoring 9-1 Owls. Grossman caught 5 TD's with Pittsburgh from 1974-81. He earned four Super Bowl rings as **Chuck Noll's** Steelers beat Minnesota in SB IX in 1975, Dallas in SB X in 1976, Dallas in SB XIII in 1979, and Los Angeles in SB XIV in 1980.

BOB GRUPP played for the Neshaminy High School Redskins in Langhorne, Pennsylvania. He was a punter at Duke from 1973-76 and with Kansas City from 1979-82 where he was All-Pro.

DICK GUESSMAN was a tackle for Brownsville High School Brownies under **Warner Fritsch** and at West Virginia 1956-58. He was with Detroit 1959, NY Titans/Jets 1960-63, Denver 1964.

MIKE GUMAN played for the Bethlehem Catholic Golden Hawks under **Jim Mazza**. The Lehigh Valley's scholar-athlete turned down a Major League Baseball contract with the Texas Rangers and was a running back at Penn State from 1976-79. Guman was a 1979 Academic All-American for **Joe Paterno's** Nittany Lions. He played for the LA Rams 1980-88. The versatile Guman, who was a crushing blocker out of the backfield for **Eric Dickerson**, rushed for 1,286 yards and 11 TD's, caught 151 passes for 1,433 yards and 4 TD's, and threw 2 TD passes.

JOHN GURSKI played for Coal Township near Shamokin and the University of Pennsylvania from 1952-54. He coached Minersville High School 1958-

GUMAN

63 and went 47-13-2 and Wilson High School of West Lawn 1964-82 and went 151-44-4. His over-all record was 198-57-6 in 25 years.

AL GURSKY was a halfback for the Governor Mifflin High School Mustangs in Shillington, Pennsylvania under **Ray Linn**. He played at Penn State from 1960-62 for **Rip Engle** and was a linebacker with New York in 1963 as **Allie Sherman's** Giants lost the NFL title to Chicago.

ANDY GUSTAFSON from Pittsburgh was the leading scorer at Pitt from 1923-25 for **Jock Sutherland**. He was an assistant to **Earl "Red" Blaik** at West Point when he took over as head coach of Miami of Florida in 1948. Gustafson coached the Hurricanes for 16 years from 1948-63 and went 93-65-0. During Gustafson's "Glory Years," he produced nine first team All-Americans including five Pennsylvanians in **Nick Chickillo, Fran Curci, Bill Miller, Dan Connors** and **Ed Weisacosky**. Gustafson went into the College Football Hall of Fame in 1985.

JOHN GUTKUNST was a quarterback for the Pennridge High School Rams in Perkasie, Pennsylvania under **Wayne Helman**. He played at Duke from 1963-65 for **Bill Murray**. The Blue Devils' captain was coach of University of Minnesota from 1986-91 and went 29-36-2.

MELWOOD "BUZZ" GUY was a fullback for the Ellwood City High School Wolverines under **Al Como**. He was a guard at Duke from 1955-57 for **Bill Murray's** nationally ranked Blue Devils. "Buzz" played for New York in 1958 and 1959 as **Jim Lee Howell's** Giants lost two straight NFL titles to Baltimore. He finished at Dallas 1960-61 and Denver 1962.

JOHN "BULL" GUZIK from Lawrence played for Cecil Township High School. He was a guard at Pitt 1956-58 for **John Michelosen** and was a 1958 All-American and Academic All-American for the Panthers. "Bull," already drafted by Los Angeles as a junior, was with the Rams 1959-60 and Houston 1961. **Wally Lemm's** Oilers beat San Diego for the 1961 AFL crown.

GUZIK

DICK HALEY played at Midway High School and was a versatile halfback at Pitt from 1956-58 for **John Michelosen's** Panthers. Haley spent six years in the NFL secondary from 1959-64 with Washington, Minnesota and Pittsburgh. He had 14 interceptions and scored 2 TD's.

ED HALICKI played for Hanover High School near Wilkes-Barre and was **Carl Snavely's** line smashing fullback at Bucknell 1926-28. He had 10 TD's for Frankford Yellow Jackets 1929-30.

CHARLIE HALL played for the Lower Merion High School Bulldogs near Philadelphia and was a defensive back at Pitt from 1968-70. He had 2 picks with Green Bay from 1971-76.

GALEN HALL quarterbacked Williamsburg High School and Penn State from 1959-61 for **Rip Engle**. He was with Washington in 1962 and the New York Jets in 1963. Hall was the head coach of Florida from 1985-89 as the Gators went 22-17-2 and appeared in two bowl games.

HAM

JACK HAM played for Johnstown's Bishop McCort High School Crushers under **Al Fletcher**. After attending Massanutten in Virginia, Ham was a linebacker at Penn State from 1968-70 as **Joe Paterno's** Nittany Lions went 29-3. He was a 1970 consensus All-American. Ham spent 12 years with Pittsburgh 1971-82. Pittsburgh appeared in four Super Bowls and Ham earned four rings when **Chuck Noll's** Steelers defeated Minnesota in SB IX in 1975, Dallas in SB X in 1976, Dallas in SB XIII in 1979, and Los Angeles in SB XIV in 1980. The three-time All-Pro had 32 interceptions, recovered 21 fumbles, and scored two TD's. Known to the Slovak Steeler fans as Dobre Shunka, "Great Ham," he played in eight straight Pro Bowls, went into the Pro Football Hall of Fame in 1988 and the College Football Hall of Fame in 1990.

HARRY HAMILTON played for the Nanticoke High School Trojans. He was a defensive back at Penn State 1980-83 and helped **Joe Paterno's** 1982 Nittany Lions go 11-1 for the national crown. Hamilton, who was a 1983 All-Amrican and two-time Academic All-American, had 23 interceptions as an eight year veteran with the New York Jets and Tampa Bay from 1984-91.

JOE HAMILTON coached at Midland, New Brighton, Hempfield and Blackhawk High Schools from 1966-99 and went 245-104-10. His Blackhawk Cougars won four WPIAL championships in 1991, 1992, 1993 and 1996.

LOU HANNA played for Slippery Rock College. He coached at Corry Area High School for 22 years and went 123-63-7. His over-all record in 30 years of coaching was 173-86-9.

HANRATTY

TERRY HANRATTY scored 16 TD's and 118 points in 1964 for the Butler High School Golden Tornadoes under **Art Bernardi**. He was Notre Dame's field general from 1966-68 for **Ara Parseghian**. As a sophomore "Baby Bomber," with end **Jim Seymour**, he helped lead the Fighting Irish to 9-0-1 season and the 1966 national title. Hanratty was a consensus 1968 All-American as he broke the immortal **George Gipp's** total yardage record at ND with 4,738 yards and 27 TD's. In three years 1966, 1967, and 1968, Hanratty finished sixth, ninth, and third, respectively, in the Heisman Trophy vote. He spent eight years with Pittsburgh 1969-75 and Tampa Bay 1976. Hanratty earned two Super Bowl rings as **Chuck Noll's** Steelers beat Minnesota in SB IX in 1975 and Dallas in SB X in 1976. He had 165 completions for 2,510 yards and 24 TD's.

JACK HARDING from Pittsburgh was a halfback at Pitt from 1923-25 under **Jock Sutherland**. He was AD and head coach at Miami of Florida 1937-42, 1945-47 and moved the new school into major college gridiron status. Harding went 54-32-3 in nine years and became Miami's first football legend. He chose **Andy Gustafson**, who was his teammate at Pitt, as his successor in 1948. Harding was inducted into the College Football Hall of Fame in 1980.

HARVEY HARMAN from Selinsgrove was a four-year starting tackle at Pitt from 1918-21 for **Glenn "Pop" Warner**. He was head coach at Haverford, Sewanee, Pennsylvania from 1931-37 and Rutgers 1938-41, 1946-55 with an over-all record of 140-104-7. The popular Harman was Executive Director of the National Football Foundation and Hall of Fame from 1956 until his death in 1969. He was inducted into the College Football Hall of Fame in 1981.

MARVIN HARRISON was an all-purpose performer with 3,266 total yards and 36 TD's from 1988-90 for Philadelphia's Roman Catholic High School Cahillites under **Ed Brodbine**. He played at Syracuse from 1992-95 for **Paul Pasqualoni**, was a 1995 All-American and became the Orangeman's all-time top receiver with 135 receptions for 2,728 yards and 20 TD's. "Marvelous Marvin" was the #1 draft choice of Indy and has been with the Colts since 1996. All-Pro 1996.

LEON HART played for the Turtle Creek High School Creekers under **Ben Haldy**. He was a four-year starting end at Notre Dame 1946-49 and was a major force as **Frank Leahy's** Figthing Irish won three national crowns in 1946, 1947, and 1949. The Irish were ranked #2 in 1948. Hart, a three-time All-American in 1947, 1948, 1949, won both the Heisman Trophy and Maxwell Award in 1949 and was also the AP's Athlete of the Year. He was the #1 over-all draft pick of Detroit and spent eight years with the Lions 1950-57. The Lions played in four NFL title games and won three as **Buddy Parker's** Lions beat Cleveland in 1952, 1953 and **George Wilson's** Lions beat Cleveland in 1957. Hart, a 1951 All-Pro on both offense and defense, had 172 receptions for 2,499 yards and 26 TD's. He went in the College Football Hall of Fame in 1973.

DICK HART played for Morrisville High School, but did not play college football. He was an offensive guard for the Philadlphia Eagles from 1967-70 and Buffalo Bills in 1972.

MAJOR HARRIS quarterbacked Pittsburgh's Bradshear High School Bullets, now called Bulls, under **Ron Wabby**. He played at West Virginia from 1987-89 and led **Don Nehlin's** 1988 Mountaineers to a 11-1 record and the #2 national ranking. Harris, who set a WV career total offense record of 7,334 yards, was a two-time All-American in 1988 and 1989 and finished fifth and third in the in the Heisman Trophy vote. He left school after his junior year when drafted by the LA Rams, but he played for CFL's British Columbia in 1990 and five years in the Arena League.

MIKE HARTENSTINE caught 4 TD's in 1970 for Bethlehem's Liberty High School under **Bob Buffman**. He was a defensive end at Penn State 1972-74 for **Joe Paterno** and was a 1974 All-American and Chevrolet's Defensive Player of the Year for the Nittany Lions. Hartenstine was the #2 draft choice of Chicago and was with the Bears 1975-86 and Minnesota 1987. The 13 year veteran earned a Super Bowl ring as **Mike Ditka's** Bears beat New England in SB XX in 1986.

RON HATCHER was a fullback for Carnegie High School and at Michigan State from 1959-61 for **Duffy Daugherty**. He was with Washington in 1962 and Tornoto in Canada in 1963-64.

HARTENSTINE

L. HART

CARLTON HASERIG played for Johnstown High School Trojans under **Bob Arcurio**. He did not play college football at the University of Pittsburgh-Johnstown campus, but was a six-time NCAA heavyweight wrestling champion. He was drafted in the 12th round by Pittsburgh and spent five years as defensive end with the Steelers 1990-93 and NY Jets 1995.

JIM HASLETT played for the Avalon High School Panthers and at Indiana State, Pennsylvania where he was a three-time All-American defensive end in 1976, 1977 and 1978 for **Bill Neal's** Indians. He spent eight years with Buffalo and New York Jets from 1979-85. Haslett, who was the NFL's 1979 Defensive Rookie-of-the-Year, was a 1980 All-Pro linebacker with the Bills. He took over as head coach of the New Orleans Saints in 1999 and was named NFL's Coach of the Year in 2000. Haslett was inducted into the College Football Hall of Fame in 2001.

SAM HAVRILAK played for the Monessen High School Greyhounds under **Joe Gladys**. He was a quarterback at Bucknell 1966-68 where he set a single-game total offense record of 397 yards and was a 1968 All-American honorable mention. Havrilak was a halfback with Baltimore from 1969-72 and scored 7 TD's. **Don Shula's** Colts lost Super Bowl III to the NY Jets in 1969, but **Don McCafferty's** Colts beat Dallas in Super Bowl V in 1971.

ARTRELL HAWKINS was a halfback for the Johnstown High School Trojans and was a defensive back at the University of Cincinnati from 1994-97. He has been with the Bengals since 1998.

GEORGE HAYS was a lineman for the Glassport High School Gladiators and St. Bonaventure from 1946-49. He spent four years in the NFL with Pittsburgh 1950-52 and Green Bay 1953.

JONATHAN HAYES played for the South Fayette High School Lions under **Bob Babich**. He was at Iowa 1981-84 and was a 1984 All-American tight end for **Hayden Fry's** 8-4-1 Hawkeyes. Hayes was a 12 year vet with Kansas City 1985-93, Pittsburgh 1994-96. **Bill Cowher's** Steelers lost Super Bowl XXX in 1996 to Dallas. Hayes had 153 receptions for 1,718 yards and 13 TD's.

HAZLETON'S JAW BREAKING NAMES or as **Knute Rockne** once quipped about talent, "If you can't pronounce'em, they're good ones." Hazleton High School went undefeated in 1938 and 1939 under coach **Stan Oleniczak** who had good players such as backs **Joe Anrdejco, George Cheverko, Mike Vuksanovich**, and guard **John Yackanich**. The fab four then played together with nationally ranked Fordham. The four Rams from the same PA high school gained fame when their photograph with their jaw breaking names appeared in the New York Journal-American. Another Hazleton player was **Vladimir Palanuik**, who went to North Carolina for football, but later graduated from Stanford in 1946 and then became an Academy Award winning actor, better known to cinema fans as **Jack Palance**.

JO JO HEATH played for the Monessen High School Greyhounds under **Joe Gladys**. A corner back at Pitt 1976-79, Heath was a freshman on **Johnny Majors** 1976 Panther national title team. Heath spent eight years in pro ball with Cincinnati 1980, Philadelphia 1981, British Columbia in Canada 1983-86 and the NY Jets in 1987. The BC Lions lost the 1983 Grey Cup to Toronto.

RALPH HECK played for the Penn Hills High School Indians. He was a guard at Colorado in 1960-61 for **Sonny Grandelius'** 15-6 Buffaloes. Heck had 5 interceptions and one TD as a nine year veteran linebacker with Philadelphia, Atlanta and NY Giants from 1963-71.

VEL HECKMAN was a lineman for the Allentown High School Canaries under **Perry Scott** and at Florida 1954-58 where he was a 1958 All-American. He was drafted by San Francisco 1959.

GENE HEETER played for the Windber High School Ramblers under **John Kawchak**. Heeter went to West Virginia 1960-62 and as a tight end caught 2 TD's with the NY Jets from 1963-65.

HEISMAN TROPHY, which is officially called the **John W. Heisman** Memorial Trophy, has been awarded each year since 1935 to to the nation's outstanding college football player by the Downtown Athletic Club of New York. The trophy was named in honor of Heisman who was born in 1869 in Cleveland, Ohio and went to Titusville High School in Pennsylvania Heisman played at Brown and at Penn from 1887-1891 and then coached college football for 36 years at Oberlein, Akron, Auburn, Clemson, Georgia Tech, Penn, Washington and Jefferson and Rice. After his coaching days, Heisman became the first athletic director of the Downtown Athletic Club in New York and was inducted into the College Football Hall of Fame in 1954. Heisman Trophy winners from Pennsylvania are: 1936-**Larry Kelly** end from Williamsport High School and Yale; 1947-**Johnny Lujack** quarterback from Connellsville High School and Notre Dame; 1949-**Leon Hart** end from Turtle Creek High School and Notre Dame; 1973-**John Cappelletti** running back from Monsignor Bonner High School and Penn State; 1976-**Tony Dorsett** running back from Hopewell High School and Pitt; 1995-**Eddie George** running back from Abington High School (he did not play football in high school) and Ohio State. Two other Heisman Trophy winners were born in Pennsylvania, but moved to other states in their youth were 1942-**Frank Sinkwich** halfback from Georgia, was born in McKeesport, Pennsylvania, but went to high school in Youngstown, Ohio and 1961-**Ernie Davis** halfback from Syracuse, was born in Uniontown, Pennsylvania, but moved to Elmira, New York, at age 13 and played for Elmira's Free Academy.

WARREN HELLER was a triple-threat halfback for the Steelton High School Steamrollers under **J. Paul Rupp**. "The Steelton Thunderbolt" played at Pitt from 1930-32 and was a 1932 consensus All-American as he paced **Jock Sutherland's** Panthers to a 8-1-2 record and the Rose Bowl against USC. Heller scored 3 TD's with the Pittsburgh Steelers from 1932-35.

WAYNE HELMAN was an end for the Lansdale High School Huskies under **Ken Poust** and at Penn from 1944, 1946-48 for **George Munger's** nationally ranked Quakers. He coached the Pennridge High School Rams in Perkasie, Pennsylvania from 1955-80 and went 168-90-2 in 26 years. He developed four pros in **Jake Crouthamel**, **Tim** and **Will Lewis** and **Robb Riddick**.

JON HENDERSON played for Pittsburgh's Westinghouse High School under **Pete Dimperio**. He was an end at Colorado State and had 6 TD's with Pittsburgh 1968-69 and Washington 1970.

JOHN HENZES, SR. played at St. Procopius Boys School in Illinois and at East Stroudsburg State. "Papa Bear" coached the Blakely High School Bears for 33 years with 251-51-14 record.

JOHN "JACK" HENZES, JR. played for his father, **John Henzes, Sr.**, at Blakely High School and then at George Washington University. He coached at Wyoming Area High School from 1966-69 and went 31-12-0 and at Dunmore High School since 1971 with a 225-106-8 record and the 1989 PIAA 1A state championship led by pro **Tim Ruddy**. His over-all record is 256-118-8.

KEN HEROCK played for the Munhall High School Indians under **Nick Kliskey** and at West Virginia from 1960-62. He caught 4 TD's as a tight end and linebacker for seven years from 1963-69 in the AFL with Oakland, Cincinnati and Boston. **John Rauch's** Raiders defeated Houston for the 1967 AFL title, but lost Super Bowl II in 1968 to Green Bay.

BILLY HESS played for the Parkland High School Trojans in Orefield, Pennsylvania under **Tom Filipovits**. He was a 1988 Little All-American wide receiver at West Chester U. for **Danny Hale**. He was with the Eagles, Cardinals, and the CFL's San Antonio and Ottawa from 1989-96.

ERIC HICKS played for Erie's Mercyhurst Prep Lakers. He was a star defensive end at Maryland 1994-97 and has been one of the NFL's top sack leaders with Kansas City since 1998.

JACK HINKLE played for Milton Hershey High School and at Syracuse 1937-39. He scored 7 TD's with New York 1940 and Philadelphia 1941-47 as the Eagles lost the 1947 championship.

DICK HOAK played for the Jeannette High School Jayhawks under coach **A. Markley Barnes**. He was a halfback at Penn State for **Rip Engle** from 1958-60. The versatile Hoak spent 10 years with Pittsburgh from 1961-70. He gained 3,965 yards, scored 25 TD's plus had 142 receptions for 1,452 yards, 8 TD's for 33 TD's. He's been an assistant coach with Pittsburgh since 1971 and earned four Super Bowl rings as the Steelers were the NFL's Team of the Decade in 1970's.

NATE HOBGOOD-CHITTICK played for Allentown's William Allen High School Canaries under **Rich Snisack**. He was a defensive lineman at North Carolina for **Mack Brown** 1994-97. "Hobby" has been in with NY Giants, St. Louis and San Francisco since 1998 and earned a Super Bowl ring when **Dick Vermeil's** Rams beat Tennesse in SB XXXIV in 2000.

BILL HOLLENBACK from Phillipsburg, Pennsylvania played at the University of Pennsylvania where he was captain and 1908 All-American halfback for **Sol Metzger's** Quakers who went 11-0-1 and were national champions. Hollenback coached at Penn State, Missouri and Syracuse and was inducted into the College Football Hall of Fame.

RANDY HOLLOWAY was a two-way end for the Sharon High School Tigers. A defensive tackle at Pitt 1974-77, he helped lead **Johnny Majors'** Panthers to the 1976 national title. Holloway was a consensus 1977 All-American. He was the #1 draft pick of Minnesota and spent seven years with the Vikings 1978-84 and St. Louis 1984. He had 7 picks and scored one TD.

HOLOVAK

MIKE HOLOVAK was the hard-charging fullback of the Lansford High School Panthers under coach **Ken Millen** and at Boston College from 1940-42 for **Frank Leahy** and **Denny Myers**. Leahy's 1940 Golden Eagles went 11-0 for the #5 ranking in the nation. With 2,011 career yards and 23 TD's, Holovak was a 1942 consensus All-American and was fourth in the Heisman Trophy vote which was won by Georgia's **Frank Sinkwich**. He was the #1 draft choice of Cleveland in 1943, but after his military service, Holovak played for LA Rams and Chicago Bears from 1946-48. He was head coach of Boston College from 1951-59 with a 49-29-3 record. Holovak was also the head man of the Boston Patriots of the new American Football League from 1961-68 and posted a 53-47-9 record. Holovak, who was the 1964 AFL Coach of the Year, became the GM of the Houston Oilers. He went in the College Football Hall of Fame in 1979.

JEFF HOSTETLER from Hollsopple played for Conemaugh Township High School Indians in Davidsville, Pennsylvania under **Joe Badaczewski**. He played at Penn State in 1980, but transferred to West Virginia for the 1982-83 seasons and was a 1983 Academic All-American for **Don Nehlen's** 8-4 Mountaineers. He was a 14 year veteran signal caller in the NFL with the New York Giants 1984-92, Oakland 1993-96 and Washington 1997-98. Hostetler earned two Super Bowl rings as **Bill Parcells'** Giants defeated Denver in SB XXI in 1987 and Buffalo in SB XXV in 1991. He had 1,278 completiions for 15,531 yards and 89 TD's.

HOSTETLER

BOBBY HOWARD was the top running back for Pittsburgh's Langley High School Mustangs and for the Indiana University Hoosiers from 1982-85. He played for Tampa Bay from 1986-88.

GARY HRIVNAK played for the Johnstown High School Trojans under **Francis Mihalic**. He was a defensive end at Purdue 1970-72 and was All-Big Ten in 1971 for coach **Bob DeMoss'** Boilermakers. Hrivnak spent five years with the Chicago Bears from 1973-77.

MIKE HUDOCK was a center for the Tunkhannock High School Tigers under **George Bunnell**. He starred at Miami of Florida for **Andy Gustafson's** powerful Hurricanes from 1954-56. Hudock spent eight years in the AFL from 1960-67 with the NY Titans/Jets, Miami and KC.

JOHN HUFNAGEL from McKees Rocks quarterbacked the Montour High School Spartans under **Charles Connor**. He was a Penn State signal-caller from 1970-72 for **Joe Paterno**. Hufnagel was a 1972 All-American as he threw for 2,039 yards and 15 TD's and was sixth in the Heisman Trophy vote which was won by Nebraska's **Johnny Rodgers**. He spent 15 years in the pros with Denver 1974-76 and Saskatchewan in Canada 1977-88.

TOM HULL played for Uniontown High School under **Leon Kaltenbach** and was a linebacker at Penn State from 1970-73 for **Joe Paterno**. He was a SF 49er 1974 and a Packer 1975.

JOHN HUZVAR was a fullback for Milton Hershey High School and North Carolina State from 1949-51 for **Beattie Feathers**. "Jumbo" scored 6 TD's for Philly and Baltimore from 1952-54.

HENRY HYNOSKI scored 36 TD's and 224 points from 1968-70 for the Mt. Carmel High School Red Tornadoes under **Joe "Jazz" Diminick**. He starred at Temple from 1972-74 for **Wayne Hardin's** powerful Owls and was a 1974 All-American honorable mention as the school's all-time leading rusher with 2,218 yards and 21 TD's. He was with Cleveland in 1975.

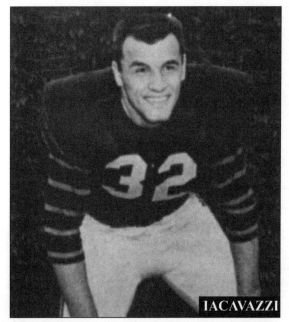

IACAVAZZI

COSMO IACAVAZZI was the "bread and butter" fullback in 1960 for the West Scranton High School Invaders under **Sam Donato**. At Princeton, Iacavazzi was a two-time All-American in 1963 and 1964 as he rushed for 1,895 yards and led **Dick Coleman's** Tigers to two Ivy League titles. The Tiger captain was ninth in the 1964 Heisman Trophy vote, won by Notre Dame's **John Huarte**. He was a NY Jet in 1965.

INDIANA UNIVERSITY INDIANS in Indiana, Pennsylvania started football in 1927 under the legendary **George Miller**. IUP was a national power under **Frank Cignetti** who took over the Crimson and Gray grid program in 1986. Cignetti, who is from Apollo, went to Washington Township High School and IUP where he graduated in 1960. He was head coach of the Leechburg High School Blue Devils from 1962-65 and went 32-9 and at West Virginia University from 1976-79 with a 17-27 record. At IUP, Cignetti went 124-30-1 from 1986-98, led the Indians to nine NCAA Division II playoffs and was Chevrolet's NCAA Division II Coach of the Year in 1991. Cignetti's Indians twice played in the NCAA Division II national championship game. In 1990, IUP went 12-2 and lost the crown to North Dakota State. Featured Indians were QB **Tony Aliucci**, WR **Jai Hill**, RB **Mike Mann**, C **Shawn Kunes** and LB **Nick Pascarella**. In 1993, IUP went 13-1 and lost the title to North Alabama. The Indians were led by RB **Mike Mann**, WR **JeMone Smith**, G **Matt Dalverny**, LB **Omar Stuart** and CB **Harold Brister**.

R. ISMAIL

RAGHIB "ROCKET" ISMAIL had 7,376 career all-purpose yards and 74 career TD's in 26 games from 1984-86 for Wilkes-Barre's Elmer L. Meyers High School Mohawks under **Mickey Gorham**. As a freshman flanker at Notre Dame, Ismail helped lead **Lou Holtz's** Fighting Irish to a 12-0 record and the 1988 national championship. "The Rocket" was a two-time All-American in 1989 and 1990 when he also was second in the Heisman Trophy vote which was won by **Ty Detmer** of BYU. Ismail skipped his senior year at Notre Dame and spent two years with Toronto in the Canadian Football League in 1991-92. He was All-CFL and earned a 1991 Grey Cup ring with **Adam Rita's** Argonauts. Ismail has been in the NFL since 1993 with Oakland, Carolina and Dallas and has 310 receptions for 4,461 yards and 26 TD's.

QADRY "MISSLE" ISMAIL played for Wilkes-Barre's Elmer L Meyers High School Mohawks under **Mickey Gorham**. Ismail had 4,041 all-purpose yards as a wide receiver and kick returner at Syracuse from 1989-92. He was a 1991 All-American for **Paul Pasqualoni's** 10-2 Orangemen ranked #11 in the nation. "The Missle," who had has been in the NFL since 1993 with Minnesota, Green Bay and Baltimore, earned a Super Bowl ring as **Brian Billick's** Ravens beat the NY Giants in SB XXXV in 2001. He has 235 receptions for 3,616 yards and 23 TD's.

RAY ISOM threw for 2,329 yards and 17 TD's in 1981-82 for the Harrisburg High School Cougars under **John "Jet" Johnson**. He was a top defensive back at Penn State 1984-86 and helped lead **Joe Paterno's** Nittany Lions to 12-0 record and the 1986 national championship.

Isom spent two years in the NFL with Tampa Bay in 1987-88.

GEORGE "LEFTY" JAMES from New Cumberland played for Bellefonte Academy and at Bucknell from 1927-29 for legendary **Carl Snavely**. He was head coach at Jersey Shore High School from 1931-34 and at Cornell 1947-60 where he went 66-58-2 in 14 years.

R. JAMES

RON "PO" JAMES set a Beaver County record when he scored 200 points in 1967 for the New Brighton High School Lions. He rushed for 3,885 yards and 33 TD's at New Mexico State from 1968-71 for **Jim Wood**. "Po" scored 6 TD's with Philadelphia from 1972-75.

CHUCK JANERETTE was a tackle for Philadelphia's Germantown High School Bears under coach **Wilbert Augustin** and at Penn State 1957-59 for **Rip Engle**. The 1959 All-America spent six years in the pros from 1960-65 as a defensive tackle with Los Angeles, New York Giants as they lost the 1961 and 1962 NFL titles to Green Bay, New York Jets, and Denver.

VALERIO JANSANTE played at Bentleyville High School and for Duquesne and at Villanova in 1943. Jansante, a two-way end, caught 14 TD's with Pittsburgh and Green Bay from 1946-51.

MIKE JARMOLUK was on the AP's first-ever All-State team as a tackle for Philadelphia's Frankford High School Pioneers in 1939 under **Elwood Geiges**. He played at Temple 1942-45 and was a 1945 All-American honorable mention for **Ray Morrison's** 7-1 Owls. "Big Mike" spent 10 years with Chicago 1946-47, Boston 1948 and Philadelphia 1949-55. Jarmoluk earned a 1946 NFL championship ring with **George Halas'** Bears and a 1949 title ring with **Greasy Neale's** Eagles. Jarmoluk had 7 interceptions and 3 TD's.

DIETRICH JELLS played for the Erie Tech Memorial Centaurs

JARMOLUK

58

under coach **Paul Petianni**. He played at Pitt from 1991-95 and was the all-time receiver in Panther history with 160 receptions for 3,003 yards and 24 TD's. Jells spent five years with New England 1996-98 and Philadelphia 1998-99. **Bill Parcells** Patriots lost Super Bowl XXXI in 1997 to Green Bay.

JIM JENSEN played for Central Bucks West High School in Doylestown, Pennsylvania under **Mike Pettine**. Jensen was at Boston University 1978-81 and was a 10 year veteran wide receiver for Miami 1981-92. **Don Shula's** Dolphins lost Super Bowls XVII to Washington in 1983 and XIX to San Francisco in 1985. Jensen had 229 receptions for 2,171 yards and 19 TD's.

STEVE JOACHIM threw for 4,056 career yards and a Pennsylvania record of 62 TD's from 1967-69 at Haverford High School. The nation's #1 school-boy quarterback played at Penn State in 1971, but then transferred to Temple where he played for **Wayne Hardin** in 1973-74. Joachim threw for 1,950 yards and 20 TD's as a 1974 All-American QB and won the Maxwell Award as the nation's most outstanding player when he directed the Owls to a 9-1 season. He was drafted by Baltimore in 1975, but played for Toronto in CFL, and the New York Jets in 1976.

JOACHIM

BILLY JOE was a fullback for the Coatesville High School Red Raiders under coach **Al Black**. He played at Villanova from 1960-62 for **Alex Bell's** powerful Wildcats and scored 19 pro TD's with Denver, Buffalo, Miami and New York Jets from 1963-69. **Lou Saban's** Bills defeated San Diego for the 1965 AFL title. Joe earned a Super Bowl ring as **Weeb Ewbank's** Jets beat Baltimore in SB III in 1969. He was the head coach of Central State in Ohio which lost the 1983 Division II national championship to North Dakota State. Joe is now the coach at Florida A&M.

JOE

B. JOHNSON

BILLY "WHITE SHOES" JOHNSON played at Chichester High School in Chester, Pennsylvania. He played at Widener University (was Pennsylvania Military College until 1972) 1971-73 and rushed for 3,737 career yards, had 5,404 all-purpose yards and scored 62 TD's. The 1973 Little All-American spent 15 years in pro ball with Houston 1974-80, Montreal 1981, Atlanta 1982-87 and Washington 1988. "White Shoes" rushed for 316 yards and 2 TD's, had 337 receptions for 4,211 yards and 25 TD's, returned 123 kick-offs for 2,941 yards and 2 TD's and returned an all-time NFL record 279 punts for 3,291 yards and 6 TD's. Johnson had a total of 35 TD's and was inducted into the College Hall of Fame in 1996.

JACK JOHNSON played for Pittsburgh's Carrick High School Raiders and at Miami of Florida for **Andy Gustafson**. He was as a defensive back with Chicago 1957-59 and Buffalo 1960-61.

DON JONAS scored 112 points and threw 5 TD's as a do-everything quarterback in 1956 for the West Scranton High School Invaders under **Sam Donato**. He played for Rip Engle at Penn State in 1958, 1960-61. Jonas spent 1962 with Philadelphia and then was a star quarterback in the Continental Football League with the Harrisburg Capitals 1963-64, Newark Bears who won the 1965 CFL tile for **Steve Van Buren**, and the Orlando Panthers 1966-69. Jonas was MVP of the CFL from 1966-68 as he led **Perry Moss'** Panthers to three straight CFL championship games and two league crowns in 1967 and 1968. He finished his pro career in Canada with Toronto 1970 and Winnipeg 1971-75. Jonas was an All-CFL QB in 1971 and 1972 for the Blue Bombers.

EDGAR "SPECIAL DELIVERY" JONES was a halfback for the Scranton Tech Red Raiders under **Fiore Cesare**. He played at Pitt from 1939-41 and was a 1941 All-American and seventh in the Heisman Trophy vote. Jones was drafted by Chicago in 1942 and played for the Bears in 1945 after his military service in World War II. "Special Delivery" then played for Cleveland in the All-American Football Conference from 1946-49 and finished his career in Canada as an All-CFL back with the Hamilton Tiger-Cats. With **Paul Brown's** Browns, Jones earned four straight AAFC championship rings from 1946-49. He rushed for 18 TD's and caught 10 TD passes.

GORDON JONES played for the East Allegheny High School Wildcats in Versailles, Pennsylvania under **James Botti**. He played at Pitt 1975-78, as **Johnny Majors'** Panthers won the 1976 national title. Jones, a 1978 All-American, had 133 career receptions for 2,230 yards and 21 TD's. He caught 8 TD's with Tampa Bay and Los Angeles from 1979-82.

J. JONES

JIMMY JONES threw for over 2,000 yards and 35 TD's in 1967 for Harrisburg's John Harris High School as he led **George Chaump's** Pioneers to a 35 game win streak from 1965-67. He was the University of Southern California QB from 1969-71 for **John McKay**. Jones paced the 1969 Trojans to a 10-0-1 season, a Rose Bowl win and the #3 ranking in the nation. The *Sports Illustrated* cover boy, spent eight years in Canada with Montreal 1973-75, Hamilton 1976-78 and Ottawa 1979-80. Jones, a 1974 CFL All-Star, led **Marv Levy's** Alouettes to two straight Grey Cups against Edmonton in 1974 and 1975 and won the 1974 game over the Eskimos.

STAN JONES played for the Lemoyn High School Trojans under **Henry "Shorty" Gasull**. He was a guard at Maryland from 1951-53 as **Jim Tatum's** Terrapins went 29-2 and won the 1953 national championship with a 10-1 record. Jones, who was a 1953 All-American and named Lineman of the Year, was well-known for his enormous strength from his 6-0, 255 pound frame, yet he was only a "little fellow" in the Jones family, as his grandfather in Altoona weighed 375 pounds. Jones was an offensive guard in the NFL for 13 years with Chicago from 1954-65 and then at Washington in 1966. Chicago lost the 1956 NFL title to New York, but Jones earned a 1963 NFL championship ring when **George Halas'** Bears defeated the Giants for the crown. Jones, a four-time All-Pro guard with the Bears, went in the Pro Football Hall of Fame in 1991.

S. JONES

DAVE JOYNER played for the State College High School Little Lions. He was a tackle at Penn State from 1969-71 for **Joe Paterno**. The 1971 co-captain was an All-American and Academic All-American for the 11-1 Nittany Lions. Joyner, one of Pennsylvania's most prominent orthopedic surgeons, went in the GTE/CoSIDA Academic Football Hall of Fame in 1991.

JUNIATA COLLEGE EAGLES in Huntingdon, Pennsylvania started football in 1920. The "Glory Years" of Juniata football was a seven year stretch from 1953-59 as the Eagles posted a 50-2-2 record under three different head coaches in **Bill Smaltz**, Penn State 1942, **Bob Hicks**, Penn State 1950, and **Ken Bunn, Jr.**, Penn State 1951. Hicks' 1955 Eagles went 8-0-1 and tied Missouri Valley State in the Tangerine Bowl. Juniata All-Americans of this era included half backs **Bill Berrier** and **Pat Tarquino** plus linemen **Barry Drexler**, **Al Dungan**, **Bill Haushalter**, **Bernie McQuown**, **"Moon" Mullen**, **Bob Soloman**, **John Staley**, and **Joe Veto**. Juniata went 10-2 in 1973 under coach **Walt Nadzak, Jr.**, and played in the NCAA Division III national championship game which they lost to Wittenberg of Ohio. Seniors pacing the Yale Blue and Old Gold included the all-star backfield of **Lou Eckerl**, **Mike McNeil** and **Gary Shope**, plus center **Don Myers**. Juniata plays its home games in Knox Stadium, which is named for **Chuck Knox**, class of 1954, and former NFL head coach of the LA Rams, Buffalo Bills, and Seattle Seahawks.

BOB JUNKO from Washington played for Trinity High School. He was a linebacker at Tulsa 1965-67 under **Glenn Dobbs'** and was a 1967 captain and All-American honorable mention for the Hurricanes.

BOB JURY from Library played at Lawrence High School for **Dave McLaughlin**. He was a safety at Pitt 1975-77 and helped lead **Johnny Majors'** 1976 Panthers to a 12-0 record and the national championship. Jury, who set an all-time Pitt record of 21 career interceptions, was a 1978 consensus All-American for **Jackie Sherrill's** Panthers. He was with San Francisco in 1978.

TOMMY KALAMANIR played for Conemaugh Township High School, at Pitt and Nevada-Reno. Kalamanir scored 3 TD's with Los Angeles 1949-51 and Baltimore 1953. The Rams played Cleveland in two straight NFL championship games in 1950 and 1951 and Kalamanir earned a NFL title ring with a 1951 win.

EMIL KARAS played for the Swissvale High School Golden Flashes and the University of Dayton Flyers. He had 3 interceptions as a defensive end and linebacker with Washington 1959 and San Diego 1960-66. **Sid Gilman's** Chargers appeared in five AFL championship games and defeated Boston for the 1963 AFL title.

KEN KARCHER quarterbacked Pittsburgh's Shaler High School Titans for **Jerry Matulevic**. He was at Notre Dame 1981-82 and Tulane 1984-85. Karcher was a back-up to **John Elway** at Denver in 1986-88 as **Dan Reeves'** Broncos lost Super Bowl XXI in 1987 to the NY Giants.

JOHN "BULL" KARCIS was the a fullback for the Monaca High School Indians and at Carnegie Tech 1929-31. "Five Yards Karcis" scored 11 TD's with Brooklyn

1932-35, Pittsburgh 1936-38 and New York 1938-39, 1943. **Steve Owens'** Giants appeared in two straight NFL title games against Green Bay in 1938 and 1939 and beat the Packers in 1938. "Bull" coached the Detroit Lions in 1942.

JIM KATCAVAGE was a tackle for Philadelphia's Roman Catholic High School Cahillites under **Joe "Goldie" Graham**. He played at Dayton from 1953-55 and was a 1955 All-American for the Flyers. Katcavage spent 13 years with the NY Giants from 1956-68 and was a three-time All-Pro. As a one of the Giants famed defensive unit with **Rosie Grier, Andy Robustelli, Dick Modzelewski, Sam Huff** and **Dick Lynch**, "Kat" appeared in six NFL title games in 1956, 1958, 1959, 1961, 1962, 1963 and earned the 1956 ring when **Jim Lee Howell's** Giants beat Chicago.

JAMES STANDON KECK played at Kiski Prep and went to Princeton where he was a captain and a two-time All-American tackle in 1920 and 1921 for **Bill Roper's** mighty Tigers. He was All-Pro at Cleveland in 1922-23 and was inducted into the College Football Hall of Fame in 1959.

K. C. KEELER played for the Emmaus High School Green Hornets under coaches **Allen Fields** and **Gene Legath**. He was a linebacker at Delaware 1977-80 as **Harold "Tubby" Raymond's** Blue Hens appeared in two straight NCAA Division II championship games in 1978 and 1979. Delaware lost the 1978 title game, but beat Youngstown State in 1979 for the crown. Keeler has been head coach of Rowan College in Glassboro, New Jersey since 1993 with a 77-19-1 record. The Profs appeared in five NCAA Division III title games in 1993, 1995, 1996, 1998 and 1999.

JAKE KELCHNER threw for 23 TD's and was the AP's Player of the Year in 1988 for Berwick High School as **George Curry's** Bulldogs won the PIAA 3A state championship. He went to Notre Dame in 1989-90, but transferred to West Virginia where he played for **Don Nehlen** in 1992-93. As a senior in 1993, Kelchner led the Mountaineers to a 11-1 record and the #8 ranking in the nation with 1,854 total yards and 17 TD's. He played in the CFL in 1994.

ALLEN "BUTCH" KELLER coached Honesdale High School and went 158-105-4 and Western Wayne High School and went 22-19. His over-all record was 180-124-4.

KEN KELLER rushed Bell Township High School to a 28 game win streak from 1948-51 and then was a four year star at North Carolina 1952-55. He scored 4 TD's with the Eagles 1956-57.

LARRY KELLEY was a star end for the Williamsport High School Millionaires under coaches **Dave Steumpfle** and **Harold Rock**. He went to Peddie in New Jersey in 1932 and then played for Yale 1934-36. Kelley, who had 49 career receptions, was the 1936 captain, a consensus All-American and won the Heisman Trophy for coach **Raymond Pond's** 7-1 Bulldogs. He chose not to play professional football when he turned down $11,000, an unheard of amount of money for the time, to play for Detroit in 1937. Kelley went in the College Football Hall of Fame in 1970.

L. KELLEY

J. KELLY

JIM KELLY was an end for the Clairton High School Bears and at Notre Dame where he caught 7 TD's as a two-time All-American in 1962 and 1963 for the Fighting Irish. Kelly was the #2 round draft choice of Pittsburgh and caught 5 TD's with the Steelers and Eagles in 1964-66.

JIM KELLY threw for 3,915 yards and 44 TD's for the East Brady High School Bulldogs under coach **Terry Henry** from 1976-78. He was the first in a long-line of recent great passers at Miami of Florida as he threw for 5,228 yards and 33 TD's from 1979-82 for **Howard Schnellenberger's** Hurricanes. Although drafted in the first round by Buffalo in 1983, Kelly played with the Houston Gamblers in the United States Football League from 1983-85 where he threw 83 TD passes in two years and was the 1984 USFL Player of the Year. Kelly then spent 11 years in the NFL with Buffalo from 1986-96. He led **Marv Levy's** Bills to four straight AFC championships and four consecutive Super Bowls 1991-94. Kelly, a future Hall of Famer, was a three-time All-Pro and had 2,874 completions in 4,779 attempts for 35, 467 yards and 175 TD's.

LEROY KELLY was a halfback for Philadelphia's Simon Gratz High School Bulldogs under **Lou DeVicaris** and then for the Morgan State Bears in Baltimore, Maryland from 1961-63. He was a 10 year veteran running back in the NFL with Cleveland from 1964-73. Kelly earned a 1964 NFL championship ring when **Blanton Collier's** Browns defeated Baltimore. In 10 seasons, the versatile Kelly rushed for 7,274 yards and 74 TD's, caught 190 passes for 2,281 yards and 13 TD's for a total 90 TD's. He went in the Pro Football Hall of Fame in 1994.

L. KELLY

MARK KELSO played for Pittsburgh's North Hills High School Indians. He was a defensive back at William and Mary where he was a 1985 Academic All-American for the Tribe. Kelso spent eight years in the NFL secondary with Buffalo from 1986-93. **Marv Levy's** Bills appeared in four straight Super Bowls from 1991-94. Kelso had 30 career interceptions and one TD.

PERRY KEMP played for the Fort Cherry High School Rangers in McDonald, Pennsylvania under **Jim Garry**. He was a wide receiver at California, PA, 1983-86. Kemp spent five years with Cleveland 1987 and Green Bay 1988-91. He had 194 receptions for 2,565 yards and 8 TD's.

KILROY

DAN KENDRA threw for a Lehigh Valley record 5,003 yards and 40 TD's from 1971-73 for the Allentown Central Catholic High School Vikings under coaches **George Kinek** and **Walt King**. He was a record-setting quarterback at West Virginia as he threw for 4,465 yards and 28 TD's from 1975-77 for **Bobby Bowden** and **Frank Cignetti**. The 1977 All-American honorable mention QB was with the LA Rams 1978 and Saskatchewan in the CFL 1980-81.

BILL KERN went to Wyoming Valley Seminary in Kingston and was a guard at Pitt 1925-27. He was a 1927 All-American for **Jock Sutherland's** Panthers who lost to Stanford in the Rose Bowl. Kern spent 1929-30 with **Curley Lambeau's** Green Bay Packers. He coached West Virginia from 1940-42, 1946-47 and went 24-23-1 in four seasons.

ANDREW KERR was born in Cheyenne, Wyoming, but graduated from Carlisle High School and then Dickinson College in 1900. Although he did not play football, Kerr coached football at Johnstown High School and joined **Pop Warner's** staff at Pitt in 1914. He was head coach of Stanford 1922-23 and went 11-7, at Washington and Jefferson 1926-28 and went 16-6-5 and at Colgate 1929-46 and went 95-53-7. Kerr's famous 1932 Red Raider team that went 9-0 and held their opponents scoreless through the season, gained gridiron notoriety when the press said Colgate was, "Unbeaten, Untied, Unscored upon and Uninvited," to the Rose Bowl. Kerr's over-all record was 122-66-12 in 23 years and he went in the College Football Hall of Fame in 1951.

GLENN KILLINGER played for Harrisburg Tech. He went to Penn State 1918-21 and was a 1921 All-American halfback for **Hugo Bezdek's** 8-0-2 Nittany Lions. "Killy" spent 1926 with the NY Giants. He coached at Dickinson, Rensselear Poly Institute, Moravian and West Chester State 1934-59 and went 146-31-6. Killinger went into the College Football Hall of Fame in 1966.

FRANCIS "BUCKO" KILROY was a tackle for Philadelphia's Northeast Catholic High School under **Kenneth "Si" Simendinger** and helped lead the Falcons to the 1937 Philadelphia Catholic League title. He played at Temple 1939-41 and was a 1941 All-American honorable mention for **Ray Morrison's** 7-1 Owls. "Bucko" spent 13 years with Philadelphia 1943-55 and appeared in three straight NFL title games as **Greasy Neale's** Eagles beat the Chicago Cards in 1948 and LA Rams in 1949. The seven-time All-Pro defensive lineman had 5 interceptions.

GEORGE KINEK from Palmerton scored 23 TD's in 1945-46 for Allentown Central Catholic High School Vikings under **Leo Crowe**. He played at nationally ranked Tulane from 1947-50 for **Henry Frnka**. Drafted by the LA Rams in 1951, Kinek had 2 picks for Chicago Cards in 1954.

CHUCK KLAUSING was an All-State lineman for Wilmerding High School and was a center at Penn State and Slippery Rock. He started coaching in 1948 and had over 300 victories and ten undefeated teams in 44 years at Pitcairn High School, Braddock High School, Indiana University of Pennsylvania, Carnegie-Mellon University and the Kiski School. Klausing's Braddock High School teams won a record 46 games in a row and a 56 game undefeated streak from 1953-60 behind quarterbacks **Mark Rutkosky** and **John Jacobs**, won six straight WPIAL titles in 1954 (co-champion with Midland), 1955, 1956, 1957, 1958, 1959 and was featured in a *Sports Illustrated* article in 1959. He went 47-10 at IUP and then 77-15-2 at Carnegie-Mellon as the Tartans made four trips to the NCAA Division III play-offs. Klausing, Division III Coach of the Year in 1979 and 1983, was inducted into the College Football Hall of Fame in 1998.

KLECKO

JOE KLECKO played for Chester's St. James High School Bulldogs under **Joe Logue**. As a nose guard at Temple from 1973-76, he led **Wayne Hardin's** Owls in tackles three straight years and was a two-time All-American honorable mention in 1975 and 1976. Klecko spent 12 years in the NFL as a defensive end with the Jets 1977-87 and Indy in 1988. He was a three-time All-Pro.

JACK KLOTZ played for Chester's Pennsylvania Military College Prep and then at PMC from 1953-55 for coach **George Hansell**. The big offensive tackle helped lead PMC to a 7-0 record in 1954. Klotz spent six years with LA 1956, NY Titans 1960-63 and Houston in 1964.

CHUCK KNOX from Sewickley was a tackle at Juniata College 1951-53 under **Bill Smaltz**. He coached Ellwood City High School before he was the head man of the Buffalo Bills 1978-82, Seattle Seahawks 1983-91 and the Los Angeles Rams 1992-94. Knox's over all NFL record was 136-138-0 in 17 years. Juniata named their 3,000 seat stadium Knox Stadium.

ROGER KOCHMAN played for the Wilkensburg High School Tigers under **Clarke Miller**. He was a star halfback at Penn State for **Rip Engle** from 1959-62. Kochman scored 4 TD's as a 1962 All-American for the 9-2 Nittany Lions. He had a career ending injury at Buffalo in1963.

BILL KOMAN from Aliquippa played for the Hopewell High School Vikings and at North Carolina from 1953-55 for **George Barclay's** Tar Heels. Koman had 7 interceptions in 12 years as a NFL linebacker with Baltimore 1956, Philadelphia 1957-58, and St. Louis 1959-67.

RON KOSTELNIK played for Ebensburg Central Catholic High School and was a star tackle at the University Cincinnati from 1958-60 for **George Blackburn**. He was a nine year veteran defensive tackle with Green Bay from 1961-68 and Baltimore in 1969. Kostelnik earned five NFL championship rings with **Vince Lombardi's** Packers in 1961, 1962, 1965, 1966, 1967 and two Super Bowl rings as Green Bay beat Kansas City in SB I in 1967 and Oakland in SB II in 1968.

KOSTELNIK

DOUG KOTAR from Muse scored 22 TD's in 1969 for the Canon-McMillan High School Big Macs in Canonsburg, Pennsylvania under **Ray Campanelli**. He was a Kentucky Wildcat from 1971-73. Kotar spent seven years with the New York Giants 1974-80. He rushed for 3,380 yards and 20 TD's, caught 126 passes for 1,022 yards and one TD, for a total of 21 TD's.

BOB KOWALKOWSKI played for the Arnold High School Lions under coach **Frank Martin**. He was a three-time All-ACC guard at Virginia from 1963-65 for **George Blackburn's** Cavaliers. Kowalkowski spent twelve years in the NFL with Detroit 1966-76 and Green Bay 1977.

BRUCE KOZERSKI from Plains played for Wilkes-Barre's James M. Coughlin High School Crusaders under **J.P. Meck**. He was a center at Holy Cross and was a 1983 All-American and Academic All-American for **Rick Carter's** Crusaders. Kozerski started for 12 years at Cincinnati from 1984-95 at center, guard and tackle. **Sam Wyche's** Bengals lost Super Bowl XXIII to San Francisco in 1989.

KOZERSKI

GEORGE KRACUM from Tresckow was a fullback for Hazleton High School under **Hugh McGeehan** and was a 1940 All-American at Pitt. He scored 3 TD's with Brooklyn in 1941.

RICH KRAYNAK played for the Phoenixville High School Phantoms under **Marty Moore**. He was a linebacker at Pitt from 1979-82 for **Jackie Sherrill** and **Foge Fazio's** nationally-ranked Panthers. He spent nine years in the NFL from 1983-91 with Philly, Atlanta, and Indianapolis.

KREIDER

STEVE KREIDER from Reading was a quarterback for the Schuylkill Valley High School Panthers in Leesport, Pennsylvania under **Mark Snyder**. He went to Lehigh where he was a record-setting wide receiver with 24 career TD's. As a 1977 All-American, Kreider helped lead **John Whitehead's** Engineers to a 12-2 record and the NCAA Division II national championship. Kreider caught 9 TD's with Cincinnati from 1979-86. **Forrest Gregg's** Bengals lost Super Bowl XVI to San Francisco in 1982.

ALEX KROLL played for the Leechburg High School Blue Devils who won the 1953 WPIAL title. He was a center at Yale, 1956 Ivy League champs, and then at Rutgers in 1960-61. Kroll, a 1961 All-American, helped lead **John Bateman's** Scarlet Knights to a 9-0 season. He spent 1962 with the AFL's New York Titans. Kroll, who became Chairman of Young & Rubicam, one of the world's largest advertising agencies, was inducted into the College Football Hall of Fame in 1997.

GENE KRUIS played for Altoona High School and St.

KROLL

72

Francis College. He coached 30 years at Lancaster Catholic and Manheim Township High Schools with a 180-75-5 record from 1950-79.

LARRY KRUTKO played for Cumberland Township High School and was a powerful fullback at West Virginia from 1955-57. He scored 4 TD's as a Pittsburgh Steeler from 1958-60.

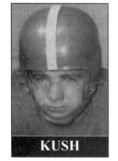

KUSH

FRANK KUSH played for the Windber High School Ramblers under **John Kawchak**. He played at Michigan State from 1950-52 and was a 1952 All-American guard as he helped lead **Biggie Munn's** 9 - 0 Spartan's to the national championship. Kush was the head coach at Arizona State for 22 years from 1958-79 with a 176-54-1 record and he won 6 out of 7 bowl games. With numerous Pennsylvanians on the Sun Devil rosters, Kush put ASU in the national grid spotlight. He was also the head coach of the Indianapolis Colts in the NFL, the Hamilton Tiger-Cats in the CFL and Phoenix in the USFL. Kush went into the College Football Hall of Fame in 1995.

LOU KUSSEROW played for the Glassport High School Gladiators. He was a four year star halfback at Columbia 1945-48 as he set a career scoring record of 270 points for **Lou Little's** Lions. The 1948 All-American halfback played for the football Brooklyn Dodgers in 1949.

KUSSEROW

KWALICK

TED KWALICK from McKees Rocks helped lead the Montour High School Spartans to the 1963 and 1964 WPIAL titles under **Bob Phillips**. He was a tight end at Penn State from 1966-68 for **Joe Paterno**. Kwalick was a two-time All-American in 1967 and 1968 and was fourth in the 1968 Hesiman Trophy vote. He was the first round draft choice of San Francisco and spent 10 years with the 49ers 1969-74 and Oakland 1975-78. Kwalick earned a Super Bowl ring as **John Madden's** Raiders beat Minesota in SB XI in 1977. The two-time All-Pro caught 168 passes for 2,570 yards and 23 TD's. He went into the College Football Hall of Fame in 1989.

STEVE LACH was a halfback for Altoona High School and at Duke from 1939-41. He was a 1941 All-American as he led **Wallace Wade's** Blue Devils to a 9-0 record, the #2 ranking, and the Rose Bowl against Oregon State. He threw one TD pass, had 5 picks, and 109 PAT's with the Chicago Cards 1942 and Pittsburgh 1946-47. He is in the College Football Hall of Fame.

LAFAYETTE COLLEGE LEOPARDS in Easton, Pennsylvania started football in 1882, and was a major power from 1896 to 1940. Lafayette gained gridiron recognition in 1896 under coach **Parke Davis** as All-American guard **Charles "Babe" Rinehart** (Hall of Fame) led the Maroon to a 11-0-1 record and co-national championship with Princeton. Lafayette now stood at the top of the collegiate football world along with the Big Four-Yale, Harvard, Princeton and Pennsylvania. Lafayette won another national title in 1921 as they upset Pittsburgh and went 9-0 for **Dr. John Bain "Jock" Sutherland** (Hall of Fame) who was a 1917 All-American guard at Pitt. The big Maroon guns were halfback **Leonard "Botts" Brunner**, two-time All-American guard **Frank "Dutch" Schwab** (Hall of Fame) from Medera and future 1924 All-American end **Charlie Berry** (Hall of Fame). Five years later in 1926 Lafayette again beat Pittsburgh and went 9-0 for another mythical national title for coach **Herbert McCracken** (Hall of Fame). Leading the Leopards were three All-Americans - halfbacks **George "Mike" Wilson** (Hall of Fame) and **Frank Kirkleski**, plus tackle **Bill Cothran**. Lafayette was the national picture again for coach **Edward "Hook" Mylin** (Hall of Fame) who came from Bucknell. The Leopards went 8-0 in 1937 behind All-American halfback **Tony Cavallo** and 9-0 in 1940 behind All-American halfbacks **Jim Farrell, George "Sammy" Moyer**, fullback **Walt Zirinsky**, center **John Quigg** and **Harold Bellis**. Other Lafayette All-Americans include: **Tony Giglio** HB 1972-73, **Tim Gerhart** TE 1978-79, **Joe Skladany** LB 1979, 1981, **Bob Rasp** DB 1979, **Dave Shea** DB 1979, **Rick Smith** TE 1979, **Roger Shepko** HB 1981, **Tony Green** MG 1982, **Frank Novak** QB 1982, **Ryan Priest** HB 1984, **Frank Baur** QB 1988-

LACH

LAFAYETTE 1896 NATIONAL CHAMPIONS

89, **Phil Ng** WR 1988, **Ed Hudak** OG 1991-92, **Dave Pyne** OG 1993, **Erik Marsh** RB 1993-94 who starred at Bethlehem Catholic High School and was the Patriot League's all-time rushing leader with 4,834 career yards and 38 TD's from 1991-94, **Ed Sasso** DT 1995, **B. J. Gallis** DB 1996. The Leopards all-time winningest coach was **Bill Russo** who went 103-98-4 from 1981-99.

LAFAYETTE vs. LEHIGH is the most played collegiate football rivalry in the nation. The two academic institutions located five miles apart, Lafayette in Easton and Lehigh in Bethlehem, started their famous intercollegiate series in 1884 and have played 136 games through 2000.

WARREN LAHR was a halfback for West Wyoming High School and at Case Western Reserve in Cleveland, Ohio from 1945-48. He spent

LAFAYETTE vs. LEHIGH

11 years as a defensive back for **Paul Brown's** Cleveland Browns from 1949-59. The Browns appeared in eight championship games and Lahr earned four rings - one AAFL title ring in 1949 over San Francisco and three NFL title rings in 1950 over Los Angeles,

1954 over Detroit and 1955 over Los Angeles. Lahr, who was a 1951 All-Pro, had 40 career interceptions, scored 5 TD's and had one fumble recovery.

NOEL LAMONTANGE played for the Southern Lehigh High School Spartans in Coopersburg, Pennsylvania under **Bob Clark**. He went to Virginia 1996-99 and was a captain and a 1999 All-American offensive guard for **George Welsh** 7-5 Cavaliers. LaMontange was in Cleveland 2000.

RON LANCASTER played for the Clairton High School Bears who won the 1954 WPIAL title. He was a quarterback at Wittenberg College in Springfield, Ohio from 1957-59. Lancaster spent 19 years in Canada with Ottawa 1960-1962 and Saskatchewan 1963-78. The ace signal-caller was in six Grey Cups and earned two CFL title rings with Ottawa in 1960 and Saskatchewan in 1966. He became player/coach of Saskatchewan from October of 1978-80 and then Edmonton from 1991-97. Lancaster's Eskimos appeared in two Grey Cups and beat Winnipeg in 1993. He took over Hamilton in 1997 and his Tiger-Cats lost the 1998 CFL championship, but beat Calgary for the 1999 Grey Cup. Although retired since 1978, Lancaster is still the CFL's all-time career passing leader with 3,384 completions in 6,233 attempts for 50,535 yards and 333 TD's. His numerous awards include the CFL's MVP in 1970 and 1976, a four-time All-CFL QB, CFL Coach of the Year in 1996 and 1998 and inducted into the CFL Hall of Fame in 1982.

JIM LASLAVIC played for the Etna High School Rams under coach **Neil Clark**. He was a linebacker at Penn State from 1970-72 for **Joe Paterno's** nationally ranked 28-6 Nittany Lions. Laslavic had 8 interceptions with Detroit 1973-78 and San Diego 1979-82.

LINDY LAURO played for New Castle High School from 1936-39 under **Phil Bridenbaugh**. He played at Alabama in 1941 and at Pitt from 1947-49. Lauro was a Chicago Cardinal in 1951. Lauro coached the New Castle High School Red Hurricanes from 1961-92 and went 220-104-15 in 32 years with 6 undefeated teams and 3 WPIAL titles in 1967, 1973, 1975. He developed three pros in **Bruce Clark**, **Rick Ranzzano** and **Sam Manos**. With winning coaches in Bridenbaugh and Lauro, New Castle is the fourth winningest scholastic program in the state behind Mt. Carmel, Easton and Berwick with a 639-318-69 record since 1892.

TAJUAN "TY" LAW played for the Aliquippa High School Fighting Quips under coach **Frank Marocco**. He was a defensive back at Michigan from 1991-94 and was a 1994 All-American for **Gary Moeller's** 8-4 Wolverines. Law has been in the NFL with New England since 1995 and has 22 picks and 3 TD's. **Bill Parcells'** Patriots lost Super Bowl XXXI in 1997 to Green Bay.

ANDY LEH played for Allentown High School and at Muhlenberg College from 1922-25. He coached the Nazareth High School Blue Eagles for 30 years from 1926-55 and went 161-73-18.

LEHIGH UNIVERSITY ENGINEERS in Bethlehem, Pennsylvania started football in 1884 with its first-ever game against Lafayette in the start of the most played rivalry in college football. Lehigh went 9-0 in 1950 under **Bill Leckonby** who is LU's all-time winningest coach at 85-53-5 from 1946-61. The Engineers, led by halfbacks **Dick Gabriel** and **Dick Doyne**, were ranked #19 in the nation for November 6, 1950 and turned down Cigar, Salad, Sun and Tangerine Bowl invitations. Lehigh under coach **John Whitehead**, who was from Summit Hill and played for the Scotland School and at East Stroudsburg State, went 12-2 and won the 1977 NCAA Division II national championship when they beat Jacksonville State of Alabama. Leading the Brown and White attack was the All-American passing combo of quarterback **Mike Rieker** and wide receiver **Steve Kreider**. Other LU offensive stars were tight end **Don Van Orden**, tackles **Andy Vandergrift, Dave Melone**, guards **Tom Stine, Jim Schulze**, center **Rick Adams** and backs **Dave Aprill, Lennie Daniels, Matt Ricketson, John Morrisey** and **Mike Ford**. The defensive line had **Greg Clark, Tom Giodani, Eric Merril, Glen Sloka,** and **Jim Pieczynski**, linebackers **Bill Bradley, Keith Frederick, Jim McCormick, Bruce Rarig** and d-backs **Dale Visockey, Steve Hefele** and **Carl Reese**. Whitehead was named the 1977 Division II Coach of the Year. Two years later in 1979, Lehigh played in the NCAA Division I-AA national championship game, but lost to Eastern Kentucky. Lehigh's line-up had receivers **Dave Rarig, Tom Nikles, Mark Yeager**, tackles **Joe Scheuer, Dave Melone**, guards **Larry Miksiewicz, Jim Mahlbacher**, center **Mark Sitar**, quarterback **Rich Andres** and backs **Joe Rabuck, Vince Rogusky, Jeff Bernstein, Bob Romeo, Jim Evanko** and kicker **Ted Iobst**. The defensive line had **Mike Crowe, Eric Yasaemski, Rich Titus, John Butkus**, linebackers **Jim McCormick, Bruce Rarig, Dave Dorrow** and d-backs **Lou D'Annibale, Charles Marck, Jeff Dunn** and **Keith Conley**. Whitehead was named the 1979 Division I-AA Coach of the Year. Lehigh has been a power again since 1994 under coach **Kevin Higgins** who played at West Chester. The Engineers went 34-4 from 1998-00, won three straight Patriot League crowns and made three straight NCAA Division 1-AA play-off appearances Lehigh All-Americans include **Bob Numbers** C 1949, **Dick Doyne** HB 1949-50, **Bill Ciarvino** G 1950, **Dan Nolan** QB 1957, **Pete Williams** T 1957, **Walt Meincke** T 1959, **John Hill** C 1971, **Kim McQuilken** QB 1973, **Bill Schlegel** TE 1973, **Rod Gardner** RB 1975, **Joe Sterrett** QB 1975, **Mike Rieker** QB 1977, **Steve Kreider** WR 1977, **Dave Melone** OT -1979, **Jim McCormick** LB 1979, **Mark Yeager** WR 1980, **Bruce Rarig** LB 1980, **John Shigo** LB 1983, **Renie Benn** WR 1983-84-85, **Wes Walton** DT 1983-84, **Dave Whitehead** C 1984, **Marty Horn** QB 1985, **Joe Uliana** OG 1986-87, **Rob Varano** TE 1989, **Keith Petzold** OG 1990, **Horace Hamm** WR 1991, **Dave Cecchini** WR 1993, **Mark LaFeir** TE 1994, **Brian Klinerman** WR 1994-95, **Brian Bartell** OT 1996, **Ben Talbott** P 1996.

LEHIGH 1977 DIVISION II NATIONAL CHAMPIONS

J. B. LEIDIG came from Chambersburg and graduated from Dickinson College in 1912. He coached the Warren High School Dragons through four decades and had a 270-124-27 record.

CHAD LEVITT from Melrose Park played for the Cheltenham High School Panthers under **Joe Gro**. He played at Cornell 1993-96 where he set a career record of 5,036 all-purpose yards and 292 points for **Jim Hofher's** Big Red. The 1996 All-American was with Oakland 1997-98 and St. Louis 1999 as **Dick Vermeil's** Rams defeated Tennessee in Super Bowl XXXIV in 2000.

BILL LEWIS from Bristol quarterbacked East Stroudsburg State from 1960-62 for **Jack Gregory**. He was head coach at Wyoming 1977-79 and went 14-20-1 and East Carolina 1989-91 and went 21-12. Lewis' 1991 Pirates went 11-1 and he was the NCAA Division I Coach of the Year. He was at Ga. Tech from 1992-94 and went 11-19-0. His over-all record was 46-51-1.

TIM LEWIS played for the Pennridge High School Rams in Perkasie, Pennsylvania under coach **Wayne Helman**. He was a defensive back at Pitt from 1979-81 for **Jackie Sherrill** and was a 1982 All-American for **Foge Fazio's** 9-3 Panthers. Lewis, the #1 draft pick of Green Bay, spent four years with the Pack 1983-86. The 1984 All-Pro had 16 career interceptions and 2 TD's.

WILL LEWIS played for the Pennridge High School Rams in Perkasie, Pennsylvania under coach **Wayne Helman**. Lewis was a all-purpose back at Millersville State University for **Gene "Doc" Carpenter** from 1976-79. He spent his pro years in Seattle 1980-81, USFL and Canada.

BOB LIGGETT played for the Aliquippa High School Quips under **Carl Aschman**. He went to Nebraska and was a two-time All-Big 8 defensive tackle 1968-69. He was with the KC Chiefs 1970, BC Lions 1971.

JONATHON LINTON rushed for 4,118 career yards and 64 TD's from 1989-92 for the Catasauqua High School Rough Riders under **Ed Csensits**. He starred at North Carolina from 1994-97 for **Mack Brown's** Tar Heels. Linton has been in the NFL since 1998 with Buffalo.

LISCIO

GEORGE LITTLE played for the Duquesne High School Dukes. He went to Iowa and was All-Big Ten defensive end for the Hawkeyes in 1984. Little was a Miami Dolphin from 1985-87.

TONY LISCIO played for Pittsburgh's Westinghouse High School Bulldogs for **Pete Dimperio**. An offensive tackle, Liscio starred at Tulsa in 1961-62 and then for nine years with Dallas 1963-71. Liscio, who was an All-Pro in 1966, earned a Super Bowl ring as **Tom Landry's** Cowboys defeated Miami in Super Bowl VI in 1972. Dallas lost Super Bowl V in 1971 to Baltimore.

DAVID LOGAN played for Pittsburgh's Peabody High School Highlanders. He was a nose tackle at Pitt from 1976-78 and helped lead **Johnny Majors'** Panthers to the 1976 national title. Logan spent nine years in the NFL trenches with Tampa Bay 1979-86 and Green Bay 1987.

BOB LONG played for Washingtown Township High School and at Wichita State 1961-63. The wide receiver spent seven years in the NFL 1964-70 with Green Bay, Atlanta, Washington and Los Angeles. He earned two Super Bowl rings as **Vince Lombardi's** Packers beat Kansas City in SB I in 1967 and Oakland in SB II in 1968. Long had 98 catches for 1,539 yards and 10 TD's.

CARSON LONG kicked a state record 10 field goals in 1971 for North Schuylkill High School in Ashland, Pennsylvania. He went to Pitt 1973-76 and became the NCAA's all-time points leader for **Johnny Majors'** 1976 national title 12-0 Panthers. Long was with Buffalo in 1977.

LOVE

SEAN LOVE from Tamaqua played for the Marian Catholic High School Colts in Hometown, Pennsylvania under **Stan Dakosty**. Love was an offensive guard at Penn State from 1988-90 for **Joe Paterno** and was in the NFL 1991-97 with Dallas, Buffalo, Tampa Bay and Philadelphia.

RICHIE LUCAS quarterbacked the Glassport High School Gladiators under **Vince McKeeta**. He played at Penn State from 1957-59 for coach **Rip Engle** who said, "Lucas is the greatest player I have ever seen" when the 1959 All-American QB led the Nittany Lions to a 9-2 record, won Maxwell Award as the nation's most outstanding player and was runner-up to LSU's **Billy Cannon** for the Heisman Trophy. The #1 draft choice of NFL Washington and AFL Buffalo, was with the Bills in 1960-61. Lucas went in the College Football Hall of Fame in 1986.

R. LUCAS

LUCCI

MIKE LUCCI played the Ambridge High School Bridgers. He was a center at Tennessee from 1959-61 and was captain and 1961 All-SEC for **Bowden Wyatt's** Vols. Lucci was a 12 year veteran linebacker with Cleveland 1962-64 and Detroit 1965-73. He earned a 1964 NFL title ring as **Blanton Collier's** Browns defeated Baltimore. The two-time All-Pro had 21 picks and 5 TD's.

JOHNNY LUJACK played for the Connellsville High School Cokers under coach **Andy Duff**. He switched from a single-wing tailback to a T-formation quarterback at Notre Dame and led **Frank Leahy's** Fighting Irish to three national championships in 1943, 1946 and 1947. Lujack was a two-time consensus All-American in 1946 and 1947 and also won the Heisman Trophy in 1947. He was the #1 draft pick of Chicago and spent four years with the Bears from 1948-51. The three-time All-Pro set a NFL single game record of 468 yards passing in 1949. In his brief pro career, the all-around Lujack, scored 21 TD's, threw for 6,295 yards and 41 TD's plus had 12 interceptions and recovered 7 fumbles. Lujack went in the College Football Hall of Fame in 1960.

MIKE LUSH played for Allentown's Wm. Allen High School Canaries under **Les Kish**. He was a 1980 Little All-American DB at East Stroudsburg for **Denny Douds**. Lush spent five years in pro ball and had 26 interceptions 1983-87 with the USFL champion Philly/Baltimore Stars, Minnesota and Atlanta.

LYCOMING COLLEGE WARRIORS in Williamsport, Pennsylvania started football in 1947. Under coach **Frank Girardi**, who was a running back at Williamsport High School and West Chester, the Warriors have won over 200 games since 1972, won 12 MAC titles, have been in the NCAA Division III play-offs nine times and the championship game twice. Lycoming went 12-1 in 1990 and lost the

LUJACK

title to Allegheny College of Pennsylvania. The Warriors went 12-1 in 1997 and lost the crown to Mt. Union College of Ohio. Record-holding Blue and Gold during the Girardi era include quarterbacks **Larry Baretta**, **Keith Cadden**, **Ed Dougherty** and **Jason Marraccini**, running backs **Troy Erdman**, **John Grier**, **Kevin McVey**, **Joe Parsnik**, **Cory Sheridan**, and **Brian Thompson**, and receivers **Tim Dumas**, **Jim O'Malley**, and **Steve Verton**.

GARRY LYLE was a do-everything quarterback for Verona High School under coach **Joe Zelek** as he led the Panthers to the 1962 WPIAL title. He was a halfback-defensive back at George Washington University from 1964-66 and was the first African-American All-American for the Colonials. Lyle, a third round draft choice of Chicago, played for the Bears from 1967-74 with 12 picks and recovered 4 fumbles.

BILL MAAS played for the Marple Newton High School Tigers in Newton Square, Pennsylvania under **Bob Kenig**. He was a defensive tackle at Pitt from 1980-83 and was a 1982 All-American for **"Foge"** **Fazio's** 9-3 Panthers. Maas, the #1 draft pick of Kansas City, spent ten years with the Chiefs in 1984-92 and Green Bay 1993. Maas, a two-time All-Pro, scored 2 TD's and 2 safeties.

BILL "RED" MACK from Allison Park played for the Hampton Township High School Talbots near Pittsburgh under **Ed Fay**. He was a halfback at Notre Dame 1958-60 and spent six years with Pittsburgh, Philly, Atlanta and Green Bay 1961-66. "Red" earned a Super Bowl ring as **Vince Lombardi's** Packers beat Kansas City in SB I in 1967. He rushed for 1,159 yards, 8 TD's.

JOHN MACZUZAK was a lineman for the Ellsworth High School Tigers under **Joe Metro** and **Paul Lapcevic**. He played at Pitt 1961-63 for **John Michelosen** as the 1963 Panthers went 9-1 and ranked #3 in the nation. Maczuzak was with Kansas City in 1964 and later became President and COO of National Steel.

BILL MACKRIDES, who was the water boy for the Eagles as a youngster, played for the West Philadelphia High School Speedboys under coach **Wes Hackman** and at Nevada-Reno 1943-46. He was a quarterback in the NFL for seven years from 1947-53 with Philadelphia, NY Giants and Pittsburgh. **Greasy Neale's** Eagles appeared in three straight NFL championship games and Mackrides earned two title rings as a back-up to **Tommy Thompson** when the Eagles beat the Chicago Cards in 1948 and LA Rams in 1949. He completed 131 passes for 1,583 yards, 8 TD's.

DON MALINAK played for the Steelton High School Steamrollers under **Joe Shevock** and was a 1953 co-captain at Penn State for **Rip Engle**. He coached at Mt. Union in 1956 and then 27 years at Loch Haven High School from 1957-83. In 28 years, his over-all record was 183-90-10.

BILL MALINCHAK was an end for Monessen High School as **Joe Gladys'** Greyhounds won the 1961 WPIAL championship. He played at Indiana University from 1963-65 and was All-Big Ten in 1964 and captain of the 1965 Hoosiers. He caught 5 TD's in 11 years with Detroit 1966-69 and Washington 1970-76. **George Allen's** Redskins lost Super Bowl VII to Miami in 1973.

TIM MANOA from the Tonga Islands in the South Seas was a running back for the North Allegheny High School Tigers and at Penn State 1983-86. **Joe Paterno's** 1986 Nittany Lions went 12-0 and won the national title. Manoa scored 8 TD's for Cleveland and Indy in 1987-91.

GREG MANUSKY played for the Dallas High School Mountaineers under coach **Ted Jackson**. He was a linebacker at Colgate from 1984-87 and was a 1987 All-American for **Fred Dunlap's** 7-4 Red Raiders. Manusky was 11 year veteran in the NFL with Washington 1988-90, Minnesota 1991-93 and Kansas City 1994-98.

BAP MANZINI played for Monongahela High School and was captain of St. Vincent's College in 1942. He played with the Eagles and Lions and coached St. Vincent's 1946-47. Manzini was coach of Bellmar High School 1951-64 with a record of 84-38-7 and at Thomas Jefferson High School from 1965-80 with a record of 119-36-1. His over-all record in 29 years was 203-74-8.

TED MARCHIBRODA played for the Franklin High School Knights and the St. Bonaventure Brown Indians from 1949-51. He spent five years as an NFL quarterback with the Pittsburgh Steelers from 1953-56 and the Chicago Cardinals in 1957. Marchibroda completed 172 passes for 2,169 yards and 16 TD's. He was the head coach of the Baltimore Colts 1975-79 and went 41-36 and the Baltimore Ravens 1996-98 and went 16-31-1. Marchibroda had a over-all record of 57-67-1 in 8 years. With the Colts, Marchibroda was the NFL's 1975 Coach of the Year.

RON MARCINIAK played for Pittsburgh's St. Justin High School under **James "Max" Carey**. He was a guard at Kansas State 1952-54 and was a Washington Redskin in 1955.

WOODY MARCKS was a tackle for the Allentown's Dieruff High School Huskies under **Ernie Wescoe**. He did not go to college, but was with the Philly Eagles 1967-68, 70 and NY Jets 1969.

FRANK MARCHLEWSKI played for the Plum High School Mustangs. He was a center for **Murray Warmath's** Minnesota Golden Golphers from 1962-64 and then spent six years in the NFL pivot from 1965-70 with Los Angeles, Atlanta and Buffalo.

MARINO

DAN MARINO played for Pittsburgh's Central Catholic High School Vikings for **Rich Erdelyi**. Although a top Major League Baseball pospect as a fourth round draft choice of the Kansas City Royals, Marino quarterbacked Pitt from 1979-82. As a junior, he was a 1981 All-American for **Jackie Sherrill's** 11-1 Panthers ranked #2 in the nation. Marino, who was the Panther's all-time leading passer with 8,597 career yards and 79 TD's, was fourth in the Heisman Trophy vote of 1981 and nineth in the 1982 vote. Known by the fans as "a real Pittsburgh guy," Marino spent 17 years in the NFL with the Miami Dolphins from 1983-99. **Don Shula's** Dolphins lost Super Bowl XIX to San Francisco in 1985. "The Arm" broke all of **Fran Tarkington's** NFL passing records of 4,967 completions in 8,358 attempts for 61,361 yards and 420 TD's. Marino was an eight-time All-Pro QB and the NFL's Man of the Year in 1998. He is a future Pro Football Hall of Famer.

PHIL MARION played for Fordham with the legendary **Vince Lombardi** and coached Ridley Township High School from 1943-72. He compiled a 228-58-15 record in 29 years.

MARK MARKOVICH played for Greensburg Central Catholic High School and was an offensive guard at Penn State from 1971-73 for **Joe Paterno**. He was a co-captain and a 1973 Academic All-American for the 12-0 Nittany Lions who were ranked #5 in the nation. Markovich spent four years in the NFL trenches with San Diego in 1974-75 and Detroit 1975-77.

DUSAN "DUKE" MARONIC played for the Steelton High School Steamrollers under **Charles Hoy**. Maronic did not play college football, but spent eight years as a guard and linebacker with Philadelphia from 1944-50 and the NY Giants in 1951. "Duke" had 2 picks and earned two NFL title rings as **Greasy Neale's** Eagles beat the Chicago Cards in 1948 and Los Angeles in 1949.

STEVE MARONIC was a tackle for the Steelton High School Steamrollers under **Nelson Hoffman**. He played at North Carolina from 1936-38 for **Ray Wolf** and was 1938 captain and an All-American for the Tar Heels. Maronic spent two years in the NFL with Detroit in 1939-40.

PAUL MARRANCA graduated from Wyoming Area High School in 1967 and Bucknell in 1971. He coached Wyoming Area from 1976-86 and went 88-34-2, Nanticoke from 1990-91 and went 14-7 and at Wyoming Area again since 1992 and is 71-34. His over-all record is 173-75-2.

LARRY MARSHALL was a star halfback for Philadelphia's Bishop Egan High School Eagles under **Dick Bedesem** and was a defensive back and punter at Maryland from 1968-71. He spent seven years in the NFL with Kansas City, Minnesota, Philly, and Los Angeles from 1972-78.

MARTHA

PAUL MARTHA from Wilkinsburg played for Pittsburgh's Shady Side Academy Indians. He was at Pitt from 1961-63 for **John Michelson** and was a 1963 consensus All-American halfback for the 9-1 Panthers ranked #3 in the nation. Martha, the #1 draft pick of Pittsburgh, was a safety with the Steelers 1964-69 and Denver 1970. He had 21 interceptions and recovered 10 fumbles.

BEN MARTIN played for Prospect Park High School near Philadelphia and was an end at Princeton and then at Navy from 1942-44 for coaches **Billick Whelchel** and **Oscar Hagberg**. He was head coach at Virginia from 1956-57 and went 7-12-1.

Martin took over at the four-year old Air Force Academy in Colorado Springs from 1958-77 and the Falcons soared to national prominence with a 93-103-9 record. In 22 years, Martin posted an over-all record of 103-115-10.

CURTIS MARTIN rushed for 1,705 yards and 20 TD's for Pittsburgh's Taylor Allderdice High School Dragons in 1990 for **Mark Whittgartner**. He played at Pitt from 1991-93, but missed his senior year. Martin has been in the NFL with New England 1995-97 and the NY Jets since 1998. **Bill Parcells'** Patriots lost Super Bowl XXXI to Green Bay in 1997. Martin, the 1995 Rookie of the Year, has 7,754 yards rushing, 54 TD's, 2,022 yards receiving, 8 TD's, for 62 total TD's.

C. MARTIN

DAVID MARTIN played for Philadelphia's John Bartram High School Maroon Wave. He was a DB at Villanova from 1977-80. Martin was at Denver in the USFL 1983-85 and San Diego 1986.

JOHN MASTRANGELO was a guard for the Vandergrift High School Blue Lancers under **Ted Rosenweig**. At Notre Dame, he was a two-time All-American guard in 1945 and 1946 as **Frank Leahy's** Fighting Irish won the 1946 national title. He was the #2 draft choice of Pittsburgh and played with the Steelers 1947-48, NY Yankees 1949 and NY Giants 1950 where he was All-Pro.

RAY MATHEWS was a halfback for the McKeesport High Tigers under **Duke Weigle**. He played at Clemson and was 1949 and 1950 All-Southern for **Frank Howard's** Tigers. Mathews spent 11 years in the pros wth Pittsburgh 1951-59, Dallas 1960 and Calgary in Canada in 1961. He rushed for 1,057 yards and 5 TD's, caught 233 passes for 3,963 yards and 34 TD's, returned 3 punts for 3 TD's and 3 kick-offs for one TD. Mathews scored a total of 43 TD's.

FRED MAUTINO was an end for Reading High School Red Knights under **Andy Stopper** and at Syracuse from 1958-60 for **Ben Schwartzwalder**. Mautino, a 1959 All-American, was an impenetrable "Sizable Seven" linemen, along with Hanover's **Al Bemiller**, that paved the way for the Orangmen's 11-0 record and national title. The 1960 Academic All-American signed with Pittsburgh.

MAXWELL AWARD has been awarded annually since 1937 to the top college player in the nation by the Maxwell Memorial Football Club of Philadelphia. The award is named in honor of **Robert W. "Tiny" Maxwell**, a Philadelphia native who was a guard at the University of Chicago and at Swarthmore College outside of Philadelphia. Maxwell played pro football, officiated, and was sports editor of the Philadelphia Evening Record. He died at age 37 in an auto accident. Maxwell Award winners from Pennsylvania are: 1943-**Bob Odell** halfback from Penn; 1946-**Charlie Trippi** halfback from Pittston High School and Georgia; 1948-**Chuck Bednarik** center from Bethlehem High School and Pennsylvania; 1949-**Leon Hart** end from Turtle Creek High School and Notre Dame; 1950-**Francis "Red" Bagnell** halfback from Philadelphia's West Catholic High School and Pennsylvania; 1959-**Richie Lucas** quarterback from Glassport High School and Penn State; 1964-**Glenn Ressler** guard from Dorsife, Mahanoy Jointure High School and Penn State; 1969-**Mike Reid** tackle from Altoona High School and Penn State; 1973-**John Cappelletti** halfback from Upper Darby's Monsignor Bonner High School and Penn State; 1974-**Steve Joachim** quarterback from Haverford High School and Temple; 1976-**Tony Dorsett** halfback from Aliquippa, Hopewell High School and Pitt; 1978-**Chuck Fusina** quarterback from McKees Rocks, Sto-Rox High School and Penn State; 1980-**Hugh Green** defensive end from Pitt; 1994-**Kerry Collins** quarterback from Wilson High School of West Lawn and Penn State; 1995-**Eddie George** running back from Abington High School and Ohio State.

MIKE MAYOCK played at the Haverford School for his father, **Mike Mayock**, Senior. He was a defensive back at Boston College 1976-80 and a 1980 captain and All-East for the 7-4 Golden Eagles. Mayock was with Toronto in the CFL 1981 and NY Giants 1982-83.

JOHN MAZUR played for the Plymouth High School Shawnee Indians under **John "Schongie" Mergo**. He was a quarterback at Notre Dame from 1949-51 for **Frank Leahy's** Fighting Irish who won the 1949 national championship. Mazur played for British Columbia in Canada from 1952-54. He was head coach of the Boston/New England 1970-72 and went 9-21-0.

FRED MAZUREK scored 13 TD's and had 1,683 total yards as a quarterback in 1960 for the Redstone High School Blackhawks in Republic, Pennsylvania under coach **Joe Bosnic**. He directed Pitt from 1962-64 and guided **John Michelosen's** 1963 Panthers to a 9-1 record and the #3 ranking in the nation. Mazurek was with the Washington Redskins in 1965-66.

RICHIE McCABE played for Pittsburgh's North Catholic High School Trojans and was a halfback at Pitt 1951-54. He spent seven years as a defensive back with Pittsburgh, Washington and Buffalo in the AFL from 1955-61. He had 9 interceptions and was 1960 All-AFL.

ED McCAFFREY was a quarterback/receiver for the Allentown Central Catholic High School Vikings under **Dick Butler**. He caught 146 passes for 2,33 yards and 15 TD's at Stanford from 1986-90 and was both a 1990 All-American and an Academic All-American for **Dennis Green's** Cardinal. He has been in a the NFL with the NY Giants 1991-93, San Francisco 1994 and Denver since 1995. "Easy Ed" has earned three Super Bowl rings as **George Seifert's** 49ers beat San Diego in SB XXIX in 1995 and when **Mike Shanahan's** Broncos beat Green Bay in SB XXXII in 1997 and Atlanta in SB XXXIII in 1999. He has 370 receptions for 4,913 yards and 43 TD's.

MARK McCANTS played for Allentown's Dieruff High School Huskies under **Bruce Trotter**. The 1980 All-East defensive back at Temple played for the USFL's champion Philadelphia/Baltimore Stars 1983-85.

MIKE McCLOSKY played for Philadelphia's Father Judge High School Crusaders under coach **Whitey Sullivan**. He was a tight end at Penn State from 1979-82 and helped lead **Joe Paterno's** Nittany Lions to a 11-1 record in 1982 and the national crown. McClosky was the #4 draft pick of Houston and caught 3 TD's in five years from 1983-87 with the Oilers and Philadelphia.

WILLIE McCLUNG was a tackle for Philadelphia's Edward Bok Tech Wildcats under coach **Anthony "Mex" Siani**. He played tackle at Florida A&M 1952-54 and spent seven years in the NFL trenches with Pittsburgh 1955-57, Cleveland 1958-59 and Detroit 1960-61.

McCOY

VANCE McCORMICK played for the Harrisburg Academy Riversiders and at Yale 1891-92. He was the first All-American from central Pennsylvania as **Walter Camp** selected him as a 1892 All-American quarterback. McCormick was a volunteer coach at the Carlisle Indian School.

MIKE McCOY played for Erie's Cathedral Prep Ramblers under **Thomas Duff**. He was a defensive tackle at Notre Dame from 1967-69 for **Ara Parseghian's** Fighting Irish. McCoy was a 1969 consensus All-American and was sixth in the Heisman Trophy vote, which was won by Oklahoma's **Steve Owens**. He was the #1 draft pick of Green Bay and spent 11 years in the NFL from 1970-80 with the Packers, Oakland, NY Giants and Detroit. He had one fumble return TD.

DEAN McGEE played for Roaring Spring High School and Lock Haven. He coached Northern Bedford and Bedford High Schools from 1957-89 and compiled a 207-89-13 record in 35 years.

McCAFFREY

ED McGINLEY from Swarthmore was a 1924 consensus All-American tackle at Pennsylvania for **Louis Young's** 9-1-1 Quakers. "Big Ed" played for the NY Giants 1925 and went in the College Football Hall of Fame in 1979.

HUGH McKINNIS was a halfback for the Farrell High School Steelers under **Bill Gargano**. He played at Arizona State 1969-72 for **Frank Kush's** nationally ranked Sun Devils. McKinnis spent four years in the NFL with Cleveland 1973-75 and Seattle 1976.

JOE McNICHOLAS played for Ridley Township High School under **Phil Marion** and at Villanova from 1951-53. He coached the Ridley High School Green Raiders from 1973-96 and went 226-28-2, had six undefeated teams, won the 1990 PIAA 4A state title and developed three pros in **Matt Blundin**, **Joe Valerio** and **Bob Kuberski**.

McQUILKEN

BILL McPEAK played for the New Castle High School Red Hurricanes for **Phil Bridenbaugh**. He was a two-way end at Pitt from 1945-48. McPeak was a nine year veteran defensive end with Pittsburgh 1949-57. He was head coach of the Washington Redskins 1961-65 and went 21-46-3.

KIM McQUILKEN quarterbacked Allentown's William Allen High School Canaries under coach **George "Fritz" Halfacre**. He played at Lehigh 1971-73 and was a 1973 All-American for **Fred Dunlap's** 7-4-1 Engineers. McQuilken set Lehigh career records with 516 completions for 6,996 yards and 37 TD's. He spent seven years with Atlanta and Washington 1974-80 and threw for 1,135 yards and 4 TD's. McQuilken finished in the USFL with Washington in 1983.

CHARLEY MEHELICH was an end for the Verona High School Panthers under **Bob Monaca** and at Duquesne. Mehelich, an uncle to **Bill Fralic**, played for the Steelers from 1946-51.

MEILINGER

STEVE MEILINGER played for the Bethlehem High School Red Hurricanes for **John Butler**. At Kentucky, Meilinger, who played end, halfback, quarterback, was a three-time All-American 1951-53 for **Paul "Bear" Bryant's** Wildcats. He was tenth in the Heisman Trophy vote of 1953 , which was won by **Johnny Lattner** of Notre Dame. Meilinger was the #1 draft choice of Washington and after his military duty, he caught 8 TD's with the Redskins, Green Bay and Pittsburgh 1956-60. With Green Bay, **Vince Lombardi's** Packers lost the 1960 NFL title to Philadelphia.

GREG MEISNER played for the Valley High School Vikings in New Kensington, Pennsylvania under **John Lewis**. He was a defensive tackle at Pitt 1977-80 and was a 1980 Academic All-American for **Jackie Sherrill's** Panthers. Meisner spent ten years with Los Angeles and Kansas City Chiefs 1981-90.

JOHN MELLUS was a tackle for Hanover High School near Wilkes-Barre and at Villanova 1935-37. He was a 1937 All-American for **"Clipper" Smith's** undefeated Wildcats. "Big John" played for New York 1938-41, San Francisco 1946 and Baltimore 1947-50. Mellus, a two-time All-Pro with NY, earned a NFL title ring when **Steve Owens'** Giants beat Green Bay in 1938.

93

L. MICHAELS

SOL METZGER from Philadelphia played at Pennsylvania from 1901-03 for **George Woodruff** and **Carl Williams**. The former Red and Blue captain was head coach at Pennsylvania in 1908 as his Quakers went 11-0-1 and were national champions. He coached West Virginia 1914-15 and Washington and Jefferson 1916-17. Metzger later wrote a syndicated column on football.

CHARLES "MONK" MEYER was a star halfback for the Allentown High School Canaries under **Birney Crum** and then at West Point from 1934-36. Meyer was a 1935 All-American for **Gar Davidson's** 6-2-1 Cadets and was runner-up to the University of Chicago's **Jay Berwanger** in the first-ever Heisman Trophy vote. "Monk" served gallantly in World War II, Korea, Vietnam and received the National Football Foundation's Gold Medal Award in 1987.

JIM MICH played for Easton Catholic High School and East Stroudsburg State. He coached Pottstown's St. Pius X for 26 years from 1959-74 and compiled a 158-89-11 record.

LOU MICHAELS played for the Swoyersville High School Sailors under **John Yonkondy**. He was a tackle at Kentucky 1955-57 and was a two-time All-American in 1956 and 1957 for **Blanton Colliers'** Wildcats. Michaels, the #1 draft choice of LA, spent 13 years as a defensive lineman/kicker with the Rams 1958-60, Pittsburgh 1961-63, Baltimore 1964-69 and Green Bay 1970. He earned a 1968 NFL title ring when **Don Shula's** Colts beat Cleveland, but lost Super Bowl III in 1969 to the NY Jets. The three-time All-Pro scored one TD, kicked 187 FG's and 385 PAT's for 955 total points. Michaels went into the College Football Hall of Fame in 1992.

WALT MICHAELS played for the Swoyersville High School Sailors under **John Yonkondy**. He was a fullback at Washington and Lee from 1948-50 for **Rube McCray** and then was a 13 year veteran linebacker with Green Bay 1951, Cleveland 1952-61 and NY Jets 1963. Michaels, who played in the Pro Bowl 1956-60, earned three NFL championship rings when **Paul Brown's** Browns beat Detroit in 1954, Los Angeles in 1955 and Detroit in 1957. The three-time All-Pro had 11 career interceptions and 4 TD's. Michaels was the head coach of the NY Jets from 1977-82 with a 39-47-1 record. He coached the USFL's New Jersey Generals in 1984-85.

JOHN MICHELS played for Philadelphia's West Catholic High School Burrs for **Bill McCoy**. He was a guard at Tennessee from 1950-52. As a junior in 1951, he helped lead **General Robert Neyland's** 10-0 Volunteers to the national championship. As a senior, Michels was a 1952 All-American for the 8-2-1 Vols ranked #8 in the nation. He was with Philadelphia in 1953, 1956 and Winnipeg in the CFL in 1957. Michels went in the College Football Hall of Fame in 1996.

MICHELS

95

JOHN MICHELOSEN played for the Ambridge High School Bridgers under **Moe Rubenstein**. As a single-wing quarterback at Pitt, Michelosen helped lead **Jock Sutherland's** Panthers to a 8-1-1 record in 1936 and a Rose Bowl win. He was captain of the 1937 Panthers that went 9-0-1 and were national champs. Michelosen was head coach at Pitt from 1955-65 and went 56-49-7.

MIKE MICKA played for the Clairton High School Bears and was a halfback and captain at Colgate 1941-43 for **Andy Kerr's** Red Raiders. Micka spent five years with Washington 1944-45 and Boston Yanks 1946-48. **Dudley DeGroot's** Redskins lost the 1945 title to Cleveland.

SCOTT MILANOVICH quarterbacked the Butler High School Golden Tornadoes under coach **Tim Nunnes**. He played at Maryland 1993-95 for **Mark Dufner** and was a two-time All-ACC QB as he set 31 Terrapin passing records including 650 completions for 7,301 yards and 49 TD's. Milanovich has been in the NFL with Tampa Bay since 1996.

JOE MILINICHICK from Macungie was a tackle for the Emmaus High School Green Hornets under **Gene Legath** and **Joe Ortelli**. He played at North Carolina State 1982-85 and was a 1985 All-American offensive tackle for **Tom Reed's** Wolfpack. "Big Joe," 6-5, 295, spent 10 years with Detroit, 1986-89, LA Rams 1990-92 and San Diego 1993-95. **Bobby Ross'** Chargers lost Super Bowl XXIX in 1995 to the SF 49ers.

MILINICHIK

KEN MILLEN from Lansford went to the U. of Illinois. He coached at Tamaqua, Lansford and Carlisle High Schools from 1931-62. He had a 223-81-22 record, five undefeated teams and three Lansford pros in **Mike Holovak, Joe Repko, Mike Lukak** plus a fourth pro **Clyde Washington** at Carlisle.

MATT MILLEN from Hokendauqua played for the Whitehall High School Zephyrs under **Andy Melosky**. He was a defensive tackle at Penn State 1976-79 and as a junior in 1978 was an All-American for **Joe Paterno's** 11-1 Nittany Lions. Millen was the second round draft choice of Oakland and spent twelve years in the NFL as a linebacker with the Raiders 1980-88, San Francisco 1989-90 and Washighton 1991. "Matty" earned four Super Bowl rings when **Tom Flores'** Raiders beat Philadelphia in SB XV in 1981 and Washington in SB XVIII in 1984, as **George Seifert's** 49ers beat Denver in SB XXIV in 1990, and when **Joe Gibbs'** Redskins beat Buffalo in SB XXVI in 1992. Millen, a three-time All-Pro, had 9 interceptions and 11 sacks. He was named President and CEO of the Detroit Lions in 2001.

M. MILLEN

B. MILLER

BILL MILLER played for the McKeesport High School Tigers under **Duke Weigle**. He was at Miami of Florida for **Andy Gustafson** and was called, "The best end in Hurricane history," as a two-time All-American in 1960 and 1961. Miller was seven year veteran with the Dallas Texans 1962, Buffalo 1963, and Oakland 1964-68. **Hank Stram's** Texans beat Houston in 1962 for the AFL title. **John Rauch's** Raiders beat Houston in 1967 for the AFL crown, but lost Super Bowl II in 1968 to Green Bay. Miller had 141 receptions for 1,879 yards and 10 TD's.

EUGENE "SHORTY" MILLER from Harrisburg was a 1912 All-American halfback at Penn State as he led **Hugo Bezdek's** Nittany Lions to a 8-0-2 record. "Shorty" played several years of pro ball with the Massillon Tigers and went in the College Football Hall of Fame in 1974.

BRIAN MILNE from Waterford played for the Ft. LeBoeuf High School Bisons under **Joe Shesman**. After missing his senior high school season because of cancer, Milne went on to be a top running back at Penn State 1993-95. **Joe Paterno's** Nittany Lions went 12-0 in 1994 and ranked #2 in the nation. Milne has been in the NFL since 1996 with the Colts, Bengals, Saints.

RICH MILOTT from Coraopolis played for the Moon High School Tigers under **Rip Scherer**. He was a linebacker at Penn State for **Joe Paterno** in 1977-78. Milot spent nine years with Washington from 1979-87. He earned two Super Bowl rings when **Joe Gibbs'** Redskins beat Miami in SB XVII in 1983 and Denver in SB XXII in 1988. Milot had 13 interceptions.

ALVIN MITCHELL played for Philadelphia's Simon Gratz High School Bulldogs. He was a defensive back at Morgan State and with the Cleveland Browns 1968-69 and Denver in 1970.

KEVIN MITCHELL played for the Harrisburg High School Cougars under **Richard Hamilton**. He was a nose guard at Syracuse from 1990-93 and started all 48 games with 275 tackles and 21 sacks. "The Minister of Defense" was the #2 draft pick of San Francisco in 1994 and he earned a Super Bowl ring as **George Seifert's** 49ers beat San Diego in SB XXIX in 1995.

TOM MITCHELL played for the Plymouth-Whitemarsh High School Colonials in Plymouth Meeting, Pennsylvania under **Ed Charters**. He was a two-time Little All-American end in 1964 and 1965 at Bucknell for **Bob Odell's** Bison. Mitchell was a 12 year vet with Oakland

1966-67, Baltimore 1968-73 and San Francisco 1974-77. Baltimore beat Cleveland for the 1968 AFL title, but **Don Shula's** Colts lost Super Bowl III in 1969 to the NY Jets. **Don McCafferty's** Colts beat Dallas in Super Bowl VI in 1971. Mitchell had 239 catches for 3,181 yards and 24 TD's.

BOB MITINGER played for Greensburg-Salem High School and at Penn State from 1959-61. He was a 1961 All-American two-way end for **Rip Engle's** 8-3 Nittany Lions. Mitinger spent seven years with San Diego 1962-68. **Sid Gillman's** Chargers appeared in three straight AFL title games 1963-65 and beat Boston in 1963. Mitinger had 3 interceptions.

JOHN MOBLEY played for Chichester High School in Chester, Pennsylvania under coach **Ted Woolerey**. He started all four years as a linebacker at Kutztown University 1992-95, made 387 tackles, scored 5 TD's and was a 1995 All-American for **Al Leonzi's** Golden Bears. Mobley was the first player in Pennsylvania State Athletic Conference history to be drafted in the first round of the NFL draft when selected by Denver in 1996. He earned two Super Bowl rings as **Mike Shanahan's** Broncos beat Green Bay in SB XXXII in 1998 and Atlanta in SB XXXIII in 1999.

DICK "LITTLE MO" MODZELEWSKI from West Natrona played for the Har-Brack Union High School Tigers in Brackenridge, Pennsylvania under coach **Neal Brown**. He was a tackle at Maryland 1950-52 and was a two-time All-American in 1951 and 1952 for **Jim Tatum's** Terrapins. "Little Mo" won the 1952 Outland Trophy as the nation's best lineman and then spent 14 years as a defensive tackle with Washington 1953-54, Pittsburgh 1955, New York 1956-63 and Cleveland 1964-66. He appeared in eight NFL championship games and earned two title rings as **Jim Lee Howell's** Giants beat Chicago in 1956 and **Blanton Colliers'** Browns beat Baltimore in 1964. The three-time All-Pro went in the College Football Hall of Fame in 1993.

D. MODZELEWSKI

ED "BIG MO" MODZELEWSKI from West Natrona played for the Har-Brack Union High School Tigers in Brackenridge, Pennsylvania under **Neal Brown**. He was a fullback at Maryland 1949-51 and a 1951 All-American for **Jim Tatum's** 10-0 Terrapins. "Big Mo" spent six years with Pittsburgh 1952 and Cleveland 1955-59. He earned a 1955 NFL championship ring as **Paul Brown's** Browns beat Los Angeles. The Browns lost the 1957 title to Detroit. He rushed for 1,292 yards and 11 TD's, caught 38 passes for 277 yards, 3 TD's for 14 total TD's.

JOE MONTANA from Monongahela threw for 3,062 career yards and 20 TD's from 1971-73 for the Ringgold High School Rams under **Chuck Abramski**. He went to Notre Dame from 1974-78 and as a junior directed **Dan Devine's** Fighting Irish to 11-1 record and the 1977 national championship. The two-time All-American honorable mention QB in 1977 and 1978 completed 268 of 515 passes for 4,121 yards and 25 TD's in three seasons for the Irish. Montana spent 14 years in the NFL with San Francisco 1979-92 and Kansas City 1993-94. He earned four Super Bowl rings as he paced **Bill Walsh's** 49ers over Cincinnati in SB XVI in 1982 (MVP), Miami in SB XIX in 1985 (MVP), Cincinnati in SB XXIII in 1989 and **George Seifert's** 49ers over Denver in SB XXIV in 1990 (MVP). "The Comeback Kid" completed 3,409 passes in 5,391 attempts for 40,551 yards and 273 TD's and led his two NFL teams to 31 "comeback" victories. The seven time All-Pro went in the Pro Football Hall of Fame in 2000.

CLIFF MONTGOMERY was a halfback for the Har-Brack Union High School Tigers in Brackenridge, Pennsylvania under **Dick Williams**. At Columbia, Montgomery was captain and a 1933 All-American for **Lou Little's** 9-1 Lions who upset Stanford 7-0 in the Rose Bowl. He was with Brooklyn in 1934, was a long-time official and went in the College Football Hall of Fame.

BRANDON MOORE was a tackle for Philadelphia's Archbishop Carrol High School under **Kevin Clancy**. He was All-ACC Academic at Duke 1990-92 and with New England 1993-95.

BILL "RED" MOORE was a guard for the Rochester High School Rams and at Penn State where he was co-captain of the 1946 Nittany Lions. He was with the Steelers from 1947-49.

MONTGOMERY

JOE MOORE was a halfback for Pittsburgh's Schenley High School and at Penn State. He won 118 games at Towanda, Erie McDowell and Upper St. Clair High Schools. Moore developed some of the greatest college offensive lines as line coach at Pitt 1977-85, Notre Dame 1988-96.

MONTANA

L. MOORE

LENNY MOORE scored 22 TD's in 1951 for the Reading High School Red Knights under coach **Andy Stopper**. "The Reading Comet" played at Penn State from 1953-55 for **Rip Engle**. He scored 18 TD's and was a two-time All-American in 1954 and 1955 for the Nittany Lions. Moore spent 12 years with the Baltimore Colts from 1956-67. He earned two NFL championship rings as **Weeb Ewbank's** Colts defeated the NY Giants in 1958 and 1959. The Colts lost the 1964 NFL title to Cleveland. The versatile Moore rushed for 5,174 yards and 63 TD's, caught 363 passes for 6,039 yards for 48 TD's and returned 49 kick-offs for 1,180 yards and one TD. "Spats," who had 12,451 all purpose yards and scored 113 TD's, set an NFL record from 1963-65 when he scored at least one TD in 18 consecutive games. The three-time All-Pro went into the Pro Hall of Fame in 1975.

BOB MORGAN was a tackle for Freeport High School and Maryland 1951-53 for **Jim Tatum**. He was a 1953 All-American honorable mention for the national champs and was a Redskin 1954.

EUGENE "MERCURY" MORRIS rushed for over 2,000 career yards and scored 34 TD's from 1963-65 for Pittsburgh's Avonworth High School Antelopes under **Al Shriver**. He starred at West Texas State 1966-68 and as a junior in 1967 paced **Joe Kerbel's** Buffalos to an 8-3 season and a Junior Rose Bowl victory. "Mercury" was a 1968 All-American as he set NCAA records of 340 yards in a single game, 1,571 yards in a single season and 3,388 yards in a three-year career. He spent eight years with Miami 1969-75 and San Diego 1976. With **Don Shula's** Dolphins, Morris appeared in three straight Super Bowls and earned two rings as Miami beat Washington in SB VII in 1973 and Minnesota in SB VIII in 1974. Morris, a 1973 All-Pro, rushed for 4,133 yards, 31 TD's, and 3 TD's on kick-off returns for a total of 34 TD's.

MORRIS

GEORGE MRKONIC was a tackle for the McKeesport High School Tigers for **Duke Weigle**. He played at Kansas from 1950-52 and was a 1951 All-American as a junior for **J. V. Sikes'** 8-2 Jayhawks. Mrkonic was a Philadelphia Eagle in 1953 and then played in Canada.

JOE MUCCI from Bradenville graduated from St. Vincent's College in 1955. He coached Greensburg Central Catholic 1959-67 and went 34-15-2 and at Jeannette High School 1968-85 and went 150-33-3 with 3 WPIAL titles in 1971, 1981, 1983. His over-all record was 184-48-5.

JOE MUHA played for Preston High School and at VMI. The tough fullback spent five years with Philadelphia from 1946-50. He played in three straight NFL championship games from 1947-1949 as **Greasy Neale's** Eagles beat the Chicago Cards in 1948 and the LA Rams in 1949. Muha, who was an All-Pro in 1948, scored one TD.

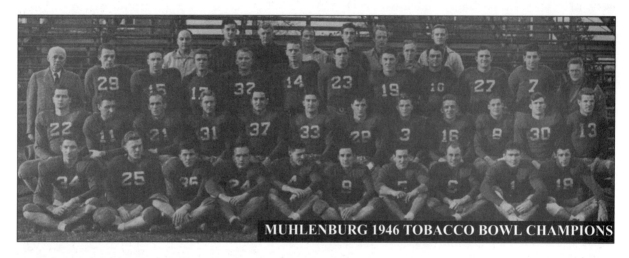

MUHLENBURG 1946 TOBACCO BOWL CHAMPIONS

MUHLENBERG COLLEGE MULES in Allentown, Pennsylvania started football in 1900 and produced many Lehigh Valley legendary scholastic coaches such as Allentown's **J. Birney Crum**, **Pauley Clymer**, **Milo Sewards**, **Perry Scott** and **John Donmoyer**, Northampton's **Al Erdosy**, **Mike Lisetski** and **Pete Schneider** and Nazareth's **Andy Leh**. Muhlenberg was a national powerhouse from 1946 to 1948 under coach **Ben Schwartzwalder** (Hall of Fame) who was from West Virginia. Schwartzwalder's 1946 Mules went 9-1, were the AP's #19 team for November 18, 1946, and defeated St. Bonaventure in the Tobacco Bowl in Lexington, Kentucky for the mythical small college championship. The 1947 Mules went 9-1, but rejected a Tangerine Bowl (today's Florida Citrus Bowl) invitation. Magnificent Mules during the Schwartzwalder golden era included ends: Little All-American **George Bibighaus**, **Irving Dean**, **Ken Moyer** the Mules future basketball coach, linemen **Bob Mirth**, **Carl Reimer**, **Mike Bogdziewicz**, **Sisto Averno** who will play for the Colts, **Carminello Sbordone**, **Prentice Beers**, centers **John Sweatlock**, **Dale Whiteman**, quarterbacks **Jack Crider**, **Marty Binder**, backs **Eddie Sikorski**, **Bill Bell**, **Hal Roveda**, **Harry Mackin**, **Russ Strait** and **Elmo Jackson**. Schwartzwalder went to Syracuse in 1949, led the Orangemen to the 1959 national title, won 153 games, developed all-time running backs in **Jim Brown**, **Ernie Davis**, **Floyd Little**, **Jim Nance** and **Larry Csonka** and went into the College Football Hall of Fame in 1982. Today, the Mules play in Division III.

ALVIN MULLEN played for the Clairton High School Bears under coach **Pat Risha**. He went to Western Kentucky and had 4 interceptions as defensive back for the NY Jets from 1983-86

MIKE MUNCHAK played for the Scranton Central High School Golden Eagles under coach **Emil DeCantis**. He was an offensive guard on **Joe**

MUNCHAK

Paterno's Penn State teams from 1979-81 and was a 1981 All-American for the 10-2 Nittany Lions who were ranked #3 in the nation. Drafted in the first round by Houston, Munchak spent 12 years in the NFL trenches from 1982-93 with the Oilers, a perennial high-powered play-off team under coaches **Jerry Glanville** and **Jack Pardee**. Munchak, a ten-time All-Pro, was inducted into the Pro Football Hall of Fame in 2001.

CHUCK MUNCIE was a running back for the Uniontown High School Red Raiders although he did not play in his senior year because of an injury. He went to Arizona Western JC and the University of California at Berkeley where he was a 1975 consensus All-American and a Heisman Trophy candidate for the 8-3 Golden Bears. Muncie spent nine years with New Orleans 1976-80 and San Diego 1980-84. He rushed for 6,702 yards and 71 TD's and caught 263 passes for 2,323 yards and 3 TD's. Muncie had 74 total TD's.

GEORGE MUNGER played for Philadelphia's Episcopal Academy under **Charles McCarty** and was a star running back at Pennsylvania from 1930-32 for **Lud Wray** and **Harvey Harman**. Munger was head coach at Episcopal Academy from 1934-36 and then at Penn from 1938-53. He went 82-42-10 in 16 years as head coach of the nationally ranked Quakers and won or tied nine unofficial Ivy League titles. Munger developed 14 All-Americans and five Hall of Famers. The popular Munger was inducted into the College Football Hall of Fame in 1976.

MUNCIE

BILL MUNSEY was a halfback for the Uniontown High School Red Raiders under **Bill Power**. He played at Minnesota 1960-62 and with Uniontown teammate, QB **Sandy Stephens**, led **Murray Warmath's** Golden Gophers to the 1960 national title. Munsey was an All-CFL safety with British Columbia as the Lions played in two Grey Cups against Hamilton in 1963 and 1964.

NELSON MUNSEY was a halfback for the Uniontown High School Red Raiders under **Leon Kaltenbach**. He played at Wyoming from 1966-70 for **Lloyd Eaton's** 27-5 Cowboys. Munsey had 7 interceptions and 2 TD's with the Baltimore Colts from 1972-77.

FRAN MURRAY was a halfback for Philadelphia's St. Joseph Prep under **Anthony "Ank" Scanlon**. He played at Pennsylvania 1936-38 and was a 1936 All-American in Penn's "Destiny Backfield" for **Harvey Harman's** 7-1 Quakers. Murray was a Philadelphia Eagle in 1939-40.

JIM MUTSCHELLER played for the Beaver Falls High School Tigers for **Leland Scharken**. He was an end at Notre Dame from 1949-51 for **Frank Leahy**. The 1949 Irish won the national championship

105

and Mutscheller was a 1951 All-American. He spent ten years with Dallas and Baltimore 1952-61. He earned two NFL title rings as **Weeb Ewbanks'** Colts beat the NY Giants in 1958 and 1959. The 1957 All-Pro had 220 career receptions for 3,684 yards and 40 TD's.

BRAD MYERS played for Quarryville High School and was a 1952 Little All-American honorable mention halfback at Bucknell. He was with the LA Rams 1953, 56, Philadelphia 1958.

MYTHICAL STATE CHAMPIONS OF HIGH SCHOOL FOOTBALL 1890-1921. In the early days of scholastic football in Pennsylvania there were few secondary schools who played football and there were no conferences or even a statewide organization to set-up a play-off system to determine a state champion. At times, a school with a good record just declared itself to the public as the state champion. Still, at other times there was a "weeding out" process as the schools, who claimed the title, challenged each other to a game with the winner being recognized as the state champion. The mythical Pennsylvania state champions are: 1890-Philadelphia Central; 1891-Philadelphia Central; 1892-Philadelphia Central; 1893-Harrisburg Central; 1894-Harrisburg Central; 1895-Harrisburg Central; 1896-Williamsport; 1897-Williamsport; 1898-Harrisburg Central; 1899-Harrisburg Central; 1900-Harrisburg Central; 1901-York; 1902-Easton; 1903-Lebanon; 1904-Williamsport; 1905-Williamsport; 1906-Johnstown; 1907-Shamokin; 1908-Williamsport; 1909-Harrisburg Central; 1910-Williamsport; 1911-Lancaster; 1912-Johnstown; 1913-Reading; 1914-Greensburg; 1915-Harrisburg Central; 1916-Greensburg; 1917-Easton; 1918-Harrisburg Tech; 1919-Harrisburg Tech; 1920-Greensburg; 1921-Greensburg.

MYTHICAL STATE CHAMPIONS OF HIGH SCHOOL FOOTBALL 1922-1940. Starting in 1922, the winners in the Eastern and Western divisions of the Central Pennsylvania Interscholastic Athletic League played a post-season game for the mythical state championship. Philadelphia and Pittsburgh high schools did not qualify to participate in these play-offs as they were not members of the CPIAL. The CPIAL East-West play-off champions for the mythical state championship are: 1922-Harrisburg Tech 47 Lock Haven 6; 1923-Harrisburg Tech 43 Lock Haven 7; 1924-Lock Haven 13 Harrisburg Tech 0; 1925-no game; 1926-Steelton 39 Johnstown 0; 1927-Mt.Carmel 7 Bellefonte 6; 1928-Harrisburg William Penn 26 Jersey Shore 0; 1929-tie Williamsport 0 Altoona 0; 1930-Williamsport 24 Johnstown 9; 1931-Harrisburg John Harris 13 Altoona 7; 1932-Harrisburg William Penn 12 Altoona 6; 1933-Windber 7 Harrisburg John Harris 6; 1934-tie Bethlehem 13 Altoona 13; 1935-Ashland 6 Altoona 2; 1936-Kingston 6 Curwensville 0; 1937-Windber 21 Steelton 0. In the next and what will be the last three years of these play-offs the mighty teams of the BIG 15 Conference withdrew from play-off consideration. 1938-Kulpmont 59 Ferndale 19; 1939-Blythe Township 12 Clearfield 0; 1940-Shenandoah 0 Tyrone 0.

JOE NAMATH threw for 1,511 yards and 12 TD's in 1960 for Beaver Falls High School as coach **Larry Bruno's** Tigers won the WPIAL championship. A Major League Baseball prospect, Namath was a three-year starting QB at Alabama for **Paul "Bear" Bryant** from 1962-64. As a 1964 All-American, Namath led the Crimson Tide to a 10-1 record and the national crown. Namath, the #1 draft choice of NFL St. Louis and AFL New York, signed a record $400,000 contract and spent 13 years in the pros with the Jets from 1965-76 and LA Rams in 1977. "Broadway Joe" first engineered New York to a 1968 AFL championship over Oakland and then earned a Super Bowl ring when he backed up his statement, "The Jets are going to win on Sunday, I guarantee it." As MVP of the game, Namath directed **Weeb Ewbanks'** Jets to an upset victory over the NFL's Baltimore Colts, an 18 point favorite, in Super Bowl III in 1969. Namath had 1,886 career completions in 3,762 attempts for 27,663 yards and 173 TD's. The five-time All-Pro QB went into the Pro Football Hall of Fame in 1985.

NAMATH

NANCE

JIM NANCE was a fullback for Indiana High School. He played at Syracuse from 1962-64 for coach **Ben Schwartzwalder** and was a 1964 All-American and a two-time NCAA heavyweight wrestling champion. "Big Jim" spent 11 years with the Boston/NE Patriots 1965-71, NY Jets 1973 and WFL Shreveport. The two-time All-AFL fullback rushed for 5,401 yards and 45 TD's.

BOB NAPONIC from Jeanette played for the Hempfield Area High School Spartans under **Bill Abraham**. He quarterbacked Illinois 1966-68 and was a Houston Oiler 1969-70.

JOHN NAPONICK played for Norwin High School Knights in Irwin, Pennsylvania under **Rip Scherer**. "Big John," 6-9, 265 pounds, was an imposing two-way tackle at Virginia for **George Blackburn's** Cavaliers 1965-67. He spent his pro career in Canada with Winnipeg and Montreal.

BILL NEILL played for Perkiomen Valley High School in Greaterford, Pennsylvania. He was a nose tackle at Pitt 1977-80 for the powerful Panthers. He was a Giant 1981-83 and Packer 1984.

MIKE NICKSICK a.k.a. NIXON from Burgettstown was a halfback at Pitt in 1933-34 for **Jock Sutherland's** powerful 16-2 Panthers. He played two years with Pittsburgh and Brooklyn. Nixon was head coach of the Washington Redskins from 1959-60 and went 4-18-2.

NIGHT FOOTBALL in the United States started on the evening of September 29, 1892 at the Mansfield, Pennsylvania Fairgrounds when Mansfield Teachers College hosted the Wyoming Seminary of Kingston, Pennsylvania. Twenty lights of two thousand candlepower each were used to illuminate the playing field. The history making nighttime game ended in a scoreless tie. The first night game in professional football occurred in 1902 in the first-ever professional grid league which called itself the National Football League. Under the lights in Elmira, New York, **Connie Mack's** Philadelphia Athletics football team defeated the Kanaweola Athletic Club 39-0.

"9-1, NO BOWL TEAM" is the inscription on the watches from the 1963 Pitt Panther team. **John Michelosen's** Panthers went 9-1 and were ranked #3 in the nation as they only lost to #2 ranked undefeated Navy, led by Heisman Trophy winner **Roger Staubach**, who in turn only lost to #1 ranked undefeated Texas. Yet, Pitt did not go to a bowl game that year. Proud Panthers included ends **Al Grigaliunas**, **John Jenkins**, **Joe Kuzneski**, **Bob Long**, tackles **Ernie Borghetti**, **John Maczuzak**, guards **Ed Adamchik**, **Ray Popp**, **Jeff Ware**, centers **Charles Ahlborn**, **Paul Cercel**, **Marty Schottenheimer**, quarterbacks **Fred Mazeruk**, **Glenn Lehner**, backs **Paul Martha**, **Rick Leeson**, **Bill Bodle**, **John Telesky**, **Bob Roeder**, and **Eric Crabtree**.

B. NOVOGRATZ

BOB NOVOGRATZ was a guard for the Northampton High School Konkrete Kids under coach **Al Erdosy**. He played at West Point for **Earl "Red" Blaik** from 1956-58. Novogratz was a 1958 All-American along with halfbacks **Bob Anderson** and **Pete Dawkins**, who also won the Heisman Trophy, as they led the 8-0-1 Cadets to the #3 ranking in the nation. He also received the Knute Rockne Award in 1958 as the "Outstanding College Lineman in the Nation."

JOE NOVOGRATZ was an end for the Northampton High School Konkrete Kids under **Al Erdosy**. He played at Pitt 1963-65 and was a 1965 All-American honorable mention for **John Michelosen's** Panthers. Drafted by the Steelers, Novogratz played for Minnesota in 1966.

OLKEWICZ

NEAL OLKEWICZ played for the Phoenixville High School Phantoms under **Paul Tompko**. He was a linebacker at Maryland 1976-78 and spent 11 years with Washington 1979-89. **Joe Gibbs'** Redskins appeared in three Super Bowls and Olkewicz earned two rings against Miami in SB XVII in 1983 and Denver in SB XXII in 1988. He had 11 interceptions, 12 sacks, one TD.

DOUG OLSON was a tackle for Emmaus High School under **Al Neff** and **Bruce Polster**. The 1972 and 1973 West Chester Little All-American was a WFL Philadelphia Bell 1974-75 and a Buffalo Bill in 1976.

JOE O'MALLEY played for Scranton Tech Red Raiders under **Pete Doyle**. He was an All-SEC defensive end at Georgia for **Wally Butts** 1952-54. O'Malley was with Pittsburgh 1955-56.

BOB O'NEILL from Bridgeville played for Lincoln High School and was an end at Notre Dame in 1950-52. He was a guard with Pittsburgh in 1956-57 and the New York Titans in 1961.

ED O'NEILL played for Warren High School Dragons under **John "Toby" Shea**. He was a linebacker at Penn State 1971-73 and was a 1973 All-American for **Joe Paterno's** perfect 12-0 Nittany Lions ranked # 5 in the nation. O'Neill was the #1 draft choice of Detroit and had 5 interceptions with 3 TD's as a seven year veteran with the Lions 1974-80 and Green Bay 1980.

PAT O'NEILL played for Red Land High School under **Jim Page**. He was a kicker and punter at Syracuse 1990-93 and was a 1993 Academic All-American for **Paul Pasqualoni's** Orangemen. O'Neill spent two years in the NFL with New England 1994-95 and NY Jets 1995.

ONKOTZ

DENNIS ONKOTZ rushed for 1,234 yards and 19 TD's in 1965 for the Northampton High School Konkrete Kids under **Al Erdosy**. The Lehigh Valley's scholar-athlete was a linebacker and punt returner at Penn State 1967-69 for **Joe Paterno**. Onkotz, who set a PSU career record of 287 tackles, also had 11 interceptions and 3 TD's as a two-time All-American and Academic All-American in 1968 and 1969 for the 22-0 Nittany Lions. He had a career ending injury in 1970 with the NY Jets. Onkotz went in the College Football Hall of Fame in 1996.

BOB ONTKO played for Wyoming Valley West High School in Plymouth, Pennsylvania and was a linebacker at Penn State 1983-86 for **Joe Paterno's** Nittany Lions. Ontko was a Colt in 1987.

TONY ORLANDINI was a tackle for Wyoming Area High School and at Pitt from 1994-97 for **John Majors** and **Walt Harris**. He was in the NFL with Chicago 1998 and Pittsburgh 1999.

JOSEPH "BO" ORLANDO quarterbacked the Berwick High School Bulldogs under **George Curry** to the USA Today national championship in 1983. He was a defensive back at West Virginia from 1985-88. "Bo" was a co-captain and a 1988 All-American for **Don Nehlen's** 11-1 Mountaineers who lost the national title to Notre Dame in the Fiesta Bowl. Orlando has been a nine year veteran in the NFL from 1990-98 with Houston, San Diego, Cincinnati, and Pittsburgh.

JERRY OSTROSKI from Collegeville played for the Owen J. Roberts High School Wildcats in Bucktown, Pennsylvania under **Hank Bernat**. He was a guard at Tulsa 1988-91 and was a 1991 All-American for **David Rader's** 10-2 Hurricanes. Ostroski has been with Buffalo since 1992 as **Marv Levy's** high-powered Bills dropped back-to-back Super Bowls in 1993 and 1994 to Dallas.

PHIL OSTROWSKI played for Wilkes-Barre's Elmer L. Meyers High School Crusaders and was a guard at Penn State for **Joe Paterno** 1994-97. Ostrowski has been a SF 49er since 1998.

A. OWENS

ARTIE OWENS rushed for Pennsylvania single season records of 41 TD's and 248 points in 1971 and 69 career TD's for the Stroudsburg High School Mountaineers under **Fred Ross**. "King Arthur" ran wild at West Virginia 1972-75, as he set WV career records of 2,648 yards and 3,971 all-purpose yards for **Bobby Bowden's** Mountaineers. He scored 4 TD's with San Diego 1976-78, Buffalo and New England 1980. Owens finished with the USFL Philly Stars in 1983.

RICH OWENS played for Philadelphia's Abraham Lincoln High School Railsplitters under coach **William "Jeb" Lynch**. He was a defensive end at Lehigh from 1991-94 for **Hank Small** and then **Kevin Higgins**. Owens has been in the NFL with Washington and Miami since 1995.

FRED PAGAC from Centerville rushed for 2,008 yards and scored 29 TD's in 1968-69 for the Beth-Center High School Bulldogs. He was a tight end at Ohio State 1971-73 under **Woody Hayes** as the Buckeyes went 9-2 in 1972 and ranked #3 in the nation and 10-0-1 in 1973 and ranked #3 again. Pagac spent four years in the NFL with Chicago 1974-75, Tampa Bay 1976-77.

JOE PAGLILI played for the Clairton High School Bears and was a fullback at Clemson from 1953-55. Paglili was with Philadelphia in 1959 and the AFL New York Titans in 1960.

LOU PALATELLA was a guard for Vandergrift High School Blue Lancers and at Pitt from 1951-54 for **Lowell "Red" Dawson**. The 1954 Academic All-American played with the San Francisco 49ers from 1955-58.

LOU PALAZZI was a center for the Dunmore High School Bucks under coach **V. J. Gatto**. He played at Penn State from 1940-42 for **Bob Higgins** and was captain of the 1942 Nittany Lions. Drafted by New York in 1943, he played for the Giants in 1946-47 after WW II. **Steve Owen's** Giants lost the 1946 NFL championship to Chicago. Palazzi was an NFL official for 30 years.

JOHN PALUCK was an end for the Swoyersvile High School Sailors under **John Yonkondy**. He played at Pitt 1953-55 and was the #2 draft pick of Pittsburgh. He spent eight years with the Steelers and Washington 1956, 1959-65. The a two-time All-Pro defensive end scored one TD.

JOHN PAPIT scored 3 TD's and passed for another TD as he paced Philadelphia's Northeast High School Archives under coach **Harold "Gus" Geiges** to the 1946 Philadelphia City League championship over West Catholic before 60,000 fans in Franklin Field. He was a record-setting fullback at Virginia from 1947-50 and was captain and a 1950 All-American for **Art Guepe's** 8-2 Cavaliers. He scored 2 TD's in the NFL with Washington in 1951-53 and Green Bay in 1954.

PARILLI

VITO "BABE" PARILLI played for the Rochester High School Rams and at Kentucky from 1949-51 for **Paul "Bear" Bryant**. He threw a career record 50 TD passes as a two-time All-American in 1950 and 1951 and was fourth and third in Heisman Trophy vote in 1950 and 1951, respectively. "Babe" was the #1 draft pick of Green Bay and spent 15 years with the Packers 1952-58, Oakland 1960, Boston 1961-67 and NY Jets 1968-69. Parilli led **Mike Holovak's** Patriots to the 1963 AFL title game and was All-AFL in 1964. He earned a Super Bowl ring as a back-up to **Joe Namath** when **Weeb Ewbank's** Jets defeated Baltimore in SB III in 1969. Parilli threw for 22,681 yards and 178 TD's and went in the College Football Hall of Fame.

BOB PARSONS from Wind Gap scored 19 TD's and 136 points as a quarterback in 1967 for the Pen Argyl High School Green Knights under **Elwood Petchel**. He did all of the punting at Penn State from 1969-71 for **Joe Paterno** and switched from quarterback to tight end as a junior. Parsons spent 12 years in the NFL with the Chicago Bears from 1972-83. He caught 4 TD's and punted for 34,180 yards and a 38.7 yard average.

HERB PATERRA played for the Glassport High School Gladiators under **Vince McKeeta**. He was a guard at Michigan State 1960-62 for **Duffy Daugherty** and spent six years in the pros with Buffalo in 1963-64 and in Canada with Hamilton from 1965-68. He earned two Grey Cup rings as **Ralph Sazio's** Tiger-Cats beat Winnipeg in 1965 and Saskatchewan in 1967.

PARSONS

FRANK PATRICK played for Derry Area High School and was a defensive end at Nebraska from 1967-69 for **Bob Devaney**. He played with the Green Bay Packers from 1970-72.

FRANK PAZZAGLIA played at Blakely High School under **John Henzes, Sr.** and at George Washington University. He has coached the Valley View High School Cougars in Archbald, Pennsylvania since 1969 and has a 279-80-8 record.

BOB PECK from Loch Haven was a center at Pitt from 1913-16 for **Joe Duff** and then **Glenn "Pop" Warner**. The Panthers went 30-3-1 in those four seasons and were national champions in 1916. Peck, a three-time All-American in 1914, 1915 and 1916, is in the College Football Hall of Fame.

B. PELLEGRINI

BOB PELLEGRINI from Yatesboro played for the Shannock Valley High School Spartans in Rural Valley, Pennsylvania under **Jim Sibley**. He was a guard/center at Maryland from 1953-55 for **Jim Tatum's** 27-4-1 Terrapins. Maryland won the 1953 national crown. Pellegrini, who was on the cover of Sports Illustrated, was a consensus 1955 All-American and was sixth in the Heisman Trophy vote. He was the #1 draft choice of Philadelphia and spent ten years with the Eagles 1956-61 and Washington 1962-65. Pellegrini earned a 1960 NFL title ring as **Buck Shaw's** Eagles beat Green Bay. He went in the College Football Hall of Fame in 1996.

GASPARE "GAMP" PELLEGRINI graduated from Philadelphia's St. Thomas More High School and coached at St. Thomas More 1967-69 with a 9-20 record, St. Joseph's Prep 1970-77 with a 50-38-1 record and the 1977 Philadelphia City League championship, Malvern Prep 1978-00 with a 155-69-8 record and 10 Inter-Ac League championships plus the Friars also had a 34 game win streak from 1979-81. His over-all record in 34 years is 214-127-9.

PENNSYLVANIA STATE ATHLETIC CONFERENCE is one of the largest NCAA Division II conferences in the nation. The PSAC was organized in 1951 to administer an athletic league of the 14 state teachers colleges. At first, each college could select it's own NCAA competitive division, but in 1980 the entire conference was classified as NCAA Division II. In 1983, all the schools were granted university status by the state. From 1934 to 1948 sportswriters chose a mythical PSAC football champion. The champions were: 1934-Indiana; 1935-Shippensburg; 1936-Loch Haven; 1937-Loch Haven; 1938-Mansfield; 1939-Slippery Rock; 1940-Indiana and Millersville; 1941-Millersville; 1942-West Chester; 1943-45-no champion; 1946-California; 1947-Mansfield; 1948-Bloomsburg. From 1949 to 1959 PSAC champions were picked by the Roger Saylor System. The champions were 1949-Bloomsburg; 1950-West Chester; 1951-Bloomsburg; 1952-West Chester; 1953-West Chester; 1954-Bloomsburg,East Stroudsburg and West Chester; 1955-Bloomsburg; 1956-West Chester; 1957-Loch Haven; 1958-California; 1959-West Chester. From 1960 to 1987 there was a PSAC championship game between the Eastern and Western Divisions. The PSAC champions were 1960-West Chester 35, Loch Haven 6; 1961-West Chester 21, Slippery Rock 0; 1962-Slippery Rock 13, East Stroudsburg 6; 1963-West Chester 36, Slippery Rock 7; 1964-East Stroudsburg 37, Indiana 14; 1965-East Stroudsburg 26, Indiana 10; 1966-Clarion 28, West Chester 26; 1967-West Chester 27, Clarion 7; 1968-tie California 28, East Stroudsburg 28; 1969-West Chester 41, Clarion 34; 1970-Edinboro 14, West Chester 6; 1971- West Chester 35, Edinboro 14; 1972-Slippery Rock 29, West Chester 27; 1973-Slippery Rock 28, West Chester 14; 1974-Slippery Rock 20, West Chester 7; 1975-East Stroudsburg 24, Edinboro 20; 1976-tie East Stroudsburg 14, Shippensburg 14; 1977-Clarion 25, Millersville 24; 1978-East Stroudsburg 49, Clarion 14; 1979-Loch Haven 48, Cheyney 14; 1980-Clarion 15, Kutztown 14; 1981-Shippensburg 34, Millersville 17; 1982-East Stroudsburg 24, Edinboro 22; 1983-Clarion 27, East Stroudsburg 14; 1984-California 21, Bloomsburg 14; 1985-Bloomsburg 31, Indiana 9; 1986-Indiana 20, West Chester 6; 1987-Indiana 21, West Chester 9. From 1988 to the present, the PSAC does not have a championship game, but declares Eastern and Western Division champions by seasonal records. The PSAC East and West divisional champions since that time were: 1988-Millersville and Shippensburg; 1989-tie Millersville, West Chester and Edinboro; 1990-Millersville and Indiana; 1991-East Stroudsburg and Indiana; 1992-West Chester and Clarion; 1993-Millersville and Indiana; 1994-tie Bloomsburg, West Chester and Indiana; 1995-tie Bloomsburg, Millersville and Edinboro; 1996-Bloomsburg and tie Clarion, Indiana; 1997-Bloomsburg and Slippery Rock; 1998-Millersville and Slippery Rock; 1999-West Chester and Slippery Rock; 2000-Bloomsburg and a tie with Clarion, Indiana, Slippery Rock.

UNIVERSITY OF PENNSYLVANIA QUAKERS in Philadelphia, Pennsylvania started football in 1876 and has won four national championships in 1895 at 14-0 and 1897 at 15-0 under **George Woodruff** (Hall of Fame), in 1904 at 12-0 under **Carl Williams** (Hall of Fame) and in 1908 at 11-0-1 under **Sol Metzger**. Penn's gridiron glory continued under **George Munger** (Hall of Fame), who was from Elkins Park, Episcopal Academy and a star at Penn in 1930-32, as the Quakers went 82-42-10 from 1938-53. Munger's Red and Blue teams were always nationally ranked and led the country in total attendance from 1938-42. Penn joined the Ivy League in 1956 and has won eight Ivy League championships in 1959 under **Steve Sebo**, in 1982, 1983, 1984, 1985 under **Jerry Berndt**, in 1986 at 10-0 under **Ed Zubrow**, and in 1993 at 10-0 and 1994 at 9-0 under **Al Bagnoli**. Quaker first team All-Americans include **John Adams** C 1891, **Harry Thayer** B 1892, **Arthur Knipe** B 1894, **Winchester Osgood** B 1894 (Hall of Fame), **Charles Gelbert** E 1894-96 (Hall of Fame), **Alfred Bull** C 1895, **George Brooke** B 1895 (Hall of Fame), **Charles Wharton** G 1896-97 (Hall of Fame), **Wylie Woodruff** G 1896, **John Outland** T/B 1897-98, **T. Truxton Hare** G 1897-00 (Hall of Fame), **John Minds** B 1897 (Hall of Fame), **Sam Boyle** E 1897, **Peter Overfield** C 1898-99, **Josiah McCracken** G 1899, **Frank Pierarski** G 1904, **Andy Smith** B 1904 (Hall of Fame), **Vince Stevenson** B 1904 (Hall of Fame), **Otis Lamson** T 1905, **Bob Torrey** C 1905 (Hall of Fame), **William**

Hollenback B 1906, 1908 (Hall of Fame), **August Ziegler** G 1906-07, **Dexter Draper** T 1907, **Hunter Scarlett** E 1908 (Hall of Fame), **Ernest Cozens** C 1910, **LeRoy Mercer** B 1910, 1912 (Hall of Fame), **Howard Berry** B 1916-17, **Henry Miller** E 1917, 1919, **Bob Hooper** E 1918, **John Thurman** T 1922, **Ed McGinley** T 1924 (Hall of Fame), **Alton Papworth** G 1924, **George Thayer** E 1925, **John Butler** C 1926, **Charles Rodgers** B 1926, **Ed Hake** E 1927, **John Smith** T 1927, **Paul Scull** B 1928, **Fran Murray** B 1936, **Harlan Gustafson** E 1939, **Ray Frick** C 1940, **Francis X. Reagan** B 1940, **Bernie Kuczynski** E 1942, **Bob Odell** B 1943 (Hall of Fame), **George Savitsky** T 1944-47 (Hall of Fame), **Anthony "Skip" Minisi** B 1947 (Hall of Fame), **Chuck Bednarik** C 1947-48 (Pro and College Hall of Fame), **John Schweder** G 1949, **Francis "Reds" Bagnell** B 1950 (Hall of Fame), **Bernie Lemonick** G 1950, **Ed Bell** E 1951-52, **Gerald McGinley** T 1951, **Jack Schanafelt** T 1953, **Marty Peterson** OT 1986, **John Zinser** OG 1988, **Bryan Keys** RB 1989, **Joe Valererio** OT 1990, **Pat Goodwillie** LB 1994, **Miles Macik** WR 1995 and **Tom McGarrity** DE 1995.

PENN STATE UNIVERSITY NITTANY LIONS in State College, Pennsylvania started football in 1887 and was led by four College Football Hall of Fame coaches in **Hugo Bezdek**, **Charles "Rip" Engle** from Salisbury and Waynesboro High School, **Dick Harlow** from Philadelphia's Episcopal Academy and Penn State, and **Bob Higgins**. Current coach, **Joe Paterno**, played scholastically in 1943-44 for **Zev Graham** at Brooklyn Prep where he and his brother, **George Paterno**, were called the "Gold Dust Twins." Paterno became a T-formation quarterback at Brown from 1947-49 under **Rip Engle** and went with him to Penn State as an assistant in 1950. Paterno followed Engle as head coach of Penn State in 1966 and has a record of 322-90-3 in 36 years with six perfect seasons in 1968, 1969, 1973, 1986, 1989, and 1994. Under Joe Pa's leadership, Penn State has won two national championships in 1982 and 1986. In 1982 the Nittany Lions went 11-1 and beat Georgia in the Sugar Bowl to earn the national title. The Blue and White attack was led by QB **Todd Blackledge**, RB **Curt Warner**, OT **Bill Contz** from Belle Vernon, TE **Mike McClosky** from Philadelphia's Father Judge HS, WR **Gregg Garrity** from North Allegheny HS, WR **Kenny Jackson**, LB **Scott Radecic** from Brentwood, LB **Walker Lee Ashley**, and S **Mark Robinson**. In 1986 Penn State went 12-0 and beat Miami of Florida in the Fiesta Bowl to win the national crown for the second time in the 1980's. Roaring Lions were QB **John Shafer**, RB **D.J. Dozier**, OT **Chris Conlin** from Bishop McDevitt HS, LB **Don Graham** from Brentwood, and LB **Bob Ontko** from Wyoming Valley West HS. Penn State has produced numerous first team All-Americans including **W.T. "Mother" Dunn** C 1906, **Bob Higgins** E 1915, 1919 (Hall of Fame), **Percy "Red" Griffiths** G 1920 Taylor, **Charley Way** HB 1920 Downingtown, **Glenn Killinger** HB 1921 Harrisburg (Hall of Fame), **"Light Horse" Harry Wilson** HB 1923 Sharon (Hall of Fame), **Joe Bedenk** G 1923 Mansfield, **Leon Gajecki** C 1940 Colver, **Steve Suhey** G 1947 (Hall of Fame), **Sam Tamburo** E 1948 New Kensington, **Lenny Moore** HB 1955 Reading (Pro Hall of Fame), **Sam Valentine** G 1956 Dubois, **Richie Lucas** QB 1959 Glassport (Hall of Fame), **Bob Mitinger** E 1961 Greensburg, **Dave Robinson** E 1962, **Roger Kochman** HB 1962 Wilkensburg, **Glenn Ressler** G 1964 Dornsife, **Ted Kwalick** E 1967-68 McKees Rocks (Hall of Fame), **Dennis Onkotz** LB 1968-69 Northampton (Hall of Fame), **Mike Reid** DT 1969 Altoona (Hall of Fame), **Charlie Pitman** HB 1969, **Neal Smith** S 1969 Port Trevorton, **Jack Ham** LB 1970 Johnstown (Pro and College Hall of Fame), **Dave Joyner** T 1971 State College, **Lydell Mitchell** HB 1971, **Charlie Zapiec** LB 1971 Philadelphia, **Bruce Bannon** DE 1972, **John Huffnagel** QB 1972 McKees Rocks, **John Skorupan** LB 1972 Beaver, **John Cappelletti** RB 1973 Upper Darby, **Randy Crowder** DT 1973 Farrell, **Ed O'Neil** LB 1973 Warren, **John Nessel** T 1974, **Mike Hartenstine** DE 1974 Bethlehem, **Chris Bahr** K 1975 Neshaminy, **Greg**

Buttle LB 1975, **Tom Rafferty** G 1975, **Kurt Allerman** LB 1976, **Keith Dorney** T 1977-78 Macungie, **Randy Sidler** MG 1977 Danville, **Matt Bahr** K 1978 Neshaminy, **Bruce Clark** DT 1978-79 New Castle, **Chuck Fusina** QB 1978 McKees Rocks, **Pete Harris** S 1978, **Matt Millen** DT 1978 Hokendauqua, **Bill Dugan** T 1980, **Sean Farrell** G 1980-81, **Mike Munchak** OG 1981 Scranton (Pro Hall of Fame), **Curt Warner** RB 1981-82, **Walker Lee Ashley** DE 1982, **Kenny Jackson** WR 1982-83, **Mark Robinson** S 1982, **Mike Zordich** S 1985, **Shane Conlan** LB 1985-86, **Chris Conlin** T 1986 Glenside, **D. J. Dozier** RB 1986, **Tim Johnson** DT 1986, **Steve Wisnieswski** G 1987-88, **Andre Collins** LB 1989, **Blair Thomas** RB 1989 Philadelphia, **Darren Perry** DB 1991, **O. J. McDuffie** WR 1992, **Lou Benfatti** DT 1993, **Kyle Brady** TE 1994 New Cumberland, **Ki-Jana Carter** RB 1994, **Kerry Collins** QB 1994 West Lawn, **Bobby Engram** WR 1994, **Jeff Hartings** G 1994-95, **Kim Herring** S 1996, **Curtis Ennis** RB 1997, **LaVar Arrington** LB 1998-99 Pittsburgh, **Brandon Short** LB 1999 McKeesport, and **Courtney Brown** DE 1999.

PERGINE

JOHN PERGINE quarterbacked the 1963 Plymouth-Whitemarsh High School Colonials in Plymouth Meeting, Pennsylvania under **Ed Charters** to the #1 ranking in the Philadelphia area. He became a linebacker at Notre Dame from 1965-67 for **Ara Parseghian** as the 1966 Fighting Irish won the national crown. The 1967 All-American spent eight years with Los Angeles 1968-72 and Washington 1973-75. **George Allen's** Redskins lost Super Bowl VII in 1973 to Miami.

ANTHONY PETERSON was a linebacker for the Ringgold High School Rams in Monongahela, Pennsylvania under **Joe Ravasio**. He played at Notre Dame 1990-93 for **Lou Holtz**. Peterson has been with San Francisco from 1994-96, 1998-99, Chicago 1997 and Washington 2000. He earned a Super Bowl ring as **George Seifert's** 49ers defeated San Diego in SB XXIX in 1995.

BOB PETRELLA played for Philadelphia's Southern High School Rams under **Anthony "Mex" Siani** and at Tennessee from 1963-65 for **Doug Dickey**. He was a safety for six years with Miami from 1966-71 and had 5 picks. **Don Shula's** Dolphins lost Super Bowl V in 1972 to Dallas.

MIKE PETTINE was a halfback for the Conshohocken High School Golden Bears under coach **Ray Weaver**. "The Conshohocken Comet" played at Villanova from 1959-61. He was coach of Central Bucks West High School in Doylestown, Pennsylvania for 33 years from 1967-99 with a 326-42-4 record, 16 unbeaten seasons, four PIAA 4A state championships in 1991, 1997, 1998, and 1999. His Bucks also established a new state winning streak record of 59 games that started in 1997 and ended in the 2000 state title game under his coaching successor and former player **Mike Carey**. Pettine developed three pros **Frank Case**, **Randy Cuthbert** and **Jim Jensen**.

PHILADELPHIA BULLDOGS were champions of Continental Football League in 1966. The CFL was the top professional minor league in the early 1960's and Philadelphia had a franchise for two years in 1965-66. **Sylvan Cohen** and **Leonard Mercer, Jr.** founded the Bulldogs with **Wayne Hardin**, ex-Navy coach, as head man. Philadelphia defeated the Orlando Panthers 20-17 at Temple Stadium for the 1966 CFL championship. Trailing 17-3 in the title game, Bulldog quarterback **Bob Broadhead**, from Kittanning, Duke,

Browns, threw TD passes to **Dewey Lincoln** and **Claude Watts** to tie the game at 17-17 at the end of regulation time. In "Sudden Death" overtime, **Jamie Caleb's** field goal won the game for the Bulldogs. Orlando was paced by QB **Don Jonas**, from West Scranton and Penn State, who threw one TD pass and kicked a field goal. When the Philadelphia franchise folded after the 1966 season, assistant coach, **Dave DiFilippo**, took sixteen of the CFL champion Bulldogs to form the nucleus of the 1968 Pottstown Firebirds, future champs of the Atlantic Coast Football League in 1969 and 1970.

PHILADELPHIA EAGLES were started in 1933 when former Penn stars **Bert Bell** (Hall of Fame) and **Lud Wray** purchased the franchise from the National Football League. Bell sold the franchise to **Alex Thompson** in 1940, became associated with **Art Rooney's** Pittsburgh Steelers, and later became Commissioner of the NFL from 1946-59. Bell died in October of 1959 and was replaced as head of the league by **Pete Rozelle**. Bell was a charter member of the Pro Football Hall of Fame in 1963. The Eagles were NFL champions in 1948, 1949, and 1960. Under coach **Earle "Greasy" Neale** (Hall of Fame), the Eagles lost the 1947 NFL title game to the Chicago Cardinals, but rebounded with two straight crowns by beating the Cardinals 7-0 in 1948 during a blizzard in Shibe Park and the Los Angeles Rams 14-0 in 1949. High-flying Eagles were receivers **Pete Pihos** (Hall of Fame), **Jack Ferrante** from Philly, **Neil Armstrong**, **John Green**; tackles **Al Wistert**, **Vic Sears**, **Mike Jarmoluk** from Philly's Frankford High School and Temple, **George Savitsky** from Penn; guards **Francis "Bucko" Kilroy** from Philly's Northeast Catholic High School and Temple, **Cliff Patton**, **Duke Maronic** from Steelton; centers **Vic Lindskog**, **Alex Wojciechowicz** (Hall of Fame) **Chuck Bednarik** (Hall of Fame) from Bethlehem High School and Penn; quarterback **Tommy Thompson**, and running backs **Steve Van Buren** (Hall of Fame), **Bosh Pritchard**, **Joe Muha** from McKees Rocks and VMI, **Russ Craft** and **Frank Reagan** from Philly's West Catholic High School and Penn. In 1960 coach **Lawrence "Buck" Shaw** guided the Eagles to their third NFL title by beating the Green Bay Packers 17-14 at Franklin Field. The Eagles soared to the top with receivers **Tommy McDonald** (Hall of Fame), **Pete Retzlaff**, **Bobby Walston**, tackles **J.D. Smith**, **Jim McCusker**; guards **Stan Campbell**, **Gerry Huth**; center **Chuck Bednarik** (Hall of Fame) who also started at linebacker; quarterback **Norm Van Brocklin** (Hall of Fame), backs **Clarence Peaks**, **Billy Ray Barnes**, **Ted Dean** from Radnor High School and Wichita State and **Tim Brown**. The defensive line was anchored by **Jess Richardson** from Philly's Roxborough High School and Alabama, **Marion Campbell**, **Ed Khayat**, and **Joe Robb**; linebackers along with Bednarik were **Maxie Baughan**, **Bob Pelligrini** from Yatesboro and Maryland, **Chuck Weber** from Abington High School and West Chester State; defensive backs **Tom Brookshier** and **Jimmy Carr**. The Eagles soared once more in 1980 under Philadelphia natives - owner **Leonard Tose** and general manager **Jim Murray** - as they brought in UCLA coach **Dick Vermeil**. Philadelphia defeated Dallas for the NFC title, but lost Super Bowl XV in 1981 to Oakland 27-10. On offense the receivers were **Harold Carmichael**, **Charlie Smith**, **Keith Krepfle**, **John Spagnola** from Bethlehem Catholic High School and Yale, tackles **Stan Walters**, **Jerry Sisemore**, guards **Woody Peoples**, **Ron Baker**, center **Guy Morriss**, quarterback **Ron Jaworski**, and backs **Wilbert Montgomery**, **Billy Campfield** and **Leroy Harris**. The defense had linemen **Carl Hairston**, **Claude Humphrey**, **Charlie Johnson**, linebackers **Bill Bergey**, **John Bunting**, **Frank Lemaster**, **Reggie Wilkes**, and a defensive secondary of **Herm Edwards**, **Randy Logan**, **Bernard Wilson** and **Roynell Young**.

117

PHILADELPHIA STARS were champions of the United States Football League in 1984. The USFL was a spring-time league that operated for three years from 1983-85. The Stars were owned by **Myles Tanebaum**, an entrepreneur, with **Carl Peterson** as president and **Jim Mora** as head coach. Philadelphia lost the first-ever USFL championship game to the Michigan Panthers in 1983 and then defeated the Arizona Wranglers the following year in 1984 to win the USFL crown. The Stars repeated as USFL champions again in 1985 by beating the Oakland Invaders, however, the franchise was no longer in Philly as it relocated to Baltimore for the final season. Stars shining brightly were receivers **Scott Fitzkee** from Red Lion High School and Penn State, **Willie Collier** from Pitt, **Steve Folsom**, **Tom Donovan** from Penn State; tackles **Brad Oates**, **Irv Eatman** and **Joe Conwell** from Lower Merion and North Carolina, guards **Rich Garza** from Bethlehem's Liberty High School and Temple, **George Gilbert**, **Chuck Comminsky**; center **Bart Oats**; quarterback **Chuck Fusina** from McKees Rocks and Sto-Rox High School and Penn State; running backs **Kelvin Bryant**, **Anthony Anderson** from Temple, **Duck Riley**, and **Jeff Rodenberger** from Quakertown High School and Maryland, and kicker **Sean Landeta**. On the Stars defensive line were **William Fuller**, **Frank Case** from Doylestown's Central Bucks West High School and Penn State, **Dave Opfar** from Penn State, **Pete Kugler** from Penn State; linebackers **Sam Mills**, **George Cooper**, **Mike Johnson**, and **George Jamison** and defensive backs **Mike Lush** from Allentown's Wm. Allen High School and East Stroudsburg State, **Mark McCants** from Allentown's Dieruff High School and Temple, **Scott Woerner** and **Antonio Gibson**, **Roger Jackson** from Penn State, **Garcia Lane**, and **John Sutton**.

PHILADELPHIA QUAKERS were the champions of the American Football League in the league's only year of existence in 1926. The AFL was created tby **Red Grange** and his manager, **C.C. Pyle**, after a contract dispute with Grange's 1925 team, **George Halas'** Chicago Bears. Other AFL franchises were the Boston Bulldogs, Brooklyn Horsemen, Chicago Bulls, Cleveland Panthers, Los Angeles Wildcats, Newark Bears, and Rock Island Independents. The Quakers went 7-2 for **Bob Folwell**, from Philly and ex-Penn star, to win the AFL title. Quakers were ends **Knute Johnson**, **Joe Kostos**, **Bill Thomas**, **George Tully**, tackles **Bob Beattie**, **Russell "Bull" Behman**, **Charles Cartin**, **Century Milstead**, guards **Ed Coleman**, **Seville Carruthers**, **Jerry Fay**, **Joe Spagna**, center **Karl Robinson**, and backs **Les Asplundh**, **Bob Dinsmore**, **Wally "Doc" Elliott**, **Adrian Ford**, **Lou Gebhard**, **Al Kreuz**, **Joe Marhefka**, **John Scott**, **George Sullivan** and **Charley "Pie" Way**.

BOB PHILLIPS was a Little All-American running back at Slippery Rock. He coached the Montour High School Spartans from 1955-65 and went 92-12-4 with four WPIAL titles in 1957, 1958, 1963, 1964. "Coach Bob" was the QB coach on **Joe Paterno's** staff at Penn State for 24 years 1966-89 and developed such outstanding field generals as **Chuck Burkhart**, who played for Phillips at Montour, **John Hufnagel**, **Chuck Fusina**, **Todd Blackledge**, and **John Shaffer**.

PIAA STATE CHAMPIONSHIPS were started in 1988 when the Pennsylvania Interscholastic Athletic Association initiated for the first time an official state-wide play-off system to decide a state champion in the state's four school enrollment classifications of 4A, 3A, 2A, and 1A. PIAA champions in 4A are: 1988-Allentown Central Catholic; 1989 Upper Saint Clair; 1990-North Allegheny; 1991-Central Bucks West; 1992 Cumberland Valley; 1993-North Hills; 1994-McKeesport; 1995-Penn Hills; 1996-Downingtown; 1997-Central Bucks West; 1998-Central Bucks West; 1999 Central Bucks West; 2000-Erie Cathedral Prep. State champions in 3A are: 1988-Berwick; 1989-Perry Traditional Academy; 1990-Bethlehem Catholic; 1991-Erie Strong Vincent; 1992-Berwick; 1993-Allentown Central Catholic; 1994-Berwick; 1995-Berwick; 1996-Berwick; 1997-Berwick; 1998-Allentown Central Catholic; 1999-Strath Haven; 2000-Strath

Haven. State champions in 2A are: 1988-Bethlehem Catholic; 1989-Hickory; 1990-Hanover; 1991-Aliquippa; 1992-Valley View; 1993-Dallas; 1994-Mt. Carmel; 1995-Bishop McDevitt; 1996-Mt. Carmel; 1997-South Park; 1998-Mt. Carmel; 1999-Tyronne; 2000-Mt. Carmel. State champions in 1A are: 1988-Camp Hill; 1989-Dunmore; 1990-Marian Catholic; 1991-Schuykill Haven; 1992-Scotland School; 1993-Duquesne; 1994-Southern Columbia; 1995-Farrell; 1996-Farrell; 1997-Sharpesville; 1998-Rochester; 1999-South Side Beaver; 2000-Rochester.

PISARCIK

JOE PISARCIK played for the Kingston Central Catholic High School Queensmen under **Bernie Popson**. He was the record-setting quarterback at New Mexico State from 1971-73 with 5,770 yards passing and 30 TD's for **Jim Wood's** Aggies. The All-Missouri Valley QB spent 11 years in pro ball with Calgary in Canada 1974-76 and in the NFL with the NY Giants 1977-79 and Philadelphia 1980-84. He was a back-up to **Ron Jaworski** as **Dick Vermeil's** Eagles lost Super Bowl XV in 1981 to Oakland. Pisarcik threw for 5,552 yards and 24 TD's in the NFL.

PITTSBURGH STEELERS were started in 1933 when **Arthur J. Rooney** obtained the franchise in the National Football League. At first, Rooney called his club the Pirates after the city's baseball team, but in 1940, he changed the nickname to the Steelers. Rooney went through 16 coaches and 26 losing seasons when he hired **Chuck Noll** in 1969. Noll, who played for the coach **Paul Brown** at Cleveland and was an assistant coach under **Don Shula** at Baltimore, turned the Steelers into the Team of the Decade for the 1970's. The Steelers won four Super Bowls when they beat Minnesota 16-6 in Super Bowl IX in 1975, Dallas 21-17 in Super Bowl X in 1976, Dallas for the second time 35-31 in Super Bowl XII in 1979, and the Los Angeles Rams 31-19 in Super Bowl XIV in 1980. Standout Steelers on offense were receivers **Lynn Swann** (Hall of Fame), **Ron Shanklin, John Stallworth, Randy Grossman** from Haverford High School and Temple; tackles **Jon Kolb, Glen Ray Hines, Gerry Mullins**; guards **Sam Davis, Bruce Van Dyke**; and **Steve Courson** from Gettysburg High School and South Carolina; centers **Ray Mansfield** and **Mike Webster** (Hall of Fame); quarterbacks **Terry Bradshaw** (Hall of Fame), **Terry Hanratty** from Butler and Notre Dame; running backs **Franco Harris** (Hall of Fame) from Penn State, **Bob "Rocky" Bleier, John "Frenchy" Fuqhua**; and kicker **Matt Bahr** from Neshaminy High School and Penn State. The "Steel Curtain" defense was led by linemen **"Mean Joe" Greene** (Hall of Fame), **L.C. Greenwood, Dwight White** and **Ernie Holmes**; linebackers **Jack Ham** (Hall of Fame) from Johnstown's Bishop McCort High School and Penn State, **Jack Lambert** (Hall of Fame), and **Andy Russell**, plus defensive backs **Mel Blount** (Hall of Fame), **Mike Wagner, Glen Edwards** and **Donnie Shell**. The Steelers were back at the top in the NFL in 1995 under coach **Bill Cowher** who was a local product out of Carlynton High School and North Carolina State. However, Pittsburgh lost Super Bowl XXX in 1996 to Dallas. Leading the Steelers were receivers **Yancy Thigpen, Ernie Mills, Mark Bruener**, tackles **Leon Searcy, John Jackson**, guards **Brendon Stai, Tom Newberry**, center **Dermonti Dawson**, quarterback **Neil O'Donnell** and running backs **Erric Pegram, J. L. Williams** and **Bam Morris**. Defensive linemen were **Brenston Buckner, Joel Steed, Ray Seals**, linebackers **Kevin Greene, Greg Lloyd, Levon Kirkland, Jerry Olsavsky** of Pitt, **Eric Ravotti** of Penn State, and defensive backs **Rod Woodson, Willie Williams, Darren Perry** of Penn State, **Carnell Lake** and **Myron Bell**. **Art Rooney** was inducted into the Pro Football Hall of Fame in 1964. Coach Noll went in the Pro Football Hall of Fame in 1993. Rooney's son, **Dan Rooney**, who played for Pittsburgh's North Catholic High School and worked for the Steelers since 1955, went in the Pro Football Hall of Fame in 2000.

UNIVERSITY OF PITTSBURGH PANTHERS in Pittsburgh, Pennsylvania, started football in 1890 and went undefeated in 1904 at 10-0 under **Arthur St. L. Mosse**. The Panthers were undefeated again in 1910 at 10-0 and were national champions under **Joe Thompson** (Hall of Fame) who starred for Pitt 1904-06. Under coach **Glenn Scobey "Pop" Warner** (Hall of Fame), who was a star tackle at Cornell and came to Pitt from the Carlisle Indian School in 1915, the Panthers went undefeated three straight years in 1915 at 8-0, 1916 at 8-0, and 1917 at 10-0 and were national champions in 1916 and 1918. Warner went 60-11-4 in eight years from 1915-23. The next great Pitt coach was **Dr. John Bain "Jock" Sutherland** (Hall of Fame), a 1917 All-American guard under Warner. Sutherland, who was from Scotland and moved to Sewickley as a teenager, went 111-20-12 in 16 years from 1924-38, took the Panthers to four Rose Bowls and won the 1937 national title. Pitt's last national crown came in 1976 when the Blue and Gold went 12-0 and beat Georgia 27-3 in the Sugar Bowl under coach **Johnny Majors**, a former 1956 All-American tailback at Tennessee. The powerful Panther attack was led by RB **Tony Dorsett**, the Heisman Trophy winner from Aliquippa and Hopewell High School, who became the NCAA's all-time leading ground gainer, E/K **Carson Long**, from Ashland and North Schuylkill High School, who became the NCAA's all-time leading scorer, QB **Matt Cavanaugh**, MG **Al Romano**, T **Randy Holloway** from Sharon, S **Bob Jury** from Lawrence and C **Tom Brzoza** from New Castle. Pitt continued as a national power under **Jackie Sherill** who went 50-9-1 from 1977-81. Pitt developed many first team All-Americans including **Robert Peck** C 1914-16 Loch Haven (Hall of Fame), **James Herron** E 1916 Beaver, **Andy Hastings** B 1916, **Claude "Tiny" Thornhill** G 1916 Beaver, **Harold "Doc" Carlson** E 1917 Pittsburgh and Hall of Fame Pitt basketball coach, **Dale Sies** G 1917, **George "Tank" McLaren** B 1917 Pittsburgh, **Leonard Hilty** T 1918 Pittsburgh, **Tom Davies** B 1918, 1920 Pittsburgh (Hall of Fame), **Herb Stein** C 1920-21 (Hall of Fame), **Ralph "Horse" Chase** T 1925 Easton, **Bill Kern** T 1927 Kingston, **Gilbert "Gibby" Welch** B 1927, **Mike Getto** T 1928 Jeanette, **Toby Uansa** B 1929 McKees Rocks, **Joe Donchess** E 1929 (Hall of Fame), **Ray Montgomery** G 1929, **Tom Parkinson** B 1929 Coal Center, **Jesse Quatse** T 1931 Greensburg, **Joe Skladany** E 1932-33 Larksville (Hall of Fame), **Warren Heller** B 1932 Steelton, **Charles Hartwig** G 1934, **George Shotwell** C 1934 Wilkes-Barre, **Isadore Weinstock** B 1934 Wilkes-Barre, **Art Detzel** T 1935, **Bill Glassford** G 1936 Pittsburgh, **Averell Daniel** T 1936 Mt. Lebanon (Hall of Fame), **Frank Souchak** E 1937 Berwick, **Bill Daddio** E 1937-38 Meadville, **Tony Matisi** T 1937, **Marshall Goldberg** B 1937-38 (Hall of Fame), **Ralph Fife** G 1941, **Bernie Barkouskie** G 1949 Kulpmont, **Eldred Kraemer** T 1952, **Joe Schmidt** LB 1952 Brentwood, **Joe Walton** E 1956 Beaver Falls, **John Guzik** G 1958 Lawrence, **Mike Ditka** E 1960 Aliquippa (Pro and College Hall of Fame), **Paul Martha** B 1963 Wilkensburg, **Ernie Borghetti** T 1963, **Tony Dorsett** RB 1973-76 Aliquippa (Pro and College Hall of Fame), **Gary Burley** MG 1974, **Al Romano** MG 1976, **Matt Cavanaugh** QB 1977, **Randy Holloway** T 1977 Sharon, **Bob Jury** S 1977 Lawrence, **Tom Broza** C 1977 New Castle, **Gordon Jones** WR 1978 Versailles, **Hugh Green** DE 1978-80 (Pro and College Hall of Fame), **Mark May** OT 1980, **Julius Dawkins** WR 1981 Monessen, **Dan Marino** QB 1981 Pittsburgh, **Sal Sunseri** LB 1981 Pittsburgh, **Jimbo Covert** OT 1981-82 Conway, **Bill Maas** DT 1982, Newton Square, **Bill Fralic** OT 1982-84 Penn Hills (Hall of Fame), **Randy Dixon** OT 1986, **Tony Woods** DE 1986, **Ezekial Gadson** LB 1987, **Craig "Ironhead" Heywood** RB 1987, **Jerry Olsavsky** LB 1988, **Mark Stepnoski** G 1988 Erie, **Marc Spindler** DT 1989 Scranton, **Brian Greenfield** P 1990, and **Ruben Brown** OT 1994.

DOUG PLANK played for the Norwin High School Knights in Irwin, Pennsylvania. He went to Ohio State where he played from 1972-74 for **Woody Hayes'** 29-4-1 Buckeyes. Plank spent eight years in the NFL as a defensive back with the Chicago Bears from 1975-82. He earned a

Super Bowl ring as **Mike Ditka's** Bears beat New England in 1986. Plank had 15 interceptions.

GERALD PLANUTIS was a fullback for the West Hazleton High School Wildcats under **Jim Horn**. He played for Michigan State from 1953-55 for **Duffy Daugherty** and was a 1955 All-American for the 9-1, #2 ranked, Rose Bowl winning Spartans. Planutis was a Redskin in 1956.

FRANK "BUCKY" POPE played for Crafton High School and was an end for the Catawba College Indians in North Carolina. "The Catawba Claw" spent four years in the NFL with Los Angeles 1964-67 and Green Bay in 1968. He had 34 receptions for 952 yards and 13 TD's.

STEVE POTTER played for Fairview High School near Erie and was a linebacker and captain at Virginia 1976-79. Potter spent five years in the NFL 1980-84 with the Dolphins, Chiefs and Bills.

POTTIOS

MYRON POTTIOS from Van Voorhis was the "hardest-hitting" fullback in the WPIAL in 1956 for the Charleroi High School Cougars under **James "Rab" Currie**. He was a guard at Notre Dame 1958-60 and was a 1960 All-American for **Joe Kuharich's** Fighting Irish. "Mo" spent 12 years as a linebacker with Pittsburgh 1961-65, Los Angeles 1966-70 and Washington 1971-74. **George Allen's** "Over the Hill" Redskins lost Super Bowl VII in 1973 to Miami. He had 5 picks.

POTTSTOWN FIREBIRDS were champions of the Atlantic Coast Football League in 1969 and 1970. The ACFL, which was in existence for 10 years from 1962-71, was the last of the great professional minor leagues. **Cosmo Iacavazzi**, owner of the defunct Scranton Miners and an uncle to Princeton All-American and NY Jet **Cosmo Iacavazzi**, was commissioner of the ACFL. The Pottstown franchise, which started in 1968 with ties to the Philadelphia Eagles, was founded by **Bob Calvario** and a small group of businessmen before **Ed Gruber**, a local textile tycoon, took financial control of the club. The head coach was **Dave DiFilippo** who was a guard for Philadelphia's West Catholic High School under **John "Jocko" McGarry**, Villanova 1937-39, the Eagles 1941 and an assistant to **Wayne Hardin** and his 1966 Continental League champion Philadelphia Bulldogs. DiFilippo brought 16 ex-Bulldogs to Pottstown in 1968 and the Firebirds immediately won two straight ACFL crowns in 1969 and 1970. Pottstown went 10-2 in 1969 and defeated Hartford for the title. The Firebirds were 11-1 in 1970 and beat Hartford in a blizzard for their second crown. Red-hot Firebirds were receivers **John Drew, Bob Tucker, Don Alley, Jack Dolbin, Ron Holliday, Ed Pyne**; tackles **Tom Sarkisian, Bruce Puterbaugh, Frank Mitchell**; guards **Ernie Adams, John Barber**; centers **Paul Cercel** and **Leo Levandowski**; quarterbacks **Benjie Dial, Jim "King" Cocoran, Jim Haynie**; running backs **John Land, Dewey Lincoln, Claude Watts**, defensive linemen **Jim Baughn, Joe Blake, Tommy Davis, Bill Stetz**; linebackers **Jerry DiPhillippo, Mark Kosmos, Dave Weedman, Harold Wells, Steve Zegalia**; defensive backs **Buddy Allen, Greg Berger, Bryan Marshall, Herb Nauss, Billy Rakow** and **Sherman Ross**.

From left Eddie Gillespie trainer, Jack Ernst, Tony Latone, Duke Osborne, F. Bucher, Frankie Racis, Russ Hathaway, Hoot Flanagan, Charlie Berry, Russ Stein, Herb Stein, 'Fungy' Lebengood, Denny Hughes, Barney Wentz, Eddie Doyle, Walter French, Dick Rauch, coach

Pottsville still fighting for 1925 NFL title

POTTSVILLE MAROONS were the "disputed" champions of the National Football League in 1925. The Maroons started as one of the top independent pro football teams in northeastern Pennsylvania that played in the rugged Anthracite League of the early 1920's against other tough coal mining clubs such as the Coaldale Big Green, Mahanoy City, Mt. Carmel, Shenandoah and the Wilkes-Barre Panthers. The team rosters consisted mainly of local hard-nosed gridders who worked in the coal mines during the week and then enjoyed rough-house football on the weekend. However, when Pottsville, who was managed by **Dr. John G. Striegel**, joined the NFL in 1925 the Maroons imported numerous All-Americans and other college stars to represent the team in pro football's top circuit, which consisted of 20 teams in one division. Pottsville played in the NFL through 1928 and had a 27-20-1 record over four seasons. In 1925 the Maroons under coach **Dick Rauch**, who was from Harrisburg, went 10-2-0 on the year and defeated the Chicago Cardinals 21-7 in Chicago to earn the NFL championship. However, Pottsville's claim of the NFL crown was later stripped from them by **Joe Carr**, the President of the League, and given to the Cardinals. The dispute started the week following the Cardinals game when Carr claimed that he informed Pottsville three different times not to play an exhibition game against a Notre Dame All-Star team in Philadelphia's Shibe Park (later Connie Mack Stadium) because that game would infringe upon the territorial rights of the Frankford Yellow Jackets who also had a home game the same day in Frankford Stadium. Pottsville, who beat the "Four Horsemen" 9-7, claimed they never received a protest from Carr prior to the Notre Dame All-Star game. After the Pottsville game in Philly, Carr immediately revoked the Maroon's membership in the NFL for that year, awarded the 1925 title to the Cardinals and a heated "dispute" started. The 15 tough-as-nails Maroons were **Jack Ernst**, **Tony Latone**, **Duke Osborn**, **Frank Bucher**, **Frank Racis**, **Russ Hathaway**, **Hoot Flanagan**, **Charlie Berry**, **Russ Stein**, **Herb Stein**, **"Fungy" Lebengood**, **Denny Hughes**, **Barney Wentz**, **Eddie Doyle** and **Walter French**. Other NFL franchises were the Akron Pros, Buffalo Bisons, Canton Bulldogs, Chicago Bears, Chicago Cardinals, Cleveland Bulldogs, Columbus Tigers, Dayton Triangles, Detroit Panthers, Duluth Eskimos, Frankford, PA Yellow Jackets, Green Bay Packers, Hammond Pros, Kansas City Cowboys, Milwaukee Badgers, New York Giants, Providence Steam Roller, and the Rock Island Independents.

BILL POWER played for Burgettstown High School and at Washington and Jefferson College. He was head coach at Point Marion High School and then Uniontown High School from 1948-62 as his Red Raiders went 107-35-2 and won the 1962 WPIAL championship. He directed pros in **Sandy Stephens**, **Ben Gregory** and **Bill Munsey**. Power's chief assistant, **Leon Kaltenbach**, who played at Clairton High School and Clemson, took over UHS from 1963-69, went 52-12-2 and won the 1965 WPIAL title. He had pros in **Nelson Munsey**, **John Hull** and **Ray Parson**.

RON POWLUS threw for 2,943 yards and 31 TD's and was Parade's 1992 Player of the Year for Berwick High School as **George Curry's** Bulldogs won the 1992 PIAA 3A state championship and was the USA Today's #1 team. He also set Pennsylvania career records of 7,339 yards passing, 9,018 total yards and 62 TD's. Powlus was a four-year starting quarterback at Notre Dame for **Lou Holtz** from 1994-97 and became the Fighting Irish's all-time career passer with 558 completions for 7,602 yards and 52 TD's. He was in Cleveland 1999 and Philly 2000.

MARC PRIMANTI from Thorndale was a 1996 All-American place kicker at North Carolina State. "Mr. Automatic" kicked 144 career points and earned the Lou Groza Placekicking Award.

STEVE PRITKO was an end for the Northampton High School Konkrete Kids under **Woody Ludwig**. He played at Villanova from 1939-41 for **"Clipper" Smith's** Wildcats. Pritko spent eight years with the NY Giants 1943, Cleveland/LA Rams 1944-47, Boston 1948-49 and Green Bay 1950. He was All-Pro with Cleveland in 1945 as **Adam Walsh's** Rams won the NFL title. Pritko caught 13 TD's and was long-time NFL official.

SCOTT RADECIC played for the Brentwood High School Spartans under **Gary Cramer**. He was a linebacker at Penn State 1980-83 and as **Joe Paterno's** Nittany Lions won the 1982 national title. He spent 12 years with Kansas City, Buffalo and Indianapolis.

RADIO and football first started in 1921 when Pittsburgh's KDKA, the country's first radio station, broadcast games of **Glenn Scobey "Pop" Warner's** University of Pittsburgh Panthers.

GEORGE RADOSEVICH played for the Brentwood High School Spartans and was a center at Pitt 1948-50. He anchored the Baltimore Colts line from 1954-56.

RAYMOND RAFFIN played for Moshannon Valley High School and at Lock Haven State. He has been the head coach of Wyalusing Valley High School since 1966 and has over 196 victories.

DAN RAINS played for the Hopewell High School Vikings. He was a linebacker at the University of Cincinnati from 1979-81. Rains spent four years with Chicago from 1982-86.

JIM RANKIN graduated from Jeannette High School in 1966 and Clarion University in 1970. He has over 150 wins in 20 years of coaching at Ellwood City High School from 1979-86 and North Allegheny High School from 1987-00. Rankin's Tigers are 95-23-1, won the 1990 PIAA 3A state championship and were nationally ranked by USA Today in 1990, 1991, 1995 and 1997.

RICK RANZZANO was a running back for New Castle High School as **Lindy Lauro's** Red Hurricanes won the 1973 WPIAL title. He was a linebacker at Virginia Tech from 1974-77 for **Jimmie Sharpe's** Gobblers. Razzano spent five years with Cincinnati 1980-84. **Sam Wyche's** Bengals lost Super Bowl XVI in 1982 to San Francisco.

JOHN RAUCH was a triple-threat tailback for the Yeadon High School Eagles and became a T-formation QB at Georgia 1945-48 for **Wally Butts**. He led the Bulldogs to four straight bowl games, threw 33 career TD passes and was a 1948 All-American. Rauch threw 8 TD's with the NY Bulldogs, NY Yankees and Pittsburgh 1949-51. He was the head coach of AFL's Oakland 1966-68 and Buffalo 1969-70 and went 40-28-2. Rauch's Raiders defeated Houston for the 1967 AFL title, but lost Super Bowl II in 1968 to Green Bay. He was 1967 AFL Coach of the Year.

ERIC RAVOTTI played for Freeport High School Yellowjackets under coach **Gary Kepple**. He was a linebacker at Penn State from 1989-93 for **Joe Paterno**. Ravotti spent two years with Pittsburgh in 1994-95. **Bill Cowher's** Steelers lost Super Bowl XXX in 1996 to Dallas.

TOM "DOC" RAYMER was a tackle for Sunbury High School, Susquehanna and the Coaldale Big Green. He coached the Coaldale High School Tigers from 1924-48 and went 162-60-17 and developed pros in **John Gildea**, **John Kuzman** and All-American **George Welsh**.

FRANCIS X. REAGAN was a halfback for Philadelphia's Northeast Catholic High School Falcons under **Ken "Si" Siemendinger**. He played at Pennsylvania 1938-40 and was a 1940 All-American for **George Munger's** 6-1-1 Quakers. Reagan was with New York 1941, 1946-48 and Philadelphia 1949-51. **Steve Owen's** Giants lost NFL title games in 1941 and 1946, but Reagan earned a 1949 title ring as **Greasy Neale's** Eagles beat Los Angeles. Reagan scored 8 career TD's and had 35 interceptions. He was head coach of Villanova 1954-59 and went 16-37.

KEN REAVES played for the Braddock High School Tigers and the Norfolk State Spartans in Virginia from 1963-65. He spent 12 years as defensive back for Atlanta 1966-74, New Orleans 1974 and St. Louis 1975-77. Reaves had 37 interceptions, scored one TD, recovered 3 fumbles.

RECHICHAR

BERT RECHICHAR from Belle Vernon played for Rostraver High School. He was a single-wing halfback at Tennessee 1949-51, All-SEC and 1951 captain of **General Robert Neyland's** 10-1 Volunteers who won the national championship. The versatile Rechichar played in the Cleveland Indians organization and was also the #1 draft choice of the Cleveland Browns. He eventually gave up baseball and became a three-way terror in pro football from 1952-61 as a halfback, defensive back and kicker with the Browns, Baltimore, Pittsburgh and NY Titans. With Baltimore, Rechichar kicked a NFL record 56 yard field goal in 1953. He also earned two NFL championship rings as **Weeb Ewbank's** Colts beat New York in 1958 and 1959. The 1955 All-Pro scored 4 TD's, kicked 31 FG's, and 62 PAT's for 179 career points.

ANDRE REED quarterbacked Allentown's Louis E. Dieruff High School Huskies under **Bruce Trotter** and **Larry Lewis**. He played at Kutztown State 1981-84 for **George Baldwin** and **Al Leonzi** and was a record setting wide receiver with 142 career receptions for 2,020 yards and 14 TD's. Reed spent 15 years with Buffalo 1985-99 and Washington 2000. He helped lead **Marv Levy's** high-powered Bills to four straight Super Bowls 1991-94. Reed, a three-time All-Pro, is the second all-time leading receiver in the NFL with 951 receptions for 13,198 yards and 87 TD's.

REED

G. REICH

GIL REICH played for the Steelton High School Steamrollers under **Sevor Toretti** and **Joe Shevock**. He went to West Point where as a sophomore halfback in 1950, he paced **Red Blaik's** #2 ranked 8-1 Cadets. Reich transferred to Kansas and was a 1952 All-American defensive back for **J. V. Sike's** 7-3 Jayhawks. Although drafted by Green Bay, he chose not to play pro football.

FRANK REICH quarterbacked the Cedar Crest High School Falcons in Lebanon, Pennsylvania under **Norbie Danz**. He played at Maryland from 1981-84 and was a 1984 Academic All-ACC. Reich has been in the NFL since 1985 with Buffalo, Carolina, NY Jets, and Detroit. He was a back-up to **Jim Kelly** as the Bills appeared in four straight Super Bowls 1990-94. Reich is the "King of the Comebacks," as he engineered the greatest "comebacks" in NCAA and NFL history. In 1984, Maryland was down 31-0 to Miami at halftime when Reich came off the bench and threw 3 TD's to lead the Terps to a 42-40 upset of the Hurricanes in the Orange Bowl. In 1993, Buffalo was losing 35-3 to Houston in the second half of a NFL play-off game when Reich came in for the injured Kelly and threw four TD's to lead the Bills to a 41-38 overtime victory over the Oilers.

MIKE REICHENBACH played for Bethlehem's Liberty High School Hurricanes for coaches **Barry Fetterman** and **Frank Gutierrez**. At East Stroudsburg State, Reichenbach was a 1983 Little All-American linebacker for **Dennis Douds'** Warriors. He had 2 interceptions with Philadelphia and Miami from 1984-91.

MIKE REID scored 107 points in only 7 games in 1964 for the Altoona High School Mountain Lions under **Earl Strohm**. Reid was a defensive tackle at Penn State. The two-time co-captain helped **Joe Paterno's** Nittany Lions go 22-0 for the #2 national ranking in 1968 and 1969. Reid, a 1969 consensus All-American, won the Outland Trophy as the nation's outstanding lineman and placed fifth in the Heisman Trophy vote. He was the #1 draft pick of Cincinnati and spent five years with the Bengals from 1970-74. The four-time All-Pro left pro football to concentrate on his music career and became a Grammy Award winning country and western songwriter and performer. The multi-talented Reid went in the College Football Hall of Fame in 1987.

JOE RESTIC from Hastings was an end for the DeLone Catholic High School Squires in McSherrystown, Pennsylvania under **Alex Bell**. He played for St. Francis College, Villanova and the Philly Eagles in 1952. Restic was head coach for the Hamilton Tiger-Cats in Canada from 1968-70 and went 22-17-3. He coached at Harvard for 23 years 1971-93 with a 117-97-6 record and won three Ivy League crowns in 1974, 1975, 1987 and shared titles in 1982 and 1983.

JOE REPKO was a tackle for the Lansford High School Panthers under **Ken Millen**. He played for powerful, nationally ranked Boston College from 1940-42. The 1942 All-American honorable mention tackle opened gaping holes for All-American fullback, **Mike Holovak**, who was also from Lansford. Repko spent four years with Los Angeles and Pittsburgh from 1946-49 and scored one TD.

REID

GLENN RESSLER from Dornsife played for Mahanoy Jointure High School for **Clyde Miller**. He was a center/middle guard at Penn State from 1962-64 for **Rip Engle**. Ressler was a 1964 All-American and won the Maxwell Award as the nation's most outstanding player. He spent ten years with Baltimore from 1965-74. Ressler was All-Pro in 1968 and earned a NFL title ring as **Don Shula's** Colts beat Cleveland, but lost Super Bowl III in 1969 to the NY Jets. Ressler earned a Super Bowl ring as **Don McCafferty's** Colts beat Dallas in SB V in 1971.

JEFF RICHARDSON was a lineman for Johnstown High School and at Michigan State from 1964-66 for **Duffy Daugherty**. He was with the New York Jets in 1967-68 and Miami 1969.

JESS RICHARDSON played for Philadelphia's Roxborough High School Indians under **Moe Weinstein** and at Alabama from 1950-53. He was a 12 year veteran defensive lineman with Philadelphia 1953-61 and Boston 1962-64. Richardson earned a 1960 NFL title ring when **Buck Shaw's** Eagles beat Green Bay. With Boston in 1963, the Patriots lost the AFL championship. Richardson, who was one of the last players to play without a face mask, was a two-time All-Pro.

RESSLER

JESS RICHARDSON

TOM RICKETTS was a lineman for the Franklin Regional High School Panthers in Murrysville, Pennsylvania and at Pitt from 1985-88 for **Mike Gottfried**. He was the #1 draft choice of Pittsburgh and spent five years with the Steelers from 1989-91 and New Orleans in 1994-95.

LOUIS RIDDICK scored 17 TD's in 1986 for the Pennridge High School Rams in Perkasie, Pennsylvania under **Frank Krystniak**. He went to Pitt where he was a two-time Academic

All-American defensive back in 1989 and 1990 for **Mike Gottfried's** Panthers. Riddick has been in the NFL since 1991 with San Francisco, Cleveland, Atlanta and Oakland.

ROBB RIDDICK played for the Pennridge High School Rams in Perkasie, Pennsylvania for **Wayne Helman**. He was a 1980 All-American all-purpose back for **Gene "Doc" Carpenter's** Millersville State Marauders. Riddick was a 10 year vet with the Buffalo Bills from 1981-89. He rushed for 1,341 yards, 21 TD's, caught 120 passes for 1,165 yards , 5 TD's, for 26 total TD's.

BOB RIGGLE was a halfback for the Washington High School Little Prexies and at Penn State 1963-65 for **Rip Engle**. He had 3 picks and one TD as a defensive back for Atlanta in 1966-67.

TIM RIMPFEL played at Bishop McDevit High School and at West Chester State. He has a 192-66-3 record in 23 years since 1977 at Trinity, Cumberland Valley and Bishop McDevit High Schools. His Cumberland Valley High School Eagles in Mechanicsburg, Pennsylvania won the 1992 PIAA 4A state title. He developed such pros as **Rickey Watters** and **Jon Ritchie**.

RAY RISSMILLER from Raubsville was considered the greatest tackle to play for Easton High School under legendary coach **Bobby Rute**. He starred at Georgia from 1962-64 and was a 1964 All-American for **Vince Dooley's** 7-3-1 Bulldogs. Rissmiller, the #2 draft choice of Philly, was an Eagle in

RISSMILLER

R. RIDDICK

Photo by Robert L. Smith

1965-66, New Orleans 1967 and Buffalo 1968.

JON RITCHIE rushed for 4,062 career yards, had 5,017 career all-purpose yards and scored 62 career TD's from 1990-92 for Cumberland Valley High School in Mechanicsburg, Pennsylvania under **Tim Rimpfel**. The Eagles went 15-0 in 1992 and won the PIAA 4A state championship. Ritchie, a National Honor Society student, played at Michigan in 1993 and then transferred to Stanford for the 1995-97 seasons. He has been with Oakland since 1998.

HARRY ROBB played for Pittsburgh's Peabody High School and was a haflback at Penn State from 1916-20. He scored 10 TD's and was an All-Pro with the Canton Bulldogs from 1921-26.

IRVIN "BO" ROBERSON played for Philadelphia's John Bartram High School Maroon Wave. He was a star halfback at Cornell from 1955-57 for **"Lefty" James**. After being a USA sprinter in the 1960 Olympics, "Bo" spent four years with San Diego, Buffalo, Oakland, Miami 1961-64.

JEFF RODENBERGER played for the Quakertown High School Panthers for **Frank Prusch**. He was a fullback at Maryland 1979-81, USFL champion Philly Stars 1983-85 and a New Orleans Saint in 1987.

FRAN ROGEL was a rugged fullback for Scott Township High School near Pittsburgh and at Penn State from 1947-49. The 1948 All-American was a nine year vet with Pittsburgh 1950-58. "The Phantom" rushed for 3,271 yards, 17 TD's and caught 150 passes for 1,087 yards, 2 TD's. He finished his career in Canada.

JIM ROMANISZYN played for the Titusville High School Rockets. He was a fullback and wide receiver at Edinboro State from 1970-72. In 1970, Romaniszyn became the only player in school history to rush for over 1,000 yards and to receive for over 1,000 yards in a single season. Romaniszyn was a linebacker in the NFL with Cleveland from 1973-74 and New England in 1976.

FRED ROSS was an end for Catasauqua High School in 1959-60 under **Bernard Kuczynski** and at Millersville State from 1962-64 for **George Katchmar**. He has been the head coach of the Stroudsburg High School since 1969 with a 223-139-4 record and developed pro **Artie Owens**.

PETE ROSTOSKY played for the Elizabeth-Forward High School Warriors for **Gordon Hayes**. He was an offensive guard at Connecticut from 1980-83 and a Pittsburgh Steeler in 1984-86.

MOE RUBENSTEIN graduated from Geneva College and coached Ambridge High School from 1929-50 with a 146-36-10 record in 22 years. His Bridgers won the 1932 WPIAL championship, won 26 games in a row from 1932-34 with 16 consecutive shutouts. Rubenstein developed six pros in **Ed** and **Harry Ulinsky**, **Len Szafaryn**, **Bob Gaona**, **George Kisiday** and **Leo Nobile**.

ANTHONY RUBINO was a guard for the Elizabeth High School Warriors for **Orrie Rockwell** and **Joe Furno**. He was a 1942 All-American at Wake Forest and a Detroit Lion in 1943, 1946.

TODD RUCCI played for the Upper Darby High School Royals under **John Shingle**. He was a tackle at Penn State from 1990-92 for **Joe Paterno's** Nittany Lions. Rucci has been with New England since 1993. **Bill Parcells'** Patriots lost Super Bowl XXXI in 1997 to Green Bay.

130

RUDDY

TIM RUDDY was a tackle for Dunmore High School as **Jack Henzes, Jr.'s** Bucks won the 1989 PIAA 1A state championship. The National Honor Society student, was a four-year starting center at Notre Dame from 1990-93 as **Lou Holtz's** nationally ranked Fighting Irish went 40-8-1. Ruddy was a 1993 All-American and has anchored the Miami Dolphins line since 1994.

AL RUSHATZ was a fullback for the Allentown High School Canaries under **Perry Scott** and at West Point from 1959-61. He scored 10 TD's as a 1961 All-American for **Dale Hall's** Cadets.

JIMMIE RUSSELL graduated from Notre Dame in 1929 and coached the Donora High School Dragons for 34 years from 1931-64 and went 178-130-27 with 3 WPIAL titles in 1944, 1945, and 1953 (co-champs with Har Brack). In a Pittsburgh newspaper poll, Russell's 1945 Dragons, led by the backfield of **Louis "Bimbo" Cecconi, Arnold Galiffa** and **"Deacon Dan" Towler**, were rated as the best WPIAL team in the last fifty years. He coached at Belle Vernon Area High School from 1965-69 and went 20-16-1. His over-all record was 198-146-28.

BOB RUTE scored 101 points as a 1939 All-State halfback for undefeated Easton High School under **Elmer Carroll** and then starred at Duke from 1941-43 for **Wallace Wade**. He was the winningest coach in the storied gridiron history of the Easton High School Red Rovers with a 138-51-9 record in 20 years from 1948-67. Future pro lineman **Ray Rissmiller**, QB **Terry Bartolet** and an All-State backfield of **Pete Americus, Billy Houston** and **Charlie Weaver**, led his undefeated 1958 team. Because of outstanding coaches such as founding fathers **Oscar Meeker** and then **Pat Reilly**, plus Carroll and his gridiron star Rute, and Rute's football pupils **Wayne Grube** and **Bob Shriver**, Easton is the second winningest high school football program in Pennsylvania behind Mt. Carmel with a 661-292-54 record since 1894.

RUTH

MIKE RUTH from Norristown played for the Methacton High School Warriors in Fairview Village, Pennsylvania under **George Marinkov**. He was a nose tackle at Boston College from 1982-85 for **Jack Bicknell**. The 1984 Golden Eagles went 10-2 and won Lambert Trophy as the #4 team in the nation. Ruth was a consensus 1985 All-American, an Academic All-American and won the Outland Trophy as the nation's best lineman. Ruth played for New England in 1986-87.

ED RUTKOWSKI scored 158 points in 1957-58 as a do-everything QB for the Kingston High School Huskies under **James Fennell**. He was a quarterback-halfback at Notre Dame from 1960-62 for **Joe Kuharich**. Rutkowski was a halfback-wide receiver with Buffalo in the AFL from 1963-68 and scored 6 TD's. **Lou Saban's** Bills appeared in three straight AFL championship games and Rutkowski earned two title rings with victories over San Diego in 1964 and 1965.

RUTKOWSKI

DANNY SACHS was a quarterback for the Emmaus High School Green Hornets under **Luke Lobb**. He became a triple-threat tailback in Princeton's famous single-wing from 1957-59 and was All-East in 1957 as he helped lead **Dick Coleman's** Tigers to the Ivy League championship. Sachs went on to graduate study at Oxford, England in 1960 as a prestigious Rhodes Scholar.

BRYANT SALTER played for Pittsburgh's South Hills High School Orioles and was a safety at Pitt from 1968-70 for **Dave Hart** and **Carl DePasqua**. He spent six years in the NFL and had 17 interceptions from 1971-76 for San Diego, Washington and Miami.

SACHS

SAMPLE

JOHNNY SAMPLE played for Philadelphia's Overbrook High School Panthers under **Len Kolenda** and **Ed Veith** and then at Maryland Eastern Shore. He spent 11 years in the pros as a defensive back with Baltimore 1958-60, Pittsburgh 1961-62, Washington 1963-65 and the NY Jets 1966-68. Sample earned two NFL championship rings when **Weeb Ewbank's** Colts beat the NY Giants in 1958 and 1959. He also earned a Super Bowl ring as Weeb Ewbank's Jets defeated Baltimore in SB III in 1969. Sample, a 1961 All-Pro, had 41 career interceptions and 6 TD's.

RON SAMS from Bridgeville played for the South Allegheny High School Gladiators in McDonald, Pennsylvania. He was a four-year guard at Pitt 1979-82 as **Jackie Sherrill** and **Foge Fazio's** powerful, nationally ranked Panthers went 42-6. Sams was with Green Bay, Minnesota, NY Jets 1983-86.

ALEX SANDUSKY played for the Sto-Rox High School Vikings and at Clarion State. He was a 13 year veteran offensive guard with Baltimore from 1954-66. Sandusky earned two NFL championship rings when **Weeb Ewbank's** Colts defeated the NY Giants in 1958 and 1959. The Colts lost the 1963 NFL title to Cleveland. Sandusky was a 1964 All-Pro.

JOHN SANDUSKY played for the South Philadelphia High School Rams under **Joe Pitt**. He was a four-year tackle at Villanova 1946-49 for **Jordan Olivar** and **James Leonard** and was a 1949 All-American. Sandusky spent seven years with Cleveland 1950-55 and Green Bay 1956. **Paul Brown's** Browns appeared in six straight NFL title games from 1950-55 and Sandusky earned three rings with wins over LA in 1950, Detroit in 1954, and LA again in 1955.

BILL SAUL, the older bother to his identical twin brothers, **Rich** and **Ron Saul**, was an end for the Butler High School Golden Tornadoes under coach **Art Bernardi**. He went to Penn State where he was a guard for **Rip Engle's** Nittany Lions 1959-61. Saul had 4 interceptions as a linebacker with Baltimore 1962-63, Pittsburgh 1964-68, New Orleans 1969 and Detroit 1970.

RICH SAUL and his identical twin brother, **Ron Saul**, played for the Butler High School Golden Tornadoes under **Art Bernardi**. He and Ron played together at Michigan State from 1967-69 for **Duffy Daugherty**. Rich was a center, guard and linebacker at Michigan State and both brothers were Academic All-Americans in 1969. He spent 12 years with Los Angeles 1970-81. **Ray Malavasi's** Rams lost Super Bowl XIV to Pittsburgh in 1980. Rich was a two-time All-Pro.

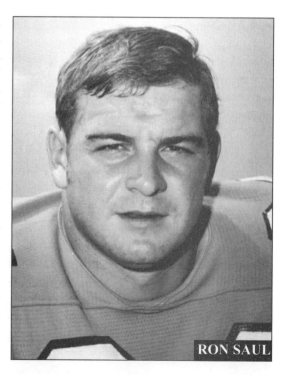
RON SAUL

RON SAUL and his identical twin brother, **Rich Saul**, played for the Butler High School Golden Tornadoes under **Art Bernardi**. He and Rich played together at Michigan State from 1967-69 for **Duffy Daugherty**. Ron was an offensive guard at Michigan State and was a 1969 All-American, and like his brother, Rich, an Academic All-American. Called "Hercules" by his teammates, Ron was a 12 year veteran with Houston 1970-75 and Washington 1976-81.

CHARLIE SCALES was a fullback for Homestead High School Steelers and at Indiana University from 1957-59. He played for Pittsburgh, Cleveland and Atlanta from 1960-66.

ANTHONY "ANK" SCANLON from Philadelphia was head coach of St. Joe's Prep from 1928-41 with a 93-14 record and the Philadelphia City League championship in 1938 and 1939.

"Ank" then took over Holy Cross and led the Crusaders to a 16-8-3 record from 1942-44. He led "The Cross" to one of the greatest upsets in gridiron history in 1942 when his 4-4-1 Crusaders demolished unbeaten and top-ranked, **Mike Holovak**-led Boston College 55-12 in the last game.

MIKE "MO" SCARRY was a center for Duquesne High School and at Waynesburg College. He played for the NFL Cleveland Rams 1944-45 and the AAFC Cleveland Browns 1946-47. "Mo" earned three championship rings when **Adam Walsh's** Rams beat Washington for the 1945 NFL title and **Paul Brown's** Browns beat the NY Yankees in 1946 and 1947 for the AAFC titles.

DON SCHAEFER played for Pittsburgh's Central Catholic High School under coach **Nick Skovich** and at Notre Dame in 1953-55. He was a 1955 All-American fullback for **Terry Brennan's** 8-2 Irish, and was a Philadelphia Eagle in 1956.

CARL SCHAUKOWITCH from McKees Rocks was a guard for the Sto-Rox High School Vikings under **George Palahunik**. He played at Penn State from 1970-72 for **Joe Paterno**. Schaukowitch was with the New York Giants 1973 and Denver 1975-77.

SCHLEICHER

STEVE SCHINDLER from Beaver was a center for Conestoga High School and at Boston College for **Joe Yukica** from 1974-76. He was All-East in 1976 and was with Denver 1977-78.

GARY SCHIPPANG played for Bethlehem's Liberty High School for **Frank Gutierrez** and was a Little All-American tackle at West Chester in 1984. He was with Vikings 1985, Giants 1987.

MAURY SCHLEICHER rushed for 1,476 yards and 19 TD's in 1954 for the Slatington High School Slaters for his brother, coach **Roy Schleicher**. He was a tight end at Penn State 1956-58 for **Rip Engle**. Schleicher was with the Chicago Cards, San Diego in the AFL and Toronto in the CFL from

SCHMIDT

1959-64. **Sid Gilman's** Chargers lost the 1960 and 1961 AFL titles to Houston.

JOE SCHMIDT was a fullback on the tough sandlots of Pittsburgh and for the Brentwood High School Spartans under **Al Crevar**. He was a guard and linebacker at Pitt 1950-52 and was a 1952 All-American for **Lowell "Red" Dawson's** Panthers. Schmidt spent 13 years in Detroit 1953-65 and helped the Lions win two NFL titles. Detroit beat Cleveland in 1953 for **Buddy Parker**, but then lost to the Browns in 1954. However, the Lions rebounded to beat the Browns again in 1957 for coach **George Wilson**. Schmidt, a five-time All-Pro, had 24 interceptions and scored 2 TD's. He was the head coach of the Lions 1967-72 with a 43-35-7 record. Schmidt went in the Pro Football Hall of Fame in 1973 and the College Football Hall of Fame in 2000.

MARTY SCHOTTENHEIMER played for the Fort Cherry High School Rangers in McDonald, Pennsylvania under **Jim Garry**. He was a linebacker at Pitt from 1962-64 for **John Michelosen**. Schottenheimer spent six years in the AFL with Buffalo 1965-68 and Boston 1969-70. **Lou Saban's** Bills defeated San Diego for the 1965 title. He was head coach of Cleveland 1984-88 and went 46-31-0 and at Kansas City 1989-98 and went 104-65-1. His over all NFL record in 17 seasons was 150-96-1. Schottenheimer took over Washington in 2001.

JIM SCHRADER was a center for Scott Township High School near Pittsburgh and at Notre Dame 1951-53 for **Frank Leahy**. He spent 11 years as the anchorman for Washington 1954-61 and Philadelphia 1962-64. Schrader was a 1961 All-Pro.

KEN SCHROY rushed for 3,181 career yards and 27 TD's in 1969-70 for the Quakertown High School Panthers under **Frank Prusch**. He played at

SCHROY

Maryland from 1972-74 and as a senior was a hard-hitting safety for **Jerry Claiborne's** ACC champion Terrapins. Schroy spent 10 years in the New York Jets secondary from 1975-84. He had 16 interceptions and scored one TD.

HARRY SCHUH from Feasterville was a fullback for the Neshaminy High School Redskins in Langhorne, Pennsylvania under coaches **Harry Franks** and **John Petercuskie**. He was a tackle at Memphis State from 1962-64 and was a 1964 All-American for **Billy "Spook" Murphy**. "Big Harry," 6-3, 260, was the #1 draft choice of Oakland and spent ten years with the Raiders, LA Rams and Green Bay 1965-74. **John Rauch's** Raiders beat Houston for the 1967 AFL title, but lost Super Bowl II in 1968 to Green Bay. Schuh was a 1969 All-Pro.

SCHWAB

SCHUH

FRANK "DUTCH" SCHWAB from Madera played at Lafayette where he was a two-time All-American guard in 1921 and 1922 for **Jock Sutherland's** Leopards. Lafayette upset both Pitt and Pennsylvania in 1921 as the Leopards went 9-0 and were named national champions. Schwab became owner of a coal company and went in the College Football Hall of Fame.

JOHN "BULL" SCHWEDER was a guard for the Bethlehem High School Red Hurricanes under **John Butler**. He played at at nationally ranked Pennsylvania for **George Munger** in 1945, 1947-49. Schweder was a 1949 All-American for the Quakers. "Bull" spent six years as the starting left guard with Baltimore in 1950 and Pittsburgh from 1951-55.

SCHWEDER

CLARENCE SCOTT played for Upper Merion High School Vikings in King of Prussia, Pennsylvania. He was a defensive back at Morgan State in Baltimore and spent four years with the Boston/ New England Patriots from 1969-72. He had 11 picks and recovered 2 fumbles.

ROBERT "BO" SCOTT was a running back for the Connellsville High School Cokers and at Ohio State in 1962 for **Woody Hayes'** Buckeyes. He left school to play in Canada with Ottawa from 1964-68 and was a four-time CFL all-star for the Rough Riders. Scott, who was drafted by Cleveland in 1965, came back to the NFL and scored 18 TD's with the Browns from 1969-74.

BOB SCRABIS was a quarterback for the Baldwin High School Highlanders and at Penn State from 1957-59 for **Rip Engle**. He was with the AFL's New York Titans from 1960-62.

LARRY SEIPLE scored 23 career TD's in 1961-62 for Allentown's Wm. Allen High School Canaries under **Perry Scott**. Seiple was a "big-play" halfback and punter (he ran for TD's from punt formation) at Kentucky 1965-67 for **Charlie Bradshaw**. He spent 12 years with Miami from 1968-79. **Don Shula's** Dolphins appeared in three straight Super Bowls 1972-74

SEIPLE

and Seiple earned two rings as Miami beat Washington in SB VII in 1973 and Minnesota in SB VIII in 1974. He scored 7 TD's and had a 40 yard punting average.

JOE SENSER played for the Hershey High School Trojans and was the leading receiver at West Chester State 1975-78 for **John Furlow's** Golden Rams with 165 receptions for 1,822 yards and 16 TD's. He was with Minnesota 1980-84 and caught 165 passes for 1,822 yards and 16 TD's.

SHAROCKMAN

PAUL SEVERIN was an end for Har-Brack Union High School in Brackenridge, Pennsylvania under **Dick Williams**. He was a two-time All-American at North Carolina in 1939 and 1940.

ED SHAROCKMAN quarterbacked the St. Clair High School Saints under **Bill Wolff**. He was a two-way halfback at Pitt 1958-60 for **John Michelosen**. Sharockman spent 12 years with Minnesota 1961-72. **Bud Grant's** Vikings beat Cleveland for the 1969 NFL title, but lost Super Bowl IV in 1970 to Kansas City. The 1964 All-Pro, had 40 interceptions and scored 6 TD's.

GREG SHELLY was a guard for the Souderton High School Indians under **Bill Yeomans**. He was a two-time All-ACC guard at Virginia in 1967-68 and was a Cleveland Brown in 1969.

TOM SHERMAN quarterbacked the Union Joint High School Golden Knights in Rimersburg, Pennsylvania under coach **Rich Vidunas**. He played at Penn State from 1965-67 for **Rip Engle** and then **Joe Paterno**. Sherman spent two years in the AFL with

Boston and Buffalo 1968-69 as he threw for 1,219 yards and 13 TD's. Sherman played for the Hartford Knights in the Atlantic Coast Football League from 1970-73, the World Football League's NY Stars in 1974 and Charlotte Hornets in 1975 and ended his career in Canada with Calgary in 1976.

JOE SHEVOCK played at Portage High School and was the captain at Loch Haven in 1935-36 for **Sol Wolf**. He was coach at Canton 1942-43, Windber 1944-45 and at Steelton High School 1948-57 where he was the winningest coach in the proud heritage (many pre-Shevock All-Americans and pros such as **Bill Shipp**, **Walt Menventhin**, **Dusan Cvivic**, **Sammy Padjan**, **Warren Heller**, **Steve** and **Duke Maronic**) of Steamroller football with a 62-30-2 record. Shevock produced numerous unstoppable 'Rollers including **Don** and **John Malinak**, **Gil** and **Dick Reich**, **Andy Padjan** and **Bill Popp**.

SHINER

DICK SHINER quarterbacked the Lebanon High School Cedars under **Henry Schmalzer**. He played at Maryland from 1961-63 for **Tom Nuggent**. Shiner was a 1962 All-American honorable mention QB for the Terrapins. He spent 11 years in the NFL with Washington, Cleveland, Pittsburgh, Atlanta, and New England from 1964-74 and threw for 4,801 yards and 36 TD's.

BRANDON SHORT was a fullback/linebacker and the AP's 1994 Player of the Year for McKeesport High School as **George Smith's** Tigers won the PIAA 4A state title. He was a four-year starting linebacker at Penn State 1996-99 for **Joe Paterno** and was a 1999 All-American. Short was with New York in 2000 as **Jim Fassel's** Giants lost Super Bowl XXXV to Baltimore in 2001.

MICKEY SHULER caught 143 passes for 1,999 yards and 14 TD's in 1973 for the East Pennsboro High School Panthers in Enola, Pennsylvania under **Jim Scible**. He was a tight end for **Joe Paterno** at Penn State from 1975-77 and caught 66 passes for 1,016 yards and 4 TD's. Shuler spent 14 years in the NFL with the NY Jets 1978-89 and Philadelphia 1990-91. He was a three-time All-Pro and caught 465 career passes for 5,100 yards and 31 TD's.

JOE SHUMOCK played for Coal Township High School and at Penn State from 1949-51. He coached Shamokin Catholic, Johnstown's Bishop McCort with a 35 game undefeated streak and Abington High Schools from 1954-75. He had a 142-50-9 record and developed **John Stoffa**.

RANDY SIDLER scored 23 TD's as a quarterback in 1973 for the Danville High School Ironmen under **Bill Wolff**. He was a guard at Penn State 1974-77 for **Joe Paterno** and was a 1977 All-American for the 11-1 Nittany Lions. Sidler was drafted by the NY Jets.

CHUCK SIEMINSKI was a tackle for Swoyersville High School under coach **John Yonkondy**. He played at Penn State from 1960-62 for **Rip Engle** and was a 1962 All-American for the 9-2 Nittany Lions. Sieminski spent six years with San Francisco, Atlanta and Detroit from 1963-68.

SHULER

CURT SINGER played for Hopewell High School and was an offensive tackle at Tennessee for from 1980-83. He spent six years in the NFL 1984-89 with Washington, Seattle and NY Jets.

JIM SIMON played for Scott Township High School and was a guard at Miami of Florida from 1960-62 for **Andy Gustafson**. He spent six years in the NFL 1963-68 with Detroit and Atlanta.

FRANK SINKWICH was a center/linebacker for Harrisburg's John Harris High School and at Duke. He had 10 interceptions and scored one TD for the Pittsburgh Steelers from 1947-52.

JOE "MUGGSY" SKLADANY played for the Larksville High School Green Wave and at Pitt from 1931-33. Skladany was a two-time consensus All-American end at Pitt in 1932 and 1933 for **Jock Sutherland's** 16-2 Panthers. "Muggsy," a defensive standout in the 1933 Rose Bowl against USC, was a Pittsburgh Steeler in 1934. He is in the College Football Hall of Fame.

LEO SKLADANY played for the Larksville High School Green Wave and was a two-way end at Pitt from 1945-48. He spent two years in the NFL with Philadelphia 1949 and the NY Giants 1950. Skladany earned a 1949 NFL title ring as **Greasy Neale's** Eagles beat the LA Rams.

TOM SKLADANY played for the Bethel Park High School Black Hawks and at Ohio State where he was a co-captain and three-time All-American punter in 1974, 1975 and 1976 for **Woody Hayes'** powerful 30-4-1 Buckeyes. Skladany spent seven years in the NFL with Detroit from 1977-82 and Philadelphia in 1983. He punted for 12,425 yards and a 42.1 yard average.

JOHN SKORUPAN was an end for Beaver Area High School under **Pat Tarquino** and helped lead the Bobcats to a 27-2-1 record from 1966-68. He played at Penn State 1970-72 for **Joe Paterno** and was a 1972 All-American linebacker with 106 tackles for the 10-2 Nittany Lions. He spent eight years in the NFL with Buffalo from 1973-77 and the NY Giants in 1978-80.

SKREPENAK

GREG SKREPENAK played for Wilkes Barre's GAR (Grand Army of the Republic) Memorial High School Grenadiers under **Charlie Fick**. He was a four year starting offensive tackle at Michigan from 1988-91. "Big Greg," 6-6, 322, was a co-captain and a two-time All-American in 1990 and 1991 for **Gary Moeller's** nationally ranked Wolverines. He was the Big Ten's 1991 Lineman of the Year and was a finalist for both the Outland Trophy and the Lombardi Award. Skrepenak has been in the NFL since 1992 with the Raiders 1992-95, 1999 and Carolina 1996-98.

STEVE SMEAR played for Johnstown's Bishop McCort High School Crushers for **Al Fletcher**. He was a two-time co-captain and All-American defensive tackle in 1968 and 1969 as he helped lead **Joe Paterno's** Nittany Lions to a 22-0 record and two #2 rankings in the nation. Although drafted by Baltimore, Smear spent his pro career in Canada with Montreal and Toronto. Smear was All-CFL in 1970 and 1971 as **Jim Duncan's** Alouettes lost the 1970 Grey Cup to Calgary.

ANDY SMITH from DuBois was a star fullback at Penn State 1901-02 and then at Pennsylvania 1903-04. He was a Walter Camp All-American in 1904 as he paced **Carl Williams** 12-0 Quakers to the national championship. Smith was head coach of Pennsylvania

1909-12, Purdue 1913-15, and California 1916-25. His 1919-24 Golden Bears were nicknamed the "Wonder Teams" as they went 44-0-4 with two Rose Bowl appearances. Smith, who had a over-all record of 116-32-13, was inducted into the College Football Hall of Fame in 1951.

PAUL SMITH coached Harrisburg Technical High School from 1918-23 and went 56-7-0 in six years. Smith's 1918-19 juggernaut had no equal in the state or in the nation. In 1918, Tech went 9-0 and outscored the opposition 597-10. In 1919, Tech had a 12-0 record, scored 701 points, for a 58.4 average, and held their 12 opponents scoreless. The "Big Maroon" defeated Portland, Maine 56-0 for the 1919 mythical high school national championship.

BRYAN SNYDER threw for 2,450 yards and 24 TD's in 1992-93 for the Nazareth High School Blue Eagles under **Joe Bernard**. He directed Albright from 1994-97 and set every Lion career passing record with 836 completions for 10,718 yards and 96 TD's for **Kevin Keisel**, **Ron Maier** and **E. J. Sandusky**. Snyder played in the German Pro League of American Football.

FRANK SNYDER played for Duncannon High School and Lenoir Rhyne College. He won 238 games at Williamstown, Upper Dauphin, Susquenita and Williams Valley High Schools.

JOHN SODASKI played for Pottstown's St. Pius X High School and at Villanova 1966-68 for **Jack Gregory**. Sodaski was a DB/LB at Pittsburgh 1970, Philadelphia 1972-73, Phila Bell 1974.

RON SOLT was a lineman for Wilkes Barre's James M. Coughlin High School Crusaders under **J. P. Meck**. He played at Maryland 1980-83 for **Jerry Claiborne** and was a 1983 All-American honorable mention for the ACC champs. Solt was the #1 draft choice of Indianapolis and spent nine years with the Colts 1984-88, 1992 and Philadelphia 1988-91. He was a 1988 Pro Bowler.

FRANK SOUCHAK was an end for Berwick High School and at Pitt from 1935-37. He was a 1937 consensus All-American for **Jock Sutherland's** national champs and a Steeler in 1938-39.

JOHN SPAGNOLA played for the Bethlehem Catholic High School Golden Hawks under coach **Jim Mazza**. Spagnola was an end at Yale 1976-78 and was a 1978 All-American honorable mention for **Carmen Cozza's** Bulldogs. He caught 15 TD's with Philadelphia, Seattle, and Green Bay from 1979-89. At Philly, **Dick Vermeil's** Eagles lost Super Bowl XV to Oakland in 1981. Spagnola was a 1985 All-Pro.

SPAGNOLA

FRANK SPANIEL was a halfback for the Vandergrift High School Blue Lancers under coaches **Ted Rosenweig** and **Johnny Karrs**. He played at Notre Dame for **Frank Leahy** 1947-49 as the 28-0-1 Irish won national titles in 1947 and 1949. Spaniel was at Washington, Baltimore in 1950.

DAN SPANISH was an end for New Castle High School under **Lindy Lauro** in 1960-62 and at Kentucky 1964-66. He has coached the Connellsville High School Falcons since 1974 and has a 175-86-8 record, the 1991 WPIAL title and a 33 game regular season winning streak.

SPINDLER

MARC SPINDLER was the USA Today's Defensive Player of the Year in 1986 for the West Scranton High School Invaders under **Joe DeAntona**. He was a defensive tackle at Pitt 1987-89 and was a 1989 All-American for **Mike Gottfried's** 8-3-1 Panthers. Spindler left Pitt after his junior year when he was drafted by Detroit. He spent ten years with the Lions 1990-94, 1997-99, New York Jets 1995-96, Tampa Bay and Seattle 1997.

BRIAN STABLEIN played for Erie's McDowell High School Trojans under **Joe Sanford**. He was a wide receiver at Ohio State from 1989-92 for **John Cooper**. Stablein has been in the NFL since 1993 with Denver, Indianapolis and Detroit and has 77 receptions for 792 yards and 3 TD's.

PHIL STAMBAUGH threw for 5,595 yards and 52 TD's from 1992-95 for the St. Pius X High School Royals in Roseto, Pennsylvania under his father, coach **Mike Stambaugh** and then **Frank Scagliotta**. He set Lehigh career passing records of 818 completions for 9,669 yards and 79 TD's from 1996-99 for **Kevin Higgins'** Engineers. Stambaugh played in the WLAF 2001.

SCOTT STANKAVAGE quarterbacked the Central Bucks East High School Patriots in Buckingham, Pennsylvania under **Chuck Rocconi**. At North Carolina, Stankavage threw for 3,363 yards and 30 TD's from 1980-83 and was a three-time Academic All-ACC QB from

1981-83 for **Dick Crum's** Tar Heels. He spent four years in the NFL with Denver and Miami 1984-87.

LES STECKEL was a halfback for the Whitehall High School Zephyrs in 1962-63 under **Carl Case** and then at Kansas. He was head coach of the Minnesota Vikings in 1984 and went 3-13-0.

BOB STEM was a linebacker for Phillipsburg, NJ High School under **Harold Bellis**. He played at Syracuse from 1959-61 as **Ben Schwartzwalder's** 1959 Orangemen won the national title. Stem was coach of Phillipsburg, NJ High School from 1973-81 and went 54-33-4. He has been the coach of the Bethlehem Catholic High School Golden Hawks since 1983 with a 165-47-2 slate and the 1988 PIAA 2A state championship. His over-all record to present time is 219-80-6. Stem developed many high-flying Hawks including prize QB **Dan Kendra III**, 1994 USA Today Player of the Year, who broke all of his father's Lehigh Valley area career records with 6,087 yards passing and 60 TD's, plus 1,969 yards rushing and 31 TD's from 1991-94.

PAUL STENKO a.k.a. STENN played for the Berwick High School Bulldogs and was a star two-way tackle for **"Clipper" Smith's** Villanova Wildcats from 1939-41. Stenko was a seven year NFL veteran in New York 1942, Washington 1946, Pittsburgh 1947 and Chicago 1948-51.

STEPHENS

SANDY STEPHENS quarterbacked the Uniontown High School Red Raiders under **Bill Power**. He started at Minnesota from 1959-61 for **Murray Warmath**. In 1960, Stephens, along with Uniontown teammate **Bill Munsey** at halfback, helped lead the Golden Golphers to a 8-2 record and the national championship. Stephens was a 1961 consensus All-American and the Rose Bowl's MVP. He played in Canada for Montreal and Toronto in 1962-63.

MARK STEPNOSKI played for Erie's Cathedral Prep Ramblers under **Mina George**. He was a guard at Pitt 1985-88 and was both a consensus All-American in 1988 and a two-time Academic All-American in 1987 and 1988 for **Mike Gottfried's** Panthers. Stepnoski, also won the Walter Camp Award. He has been a 12 year veteran with Dallas 1989-94, Houston/Tennessee 1995-99 and back to the Cowboys 1999. Stepnoski, a five time Pro Bowler, earned Super Bowl rings as **Jimmy Johnson's** Cowboys defeated Buffalo in SB XXVII in 1992 and SB XXVIII in 1993.

PETE STEVENS was a center for Pittston High School and at Temple from 1933-35 for **"Pop" Warner**. He was captain of the 1934 Owl's that

STEPNOSKI

played in the first-ever Sugar Bowl of 1935. Stevens played for Philadelphia in 1936 and then coached Temple from 1956-59 and went 4-28-0.

WALT STICKEL was a tackle for Philadelphia's Northeast High School Archives under **Gus Geiges** and at Pennsylvania in 1942-44 for **George Munger**. Stickel was with Chicago from 1946-49 and Philly in 1950-51. He earned a NFL title ring with **George Halas'** Bears in 1946.

JOHN STOFFA quarterbacked Johnstown's Bishop McCort High School Crushers under **Joe Shumock**. He played at the University of Buffalo 1963-65 and then in the AFL with Miami 1966-67, Cincinnati 1968 and Miami 1969-70. Stoffa threw for 1,738 yards and 12 TD's.

ANDY STOPPER was a halfback for the Williamsport High School Millionaires under **Hal Rock** and at Villanova from 1935-37 where he was a 1937 All-American for **Clipper Smith's** 8-0-1 Wildcats. Stopper coached the Reading High School Red Knights from 1942, 1947-61 and went 82-70-7. He had "Castle on the Hill" pros in **Lenny Moore, John Jankans** and **Fred Mautino**.

DON STROCK from Warwick quarterbacked the Owen J. Roberts High School Wildcats in Bucktown, Pennsylvania under **Hank Bernat**. He directed Virginia Tech from 1970-72 and was a 1972 All-American as he led the nation in total

STROCK

offense with 3,170 yards for **Charlie Coffey's** Gobblers. Strock spent 17 years with Miami 1973-87, Cleveland 1988 and Indianapolis 1989. **Don Shula's** Dolphins appeared in three Super Bowls and Strock earned one ring in the win over Minnesota in SB VIII in 1974. He threw for 5,349 yards and 45 TD's. Strock, who was a coach in the Arena Football League, is now the head coach of Florida International University in Miami.

EARL STROHM was a lineman for Altoona High School and Shippensburg College. He coached Bellwood High School 1948-51 and went 37-4-1 and Altoona High School 1952-71 and went 133-59-9. His over-all record in 24 years was 170-63-10. He produced many heroic Mountain Lions and four pros in **Mike Reid**, **John Ebersole**, **Brad Benson** and **Ed Flanagan**.

RICK STROM quarterbacked the Fox Chapel High School Foxes under coach **Jim Morelli**. He was at Georgia Tech from 1983-87. Strom was a two-time Academic All-ACC QB in 1986 and in 1987. He spent nine years in the NFL with Pittsburgh, Buffalo, Detroit from 1988-96.

ANDY STYNCHULA played for Latrobe High School and at Penn State from 1957-59 for **Rip Engle**. He spent nine years in the pro defensive lines of Washington 1960-63, New York Giants 1964-65, Baltimore 1966-67 and Dallas 1968. Stynchula was a 1960 All-Pro.

SUHEY

MATT SUHEY the son of **Steve Suhey**, a 1947 All-American guard for Penn State, rushed for 4,557 yards, scored 59 TD's and 365 points from 1973-75 for the State College High School Little Lions under **Jim Williams**. Like his outstanding older brothers, **Larry Suhey** and **Paul Suhey**, Matt also played at Penn State for **Joe Paterno** from 1976-79 and rushed for 2,818 yards, 3,549 all-purpose yards and 26 TD's. He was with Chicago 1980-89, scored 25 TD's and was a great blocker out of the backfield for the NFL's all-time leading rusher **Walter Payton**. Suhey earned a Super Bowl ring as **Mike Ditka's** Bears defeated New England in SB XX in 1986.

DAVE "SILKY" SULLIVAN played for the Steelton-Highspire High School Steamrollers for **Bob Perugini**. He set all of Virginia's pass receiving records including 12 TD's from 1970-72 and was a 1972 All-ACC wide receiver for **Don Lawrence's** Cavaliers. "Silky" caught 5 TD's in Cleveland 1973-74.

JOHN "WHITEY" SULLIVAN coached Philadelphia's Father Judge High School Crusaders from 1974-85 and 1987-99 with a 196-95-10 record in 25 years. His Crusaders won the 1975 Philadelphia City League crown plus four Catholic League titles in 1975, 1981, 1983, and 1984. He developed pro **Mike McClosky**.

SAL SUNSERI was a four-year letterman lineman for Pittsburgh's Central Catholic High School 1973-76 under **Joe Scully**. He was a linebacker at Pitt 1979-81 for **Jackie Sherrill's** 33-3 Panthers. The 1981 All-American was drafted by Pittsburgh, but an injury ended his career.

TOM SURLAS from Mt. Pleasant was a linebacker at Alabama from 1969-71. He was a 1971 All-American for **Paul "Bear" Bryant's** 11-1 SEC champion and #4 ranked Crimson Tide.

HARRY SWAYNE played for Philadelphia's Cardinal Dougherty High School under **George Stratts**. At Rutgers 1983-86, he was a 1986 All-East DT for **Dick Anderson's** Scarlet Knights. Swayne has been a 14 year NFL veteran offensive tackle for Tampa Bay 1987-90, San Diego 1991-96, Denver 1997-98 and Baltimore since 1999. He earned three Super Bowl rings as **Mike Shanahan's** Broncos defeated Green Bay in SB XXXII in 1998, Atlanta in SB XXXIII in 1999 and with Baltimore as **Brian Billick's** Ravens beat the NY Giants in SB XXXV in 2001.

JIM SWEENEY was a lineman for Pittsburgh's Seton-LaSalle High School as **Tom Donahoe's** Rebels won the 1979 and 1980 WPIAL titles. He was a four year starting center for the powerful Pitt Panthers that went 39-8-1 from 1980-83. Sweeney was the #2 round draft choice of the New York Jets and has spent 16 years with the Jets 1984-94, Seattle 1995 and Pittsburgh 1996-99.

SWEENEY

LARRY SWIDER played for the DuBois High School Beavers and punted at Pitt from 1973-76 as **Johnny Majors** 1976 Panthers went 12-0 for the national championship. Swider spent four years in the NFL with Detroit, St. Louis Cardinals and Tampa Bay from 1979-82.

LEN SZAFARYN played for the Ambridge High School Bridgers under **Moe Rubenstein**. He was a 1948 All-American tackle at North Carolina for **Carl Snavely's** #3 ranked Tar Heels. Szafaryn spent eight years in the pros from 1949-58 with Washington, Green Bay, Philadelphia.

DAVE SZYMAKOWSKI was an end for Bethlehem High School under **Pat Garramone**. He set every pass receiving record at West Texas State (Pittsburgh's **"Mercury" Morris** set every rushing record) from 1965-67 and was a 1967 All-American honorable mention for **Joe Kerbel's** Junior Rose Bowl winning Buffalos. "Szymo" was with New Orleans 1968-71, and in the WFL in 1974 with the Southern California Sun.

SZYMAKOWSKI

JOE TAFFONI from Nemacolin was a tackle for Carmichaels High School. He played for West Virginia in 1964-65 for **Gene Corum's** Mountaineers and at the University of Tennessee-Martin in 1966 for **Bob Carroll's** Orangemen. He was a seven year vet in the NFL 1967-73 with Cleveland and New York. **Blanton Collier's** Browns lost NFC title games in 1968 and 1969.

DICK TAMBURO played for New Kensington High School as **Don Fletcher's** Red Raiders won the 1946 and 1947 WPIAL championships. He was a center at Michigan State from 1950-52 for **Biggie Munn** and was a 1952 All-American for the 9-0 national champion Spartans.

SAM TAMBURO was an end for New Kensington High School under **Don Fletcher** and at Penn State from 1946-48. The 1948 All-American played for the New York Bulldogs in 1949.

RALPH TAMM played for Bensalem High School and at West Chester University for **Danny Hale** and **Rick Daniels**. Tamm has been a 10 year veteran offensive guard in the NFL from 1990-99 with Cleveland, Washington, Cincinnati, San Francisco, Denver and Kansas City. He earned a Super Bowl ring as **George Seifert's** 49ers beat San Diego in SB XXIV in 1995.

PAT TARQUINO was a Little All-American quarterback at Juniata College. He has coached at Ellwood City High School and Beaver Area High School where he is the all-time winningest coach in Beaver County history with over 265 wins in 39 years on the sidelines.

ROBERT TATE played for Harrisburg High School Cougars and was a defensive back at the University of Cincinnati from 1993-96. Tate has 3 interceptions with Minnesota since 1997.

TELEVISION and football were joined for the first time on September 30, 1939 when Fordham hosted Waynesburg College of Pennsylvania in Triborough Stadium on Randall's Island in New York City. This historic contest, which was produced by station W2XBS (now NBC, the National Broadcasting System), marked the first-ever telecast (in black and white) of a football game. Fordham, a national power, won the game 34-7. Famed radio announcer, Bill Stern, handled the broadcast by himself. The game's lead paragraph in Sunday's New York Times read, "Fordham's 1939 grid forces went into action for the first time with a 34-7 victory over Waynesburg. The Rams had the televised game well in hand by halftime." The first-ever televised NFL football game happened three weeks later on October 22, 1939 when NBC televised the Brooklyn Dodgers 23-14 defeat of the Philadelphia Eagles at Ebbets Field. The first-ever NFL game to be televised in "living color" was by CBS-TV on September 9, 1956 in a pre-season game between the Philadelphia Eagles and the Baltimore Colts in Louisville, Kentucky. The first-ever national telecast of a scholastic contest was on November 24, 1988 when ESPN televised the annual Thanksgiving Day battle between the Easton High School Red Rovers and the Phillipsburg, New Jersey, High School Stateliners at Lafayette's Fisher Field in Easton.

TEMPLE OWLS in Philadelphia, Pennsylvania started football in 1894 and enjoyed success under legendary coach **Glenn "Pop" Warner** (Hall of Fame) who went 31-18-9 from 1933-38. Warner's Owls went 7-1-2 in 1934 and lost to unbeaten Tulane in the first-ever Sugar Bowl on Jan.1, 1935. The Owl attack was led by ends **Elmer Anderson**, **Lloyd Wise**, tackles **Bill Docherty**, **Jim Russell**, guards **Stan Gurznyski**, **Joe Drulis**, center **Pete Stevens** and backs **"Dynamite" Dave Smuckler**, who Warner likened to **Jim Thorpe** and **Ernie Nevers**, **Bill Davidson**, **Danny Testa** and **Glenn Frey**. However, Temple's greatest gridiron era came under **Wayne Hardin**, former Navy coach, who went 80-52-3 in 13 years from 1970-82. Hardin's three best Cherry and White clubs were in 1973 at 9-1, 1974 at 8-2, and the 1979 Owls who went 10-2 and beat California in the Garden State Bowl behind quarterback **Brian Broomell**, receiver **Gerald "Sweet Feet" Lucear** and back **Mark Bright**. Owls making All-American teams include: **Bucko Kilroy** T 1941, **Phil Slosburg** HB 1947, **Doug Shobert** QB 1971, **Randy Grossman** TE 1972, **Bill Singletary** OG 1972, **Steve Joachim** QB 1973-74 who also won the Maxwell Award as the nation's most outstanding player, **Joe Klecko** NT 1974-75, **Pat Staub** OG 1974, **Henry Hynoski** RB 1974, **Anthony Anderson** RB 1976, **Mike Curcio** RB 1979, **Steve Conjar** LB 1980-81, **Ted Bowles** DB 1984, **John Rienstra** OG 1984-85, **Willie Marshall** WR 1985, **Paul Palmer** RB 1985, **Mike Hinnant** TE 1986-87, **Todd McNair** RB 1987, **Kevin Jones** OT 1987 and **Lorenzo Square** LB 1988.

JOE TERESHINSKY from Glen Lyon played for the Newport Township High School Coal Crackers in Wanamie, Pennsylvania under **Clem Rogowicz**. He was an end at Georgia 1942, 1945-46 and was 1946 All-SEC as **Wally Butt's** Bulldogs went 11-0 and ranked #3 in the nation. He spent eight years with Washington 1947-54 and scored 4 TD's.

MIKE TERRY coached the Kulpmont High School Wildcats and Mt. Carmel High School Red Tornadoes for 30 years and had a 196-94-19 record.

BLAIR THOMAS was the Philadelphia Daily News' City Player of the 1980's as he rushed for city records of 626 carriers for 3,941 yards for 53 TD's and 59 total TD's from 1982-84 for Philadelphia's Frankford High School Pioneers under **Al Angelo**. He played at Penn State from 1985-89 as **Joe Paterno's** Nittany Lions won the 1986 national title. Thomas, who rushed for 3,301 career yards and 4,512 all-purpose yards at Penn State, was a 1989 All-American and tenth in the Heisman Trophy vote. He was the #1 draft choice of the NY Jets and was a Jet 1990-93, New England and Dallas 1994 and Carolina 1995. Thomas rushed for 2,236 yards and scored 6 TD's.

JOE THOMPSON from Pittsburgh played at Pitt from 1904-06 and was captain of the 1904 Panthers that went 10-0 under coach **Arthur St. Ledger Mosse**. He was head coach at Pitt from 1908-12 and went 30-14-2. Thompson's Panthers went undefeated in 1909 at 9-0 and scored 282 points to zero for the opposition. He went in the College Football Hall of Fame.

VINCE THOMPSON was a fullback for Woodrow Wilson High School in Levittown, Pennsylvania and at Villanova from 1975-78. He scored 2 TD's with Detroit from 1981-84.

CLYDE "TINY" THORNHILL from Beaver was a guard at Pitt from 1913-16 as the Panthers went 30-3-1. He was a 1916 All-American for **Glenn "Pop" Warner**. "Tiny" was head coach of Stanford from 1933-39 and went 35-25-7 in seven years. Thornhill's 1933-35 "Vow Boys," (a vow never to lose to USC - which they kept) went 25-4-2 and to three consecutive Rose Bowls.

THORPE

Allentown Morning Call File Photo.

JIM THORPE, PENNSYLVANIA located in Carbon County came about in 1954 when the two towns of Mauch Chunk and East Mauch Chunk merged to form one town called Jim Thorpe in honor of the great athlete whose body was buried there in February of 1954. Thorpe, a native of Oklahoma, starred in athletics at the Carlisle Institute, won two Gold Medals at the 1912 Olympics in Stockholm, and played pro football and baseball. He died in March 1953 in Lomeda, California and his widow had his body buried in eastern Pennsylvania in 1954. The two area high schools - the Mauch Chunk High School Bruins and the East Mauch Chunk High School Trojans, which only played basketball and baseball before this time, now became the Jim Thorpe High School Olympians in the 1954-55 school year and started to play football the following year.

WILLIE THROWER was the big gun for New Kensington High School as **Don Fletcher's** Red Raiders won the 1946 and 1947 WPIAL championships. He was a quarterback at Michigan State 1950-52 for **Biggie Munn** as the Spartans went 9-0 in 1952 for the national title. He was one of the first African-American QB's in the NFL as a back-up to **George Blanda** at Chicago in 1953.

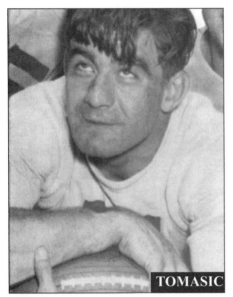

TOMASIC

ANDY TOMASIC from Hokendauqua was a triple-threat tailback for the Whitehall High School Zephyrs under **Bud Nevins** and at Temple from 1939-41. "Handy Andy" gained 1,824 yards in 1941 and was All-East for **Ray Morrison's** 7-2 Owls. "The Hokendauqua Hurricane," who is an uncle to **Matt Millen**, scored 6 TD's, and had 6 interceptions with Pittsburgh in 1942 and 1946. Tomasic left football to sign with the baseball NY Giants.

LOU "BABE" TOMASSETTI was a halfback for the Old Forge High School Blue Devils under **Danny Semenza**. He starred at Bucknell from 1936-38 and was a 1938 All-American honorable mention for the Bison. "Babe" spent eight years in pro ball with Pittsburgh 1939-40, Detroit 1941, Philly 1942 and Buffalo in the All-American Football Conference from 1946-49. The Bills lost the 1948 AAFC title game to Cleveland. Tomassetti rushed for 1,905 yards and 14 TD's.

"DEACON DAN" TOWLER was a fullback for Donora High School as **Jimmie Russell's** Dragons won the 1944 and 1945 WPIAL titles. He played at Washington and Jefferson for **Henry Luecht's** Presidents from 1946-49. With Los Angeles from 1950-56, Towler was in the Rams "Elephant Backfield" with **Dick Hoerner** and **"Tank" Younger**. LA met Cleveland in three NFL title games in 1950, 1951, 1955 and Towler earned one ring as **Joe Stydahar's** Rams beat the Browns in 1951. The two-time All-Pro rushed for 3,493 yards and 43 TD's.

JOHN TRACEY was an end for Philadelphia's Northeast High School Archives under **Charlie Martin** and at Texas A&M where he was 1956 and 1958 All-SWC for **Paul "Bear" Bryant's** Aggies. Tracey was a nine year linebacker with St. Louis 1959-60, Philly 1961, Buffalo 1962-67. He had 12 picks and two AFL title rings as **Lou Saban's** Bills beat San Diego in 1964 and 1965.

TRACEY

TRIPPI

JIM TRIMBLE played for McKeesport High School and at Indiana from 1939-41 for **Bo McMillin**. He was head coach of the Philadelphia Eagles from 1952-55 and went 25-20-3 before coaching Hamilton in Canada from 1956-62. Trimble's Tiger-Cats met **Bud Grant's** Winnipeg Blue Bombers in the Grey Cup five out of six years between 1957-62 and he won the 1957 game.

WALLY TRIPLETT was a halfback for the Cheltenham High School Panthers and at Penn State from 1946-48 for **Bob Higgins**. He was with Detroit and the Chicago Cardinals 1949-53.

CHARLEY TRIPPI played for the Pittston High School Big Red under **Cy Gallager**. He was at Georgia in 1942, 1945-46 for **Wally Butts** and led the 1946 Bulldogs to a 11-0 record. "The Pittston Flash" was a 1946 consensus All-American and won the Maxwell Award as the nation's most outstanding player. Trippi signed a record $100,000 contract and played for the Chicago Cardinals 1947-55. As a member the Cardinals "Million Dollar Backfield," Trippi helped lead **Jimmy Conzelman's** Cards to the 1947 NFL title over Philadelphia. The versatile Trippi, threw for 2,547 yards, 16 TD's, rushed for 3,506 yards, 23 TD's, caught 130 passes for 1,321 yards, 11TD's, had 2 TD's on punt returns, and a 40.3 yard punting average. Trippi, who had 52 TD's, went in the Pro Football Hall of Fame in 1968 and into the College Football Hall of Fame in 1996.

BILL TROUP quarterbacked the Bethel Park High School Black Hawks. He played for Virginia in 1970 and South Carolina in 1972. Troup was a six year veteran in pro ball with Baltimore from 1974-78 and Winnipeg in the CFL in 1979. He threw for 2,047 yards and 10 TD's.

BOB TUCKER was an end for the Hazleton High School Mountaineers under **Anthony Scarcella**. He played at Bloomsburg State 1965-67 and was the leading receiver in the Atlantic Coast Football League in 1968 with Lowell and in 1969 with the ACFL champion Pottstown Firebirds. He spent 11 yeas in the NFL with the New York Giants 1970-77 and Minnesota 1977-80. Tucker, a 1972 All-Pro, had 422 receptions for 5,421 yards and 27 TD's.

WENDELL TUCKER played for Philadelphia's Ben Franklin High School Electrons under coaches **Dave Beloff** and **Joe DiDomenic**. He played for the South Carolina State Bulldogs from 1964-66. The speedy wide receiver was with the LA Rams from 1967-70 and scored 4 TD's.

TOM TUMULTY was a tight end for the Penn Hills High School Indians under **Neil Gordon**. He was a linebacker at Pitt from 1991-95 and was the Panthers third best tackler in school history with 413 tackles. Tumulty has been a linebacker with Cincinnati since 1996.

EMLEN TUNNEL played for the Radnor High School Red Raiders, at Toledo and then at Iowa in 1946-47 for coach **Dr. Eddie Anderson**. Signed as a free agent by New York, Tunnell was a top defensive back in the NFL for 13 years with the Giants 1948-58 and Green Bay 1959-61. Emlen, "The Gremlin," appeared in four NFL championship games in 1956 and 1958 with New York and in 1960 and 1961 with Green Bay. He earned two NFL title rings when **Jim Lee Howell's** Giants defeated Chicago in 1956 and when **Vince Lombardi's** Packers beat New York in 1961. The Giants lost the 1958 title game to

155

Baltimore and the Packers lost the 1960 crown to Philadelphia. Tunnel had 79 interceptions for 1,282 yards and 4 TD's, plus 6 TD's on punt and kick-off returns. The nine-time pro bowler went in the Pro Football Hall of Fame in 1967.

JOE TYRRELL played for the Roman Catholic High School Cahillites under **Joe "Goldie" Graham**. He was a guard at Temple for **Al Kawal** from 1949-51 and a Philadelphia Eagle in 1952.

ED ULINSKY played for the Ambridge High School Bridgers under **Moe Rubenstein**. A tough-nosed guard at Marshall University in West Virginia, Ulinski spent four years with Cleveland in the All-American Football Conference from 1946-49. Ulinsky, a two-time All-AAFC guard, earned four straight AAFC title rings with **Paul Brown's** Browns from 1946-49.

HARRY ULINSKY played for the Ambridge High School Bridgers under **Moe Rubenstein**. He was a center at Kentucky from 1946-48 and was the captain and 1949 All-American honorable mention for **Paul "Bear" Bryant's** nationally ranked 9-3 Wildcats. "Hoss" spent seven years as the anchor of the Washington Redskins line from 1950-56.

JOE UNGERER was a tackle for Bethlehem High School as **Leo Prendergast's** Red Hurricanes were the 1934 state co-champs with Altoona. He played at Fordham 1938-40 for **"Sleepy" Jim Crowley's** nationally ranked Rams and was a 1940 All-American. After World War II, he played for Washington in 1944-45. **Dudley DeGroot's** Redskins lost the 1945 NFL championship game.

JOHNNY UNITAS threw 22 TD passes for Pittsburgh's St. Justin's High School in 1949-50 under **Jim Carey**. He set a University of Louisville record of 27 career TD passes from 1951-54 for coach **Frank Camp**. Although drafted by Pittsburgh in 1955, Unitas was cut in pre-season and played that year for the semi-pro Bloomfield Rams of the Greater Pittsburgh League for $6.00 a game. Unitas joined Baltimore as a free agent in 1956 and played with the Colts through 1972. He finished with San Diego in 1973. "Johnny U." led Baltimore into five NFL title games. Coach **Weeb Ewbank's** Colts won two straight NFL titles over the NY Giants in 1958 and 1959. The Colts lost the 1964 NFL crown to Cleveland. Baltimore then appeared in two Super Bowls as **Don Shula's** Colts lost to the New York Jets in SB III in 1969, but **Don McCafferty's** Colts defeated Dallas in SB V in 1971. In 18 seasons, Unitas, a five-time All-Pro, completed 2,830 of 5,186 passes for 40,239 yards and 290 TD's. He set an NFL record by throwing at least one touchdown pass in 47 consecutive games and went in the Pro Football Hall of Fame in 1979.

ANDY URBANIC from Pittsburgh played for Scott Township High School and Bethany College in West Virginia from 1956-58. He coached at Dillonvale High School in Ohio, Triadelphia High School in Wheeling West Virginia, and Penn Hills High School. Urbanic coached the Indians from 1968-81 with a 164-53-4 record and four straight WPIAL titles in 1976, 1977 (co-champs with Butler), 1978 and 1979. He developed pros **Bill Fralic**, **Tom Flynn** and **Chuck Sanders**.

TED VACTOR was a two-way halfback for the Washington High School Little Prexies under **Dave Johnston**. He played at Nebraska from 1963-65 for **Bob Devaney's** nationally ranked Cornhuskers and was All-Big 8 in 1964. Vactor had 2 picks in six NFL seasons with Washington 1970-74 and Chicago 1975. **George Allen's** Redskins lost Super Bowl VII in 1973 to Miami.

UNITAS

JOE VALERIO was a tackle for the Ridley Township High School Green Raiders in Folsom, Pennsylvania under **Joe McNicholas**. He played at Pennsylvania from 1988-90 as **Ed Zubrow's** Quakers won the 1988 Ivy title. Valerio was a 1990 All-American for **Gary Steele's** Quakers and spent six years in the NFL with Kansas City 1991-95 and St. Louis 1996. He caught 2 **Joe Montana** TD passes while with the Chiefs.

TOM VARGO coached the Williamsport High School Millionaires for 14 years with a 102-35-5 record from 1950-63. The Millionaires are the fifth winningest scholastic football program in the state behind Mt. Carmel, Easton, Berwick and New Castle with a 634-362-55 record since 1892.

GARY VENTURO was a guard for the Steelton High School Steamrollers and at Arizona State 1968-70 for **Frank Kush**. The 1970 All-American played in Canada with Calgary in 1971.

ED VEREB was a halfback for the Pittsburgh Central Catholic High School Vikings under coach **Nick Skovich**. He played at Maryland from 1953-55. **Jim Tatum's** 1953 Terrapins went 10-1 and were national champions. Vereb was a 1955 All-American as he scored 16 TD's for the 10-1 Terps who were ranked #3 in the nation. He was a CFL all-star with British Columbia in 1956-59 and was a Redskin in 1960.

VILLANOVA WILDCATS in Villanova, Pennsylvania started football in 1894 and had undefeated seasons in 1928 at 7-0-1 under **Harry Stuhldreher** (Hall of Fame) who was one of Notre Dame's famed Four Horsemen. In 1937 the Wildcats went 8-0-1 and ranked #6, and in 1938 they were 8-0-1 and ranked #18 under **Maurice "Clipper" Smith** who also played at Notre Dame. The Wildcats were paced by three All-Americans in halfback **Andy Stopper**, end **John Wysocki** and tackle **John Mellus**, plus **Jordan Oliver**, **Valentine Rizzo**, **Bill Cochrane**, and **Matt Kuber**. Villanova was a national power and bowl-bound in 1961 and 1962 under former "V" star **Alex Bell**, who was from McSherrystown, a fullback at Villanova from 1935-37 and the Detroit Lions in 1940. Bell was head coach of Delone Catholic before he came to Villanova. His 1961 Blue and White went 8-2 and beat Wichita State in the Sun Bowl, while the 1962 Wildcats went 7-3 and lost to Oregon State in Philadelphia's Liberty Bowl as **Terry Baker**, the Beavers' Heisman Trophy QB, ran 99 yards for the game's lone TD. Villanova heroes included linemen **Charles Johnson**, **Richard Ross**, **Sam Gruneisen**, **Richard Ross** and backs **Ted Aceto**, **Billy Joe**, **Larry Glueck**, **Rich Richman**, **Lou Rettino** and **Mike Pettine**. Since 1985, the Main Line school has been nationally recognized in Division I-AA under coach **Andy Talley** who is a native of Bryn Mawr and played for Haverford High School and Southern Connecticut University. Five of Talley's teams appeared in NCAA Division I-AA playoffs in 1989, 1991, 1992, 1996 and 1997. Villanova All-Americans through the years included **George Randour** HB 1933, **Ed Michaels** G 1936, **John Wysocki** E 1937-38, **John Mellus** T 1938, **Andy Stopper** HB 1938, **John Sandusky** T 1949, **Joe DeRose** C 1951, **Domenic Liotta** G 1951, **Gene Filipski** HB 1952, **Gene O'Pella** E 1958, **Charles Johnson** T 1962, **Mike Siani** WR 1971, **Paul Berardelli** G 1988, **Bryan Russo** C 1989, **Curtis Eller** LB 1991-92, **Tyronne Frazier** LB 1994, **Brian Finneran** WR 1996-97, **Chris Boden** QB 1997 and **Brian Westbrook** RB 1998.

CHRIS VILLARRIAL played for the Hershey High School Trojans under **Bob "Gump" May**. At Indiana University of Pennsylvania, Villarrial was a two-time All-American offensive tackle in 1994 and 1995 for **Frank Cignetti's** NCAA Division II national play-off Indians. Villarrial has been an "immediate impact offensive guard" with the Chicago Bears since 1996.

TROY VINCENT played for the Pennsbury High School Falcons in Fairless Hills, Pennsylvania under **Chuck Kane**. He was a defensive back at Wisconsin from 1988-91 and was a 1991 All-American for **Barry Alvarez's** Badgers. Vincent has been with Miami 1992-95 and Philadelphia since 1996. He has been a two-time All-Pro with the Eagles.

MARK VLASIC quarterbacked the Center High School Trojans in Monaca, Pennsylvania. At Iowa 1984-86, Vlasic was a 1986 Academic All-Big Ten QB for **Hayden Fry's** 9-3 Hawkeyes. He threw 4 TD's with San Diego from 1987-90 and Kansas City 1991.

CHUCK WAGNER from Oakmont, graduated from Kiski Prep and Bucknell. He has over 177 victories at Oakmont, Riverview and Fox Chapel High Schools since 1966.

ADAM WALKER played for the Steel Valley High School Ironmen in Munhall, Pennsylvania. He was a running back for **Mike Gottfried's** Pitt Panthers from 1987-89. Walker was in the NFL with San Francisco 1993-95 and Philadelphia 1996-97. He earned a Super Bowl ring when **George Seifert's** 49ers beat San Diego in Super Bowl XXIX in 1995.

ART WALKER was a quarterback at Pittsburgh's South Hills High School and for Waynesburg College. He coached Mt. Lebanon High School from 1967-87 and went 193-77-6 as his Blue Devils won the 1970 WPIAL championship and at Pittsburgh's Shady Side Academy from 1994-98 and went 34-20. His over-all record was 207-78-6. He developed pro **John Frank**.

BILL WALKER was an end for Munhall High School Indians under **Nick Klisckey** and at Maryland 1953-55 as **Jim Tatum's** Terrapins went 27-4-1. Maryland won the 1953 national crown and Walker was a two-time All-American in 1954-55. He played in Canada for Edmonton from 1956-58 as **Frank "Pop" Ivy's** Eskimos beat Montreal in the 1956 Grey Cup.

CHUCK WALKER played for Pittsburgh's North Catholic High School Trojans. He went to Duke where he was a 1963 All-ACC tackle for **Bill Murray's** 5-4-1 Blue Devils. Walker spent 12 years in the NFL trenches as a defensive tackle for St. Louis 1964-72 and Atlanta 1972-75.

WALTON

JOE WALTON, the son of **Frank "Tiger" Walton** who played for Pitt and the Redskins, was an end for the Beaver Falls High School Tigers under **Leland Schakren**. He played at Pitt 1954-56 for **John Michelosen** and was a 1956 consensus All-American and an Academic All-American for the Panthers. Walton spent six years with Washington and the NY Giants from 1957-62. The Giants lost the 1961 and 1962 NFL title games to Green Bay. He had 178 career receptions for 2,628 yards and 28 TD's. Walton was head coach of the NY Jets from 1983-89 with a 54-59-1 record. He has been the coach of Robert Morris College in Moon Township since 1994.

LARRY WALTON was an end for the Johnstown High School Trojans and at Arizona State from 1966-68 for **Frank Kush**. He caught 27 TD's with the Detroit Lions from 1969-76.

DAVE WANNSTEDT was an end for the Baldwin High School Highlanders and was an offensive lineman at Pitt from 1971-73 for **Carl DePasqua** and **Johnny Majors**. The 1973 Panther captain spent 1974 on Green Bay's injured reserve roster. Wannstedt was head coach of the Chicago Bears from 1993-98 and went 41-57-1. He took over the Miami Dolphins in 2000.

CLYDE WASHINGTON scored 122 points in 1955 for the Carlisle High School Thundering Herd under **Ken Millen**. He was a two-way halfback at Purdue 1957-59 for **Jack Mollenkopf** and had nine interceptions in seven years in the AFL with Boston 1960-61 and NY Jets 1962-66.

WASHINGTON and JEFFERSON COLLEGE PRESIDENTS in Washington, Pennsylvania started football in 1890 and was a national powerhouse in the early 1900's and again since 1984 in Division III. The Red and Black went 10-0-1 in 1913 under **Bob Folwell** who was from Philadelphia and ex-Penn star. Only a 0-0 tie with the Yale Bulldogs prevented a possible national championship for W&J. In 1921 W&J again went 10-0-1 under **Earl "Greasy" Neale** (Hall of Fame) and met mighty California in the 1922 Rose Bowl. The game ended in a 0-0 tie as W&J held coach **Andy Smith's** (Hall of Fame), from DuBois and an All-American at Penn, undefeated Golden Bears at bay. W&J's starting eleven played the entire Rose Bowl game. The W&J "Iron Horses" were ends **Herb Kopf** and **Karl Konvolinka**; tackles All-American **Russ Stein** (Hall of Fame) and **Chester Widerquist**; guards **Ray Neal** and **Ralph Vince**; center **Albert Cook**; backs **Charles "Pruner" West**, **Harold "Swede" Erickson**, **Wayne Brenkert**, and **Joe Basista**. W&J has been a Divisioin III juggernaut for coach **John Luckhardt** since he took over in 1982. Luckhardt, who went to Chartiers Valley High School and Purdue, led the Presidents to 11 NCAA Division III play-offs from 1982-97. In 1992 W&J went 11-2 and lost the NCAA Division III championship game to Wisconsin-LaCrosse. Pacing the Presidents were ends **Dave Fields**, **Mike Speca**, linemen **Tony Denuzzio**, **Kevin Pintar**, **Todd Pivinick**, running back **Chris Babirad**, and defensive stars **John Englemohr**, **Eric Tola**, **Shawn Prendergast**, **Rickey Williams**, **Mike Crawford** and kicker **Scott Lautner**. In 1994, W&J went 11-2 and lost the NCAA Division III championship game to Albion. All-Star Red and Blacks were ends **Tim McGravey**, **Chris Begley**, linemen **Lou Brungard**, **Mike Jones**, **Darren Hicks**, quarterback **Jason Baer**, running back **Jake Williams**, kicker **Mike Evans**, defense **Matt Szczypinski**, **Dan Primrose**, **Mike Brooder**, **Brian O'Malley**, **Taj Lewis**, **Ian Wagner** and punter **Darin Whitesel**.

RICKY WATTERS rushed for 4,177 career yards and 44 TD's from 1984-86 for Harrisburg's Bishop McDevitt High School Crusaders under coach **Tim Rimpfel**. He played at Notre Dame from 1987-90 for **Lou Holtz** and was a 1988 All-American flanker as he helped lead the Fighting Irish to a 12-0 record and the national championship. Watters has been in the NFL since 1991 with San Francisco 1991-94, Philadelphia 1995-97 and Seattle since 1998. He earned a Super Bowl ring as **George Seifert's** 49ers defeated San Diego in SB XXIX in 1995. Watters has rushed for 10,325 yards and scored 77 TD's, plus has 13 TD receptions for a total of 90 TD's.

CHARLES WAY rushed for 1,121 yards in 1989 for Philadelphia's Northeast High School for **Harvey "Brew" Schumer**. He played at Virginia from 1991-94 for **George Welsh**. Way scored 14 TD's with the New York Giants from 1995-99.

WATTERS

WELSH

WAYNESBURG COLLEGE YELLOW JACKETS in Waynesburg, Pennsylvania started football in 1895 when they met Washington and Jefferson. The Yellow Jackets greatest gridiron achievement came in 1966 when they won the NAIA Division I national championship as they beat Wisconsin White-Water College. The Orange and Black attack was led by quarterback **Don Paull** and running backs **Rich Dahar**, who set a record 1,186 yards rushing, and **Dallas Crable**.

CHUCK WEBER was a guard for the Abington High School Galloping Ghosts and at West Chester State from 1952-54. He was a linebacker with Cleveland 1955-56, Chicago Cards 1957-58 and Philadelphia 1959-61. He earned two NFL title rings as **Paul Brown's** Browns defeated LA in 1955 and as **Buck Shaw's** Eagles beat Green Bay in 1960. Weber had 6 picks in 1960.

HAROLD "DUKE" WEIGLE graduated from Albright College and was head coach at Windber where he went 32-0-5, Tamaqua, Johnstown and McKeesport High Schools and had an over-all record of 252-73-13. At McKeesport, "Duke" developed five Tiger pros in **Ray Mathews, George Mrkonic, Bill Miller, Jim Beirne** and **Ed Kovac**.

ISADORE WEINSTOCK was a fullback for Wilkes-Barre's James M. Coughlin High School Crusaders and at Pitt for **Jock Sutherland** from 1932-34. He was a 1934 All-American for the 8-1 Panthers. "Izzy" played for the Eagles in 1935 and Pittsburgh in 1937-38.

ED WEISACOSKY played for the Pottsville High School Crimson Tide under coach **Bill Flynn**. At Miami of Florida from 1963-65, Weisacosky set all school records for tackles as a defensive end and was a 1965 All-American for **Charlie Tate's** Hurricanes. Weisacosky spent six years in the NFL from 1967-72 with the New York Giants, Miami and New England.

JOHN WELLER from Wynnewood was a guard at Princeton from 1933-35 as **Fritz Crisler's** ferocious Tigers went 25-1. He was a consensus 1935 All-American.

GEORGE WELSH went from a single-wing halfback for the Coaldale High School Tigers under coach **Tom Raymer** to a T-formation quarterback under **Andy Kalan** from 1948-50. He went to Wyoming Seminary in Kingston in 1951 and then to the Naval Academy where in 1954 he led **Eddie Erdelatz's** Midshipmen to an 8-2 year and a Sugar Bowl win over Ole Miss. As a 1955 All-American, Welsh led the nation in passing and total offense and placed third in the Heisman Trophy vote, which was won by **Hopalong Cassidy** of Ohio State. Welsh was the head coach of Navy from 1973-81 and at Virginia from 1982-2000. In 28 years, he had a 189-132-4 record.

WESTMINSTER COLLEGE TITANS in New Wilmington, Pennsylvania started football in 1891 when they played Geneva College. **Dr. Harold Burry**, who was from New Castle and a 1935 Westminster graduate, started the Titans on the road to national gridiron success as he went 127-31-5 from 1952-71. Burry went 8-0 in 1953, 1956 and 1964. In 1970, his Blue and White went 10-0 and won the NAIA Division II national championship behind Little All-Americans quarterback **Dave Bierbach**, tackle **Mike Annarella** and linebacker **Bob Mathews**. Burry, who was the Small College Football Coach of the Year in 1967, became athletic director in 1972 and named his line coach, **Dr. Joseph Fusco**, who was a guard at Westminster from 1957-59, as the new head coach. Fusco went 154-34-3 from 1972-90 and led the Titans to four more NAIA Division II national crowns in 1976 (10-1), 1977 (11-0), 1988 (14-0), and 1989 (13-0). The Titans won a NAIA record sixth national championship in 1994 under coach **Gene Nickerson** who graduated from Slippery Rock and was the defensive coordinator under Fusco. Burry was inducted into the College Football Hall of Fame in 1996 and Fusco was inducted in the College Football of Fame in 2001. The top career "skill position" Titans include quarterbacks **Sean O'Shea** and **Joe Miccia**, backs **Brad Tokar** and **Andy Blatt**, receivers **Lamont Boykins**, **Dave Foley** and **Tim McNeil**. In 1997 the football stadium complex was named in honor of Bury.

BOB WERL was an end for Pittsburgh's South Catholic High School and at Miami of Florida for **Andy Gustafson** from 1962-65. He was a New York Jet in 1966.

PAT WEST was a fullback for Burgettstown High School and at Pitt and then USC in 1944. He scored 3 TD's with the Cleveland Rams who won the 1945 NFL championship title and then moved to Los Angeles for 1946-48 and Green Bay in 1948.

DWAYNE WHITE played for Philadelphia's Southern High School Rams under **John Pendino** and for the Alcorn State Braves in Mississippi 1986-89. The offensive guard was a seven year veteran in the NFL trenches with the New York Jets from 1990-94 and St. Louis from 1995-96

JAN WHITE played for Harrisburg's John Harris High School under **George Chaump**. He was an end at Ohio State 1968-70 and as a sophomore in 1968, helped **Woody Hayes'** Buckeyes go 10-0 for the national title. White was a co-captain and an All-American tight end in 1970 as the 9-1 Buckeyes tied for the national crown. White caught 2 TD's with the Buffalo Bills in 1971-72.

WIDENER COLLEGE PIONEERS in Chester, Pennsylvania started football in 1879 as Pennsylvania Military Academy. The school became Pennsylvania Military College in 1892 and in 1972 the named changed to Widener College. In 1977, Widener went 11-1 for **Bill Manlove** and won the NCAA Division III national championship when they beat Wabash College of Indiana. Pacing the 1977 Blue and Gold were quarterback **Mark Walter**, receivers **Gibson Ivery** and **Walker Carter**, running back **Chip Zawoisky**, defensive linemen **Jim** and **John Connor**, and defensive backs **Steve Warrington** and **Bill Johnson**. Widener won the NCAA Division III national crown again in 1981 when they went 13-0 and beat Dayton. Pioneer stars were the prolific passing combo of **Bob Cole** to **John Roche** and **Tom Kincade**, running backs **Jerry Irving** and **Gary Clofine** and Little All-American and College Football Hall of Fame defensive back **Tom Deery**. Manlove went 182-53-1 in 23 years at Widener from 1969-91.

JIM WILDMAN graduated from Clarion University and has coached the Sharon High School Tigers since 1976 with 187-55-4 record. He developed pro **Mike Archie**.

JACK WILEY from Wind Ridge was a tackle for Richill Township High School, at Waynesburg College. He spent five years with the Pittsburgh Steelers from 1946-50.

BRIAN WILLIAMS was a center for the Mt. Lebanon High School Blue Devils and at Minnesota from 1986-88 for **John Gutekunst's** Golden Gophers. Williams was with New York from 1989-99 as **Bill Parcells'** Giants defeated Buffalo in Super Bowl XXV in 1991.

ERIK WILLIAMS played for Philadelphia's John Bartram High School Maroon Wave under **Tom Bazis**. He went to Central State in Ohio. Williams has been an offensive tackle with Dallas since 1991 and earned three Super Bowl rings as **Jimmy Johnson's** Cowboys won back-to-back Super Bowls XXVII in 1993 and XXVIII in 1994 over

Buffalo, plus when **Barry Switzer's** Cowboys defeated Pittsburgh in Super Bowl XXX in 1996.

GENE WILLIAMS from Chester was a guard for the Iowa State Cyclones from 1988-91. He was an eight year veteran with Cleveland 1992-94 and Atlanta 1995-99.

JAMES "BIG CAT" WILLIAMS was a tackle for Pittsburgh's Allderdice High School Dragons and for the Cheyney State Wolves 1987-90. "Big Cat" has been an offensive tackle in the NFL trenches since the Chicago Bears signed him as a free agent in 1991.

ROBERT WILLIAMS played at Pittsburgh's Oliver High School and at Penn State 1942-43, 1946-47. He coached Kane High School 1949-54 and Greensburg High School where he was the winningest coach in the great history of the Golden Lions with a 125-67-8 record from 1955-75.

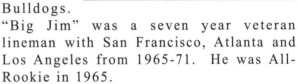

J. WILSON

JIM WILSON scored 13 TD's in only 6 games in 1959 for the Edgewood High School Vikings, near Pittsburgh, under **Art Betts**. He was a two-way tackle at Georgia 1962-64 and was a 1964 All-American for **Vince Dooley's** 7-3-1 Bulldogs. "Big Jim" was a seven year veteran lineman with San Francisco, Atlanta and Los Angeles from 1965-71. He was All-Rookie in 1965.

"LIGHT HORSE" HARRY WILSON from Sharpesville played seven years of college football. He was the top-scoring halfback at Penn State from 1921-23 for **Hugo Bezdek** and gained All-American mention. He led the 1922 Nittany Lions to 6-4-1 record and the Rose Bowl against USC. "Light Horse" then played at West Point from 1924-27. He was a 1926 All-American for **Biff Jones'** 7-1-1 Cadets and captain of the 1927 Army team that went 9-1 and beat Notre Dame. Wilson earned the Distinguished Flying Cross and Air Medal with five oak clusters as a pilot commander during WW II. He was inducted into the College Football Hall of Fame in 1973.

H. WILSON

LEO WISNIEWSKI played for the Fox Chapel High School Foxes for **Frank Rocco**. He was a nose tackle at Penn State for **Joe Paterno** from 1979-80 and with the Indianapolis Colts 1983-85.

JON WITMAN from Wrightsville was the second all-time leading rusher in York County history for Eastern York High School from 1988-90 under **Larry Nawa**. He played at Penn State from 1992-95 for **Joe Paterno**. Witman has been a Pittsburgh Steeler since 1996.

JOE WOLF was a tackle for Allentown's Wm. Allen High School Canaries under **Larry Lewis**. He played at Boston College from 1985-88 and was a team captain and a 1988 All-American for **Jack Bicknell's** Golden Eagles. Wolf was the first round draft choice of Arizona and was a ten year veteran in the NFL trenches with the Cardinals from 1989-98.

WOLF

LEE WOODALL played for the Carlisle High School Thundering Herd under **Ray Erney** and at West Chester 1990-93 for **Rick Daniels**. He has been a linebacker with San Francisco 1994-99 and Carolina 2000. Woodall earned a Super Bowl ring as **George Seifert's** 49ers beat San Diego in SB XXIX in 1995. The Pro Bowler has 6 interceptions and scored one TD.

SHAWN WOODEN from Willow Grove rushed for 2,700 yards and scored 33 TD's in 1989-90 for the Abington High School Galloping Ghosts under **Doug Mositer**. He was a defensive back at Notre Dame from 1991, 1993-95 for **Lou Holtz**. Wooden has been with Miami 1996-99 and Chicago 2000.

WOODESHICK

TOM WOODESHICK was a fullback for the Hanover Area High School Hawkeyes near Wilkes-Barre under **Ed Halicki** and at West Virginia 1960-62 for **Gene Corum's** Mountaineers. He was a 10 year veteran and scored 21 TD's with Philadelphia 1963-71 and St. Louis 1972.

JOHN WOODRING played for Springfield High School and at Brown where he was a 1980 All-American honorable mention LB for **John Anderson's** Bruins. He was a New York Jet from 1981-85.

GEORGE WOODRUFF from LeRaysville graduated from Mansfield College in 1883 and then went to Yale Law School. He was the right guard for Yale from 1885-88 as the Bulldogs went 38-1-1. His 1888 teammate at Yale was **Gifford Pinchot** who will be a two-time Governor of Pennsylvania in 1923-27 and 1931-35. Woodruff then played for Pennsylvania, where he was an instructor, and was also the coach from 1892-1901 with a 124-15-2 record. His 1895 and 1897 Quaker elevens were national champions. In one stretch from 1893 into 1897, Penn only lost one time in 68 games. Woodruff coached such legends as **John W. Heisman** for whom the Heisman Trophy is named, **John Outland** for whom the Outland Trophy is named, and **Charles Wharton** for whom the

University of Pennsylvania's Wharton School of Business is named. Woodruff, who became Pennsylvania's Attorney General, went in the College Football Hall of Fame in 1963.

JOHN WOZNIAK from Arnold City played for Fairhope High School and at Alabama from 1944-47. He was a sophomore guard on **Frank Thomas'** 1945 Bama club that went 10-0 and beat USC in the Rose Bowl. Wozniak was captain and a 1947 All-American center. He spent five years in the pros from 1948-52 with Brooklyn, NY Yankees and the Dallas Texans.

LUD WRAY went to Philadelphia's Chestnut Hill Academy and was an outstanding halfback at Pennsylvania from 1914-16 and 1918. He helped lead coach **Bob Folwell's** Quakers to a 7-3-1 record in 1916 and the Rose Bowl against Oregon. Wray played for the Massillon Tigers in 1919 and Buffalo in 1920-21. He was head coach of Penn in 1930, Boston in 1932 and the Philadelphia Eagles, which he was a co-owner with Bert Bell, in 1933-35 with a 9-21-1 mark.

FRANK WYCHECK played for Philadelphia's Archbishop Ryan High School Raiders for **Steff Kruck** and **John Quinn**. He was a tight end at Maryland from 1989-92 and was a 1991 All-ACC for **Joe Krivak's** Terps. Wycheck was at Washington 1993-94 and Houston/Tennessee since 1995. **Jeff Fisher's** Titans lost Super Bowl XXXIV to St. Louis in 2000.

FRANK WYDO played for German Township High School by McClellandtown, Pennsylvania, and then at Duquesne and Cornell. He was a 11 year NFL veteran as a rugged two-way lineman for Pittsburgh 1947-51 and Philadelphia 1952-57. Wydo, a 1953 All-Pro, intercepted one pass and recovered 3 fumbles.

WYDO

JOHN YACCINO was a halfback for the Hazleton High School Mountaineers under **Anthony Scarcella**. "Nino" played at Pitt from 1959-61 for **John Michelosen** and with Buffalo in 1962.

DON YANNESSA was a tackle for Aliquippa High School in 1956-57 under **Carl Aschman** and at New Mexico State from 1959-62 for **Warren Woodson**. He coached Aliquippa High School from 1972-88, went 142-44-5 with four WPIAL championships in 1984, 1985, 1987, 1988 and at Baldwin High School since 1989. His over-all record in 27 years is 203-83-7 and he developed pros **Sean Gilbert** and **Brian Gelzheiser**.

RAY YAKAVONIS played for the Hanover Area High School Hawkeyes near Wilkes-Bare under **Jim Moran**. He was a Little All-American defensive end at East Stroudsburg State from 1976-79 for **Denny Douds'** Warriors who went 32-6-1. Yakavonis was in Minnesota 1980-84.

YEWCIC

TOM YEWCIC played for the East Conemaugh High School Iron Horses for **Milan Gjurich**. He quarterbacked Michigan State for **Biggie Munn** from 1951-53. As a junior, Yewcic was a 1952 All-American as he threw 10 TD's and led the Spartan's to a 9-0 record and the national championship. The versatile "Kibby" first played baseball in the Detroit Tigers organization before he returned to football with Toronto in Canada. He spent six years with Boston in the American Football League from 1961-66. **Mike Holovak's** Patriots lost the 1963 AFL title to San Diego. Yewcic threw for 1,374 yards and 12 TD's and scored 4 TD's in the AFL.

DAN YOCHUM was a tackle for the Bethlehem High School Hurricanes under **Bob Buffman**. He starred at Syracuse from 1969-71 for **Ben Schwartzwalder** and was a 1971 All-American. Although drafted #1 by Philadelphia, Yochum spent ten years in Canada as an offensive tackle with Montreal and Edmonton from 1972-81. He earned three Grey Cup rings with **Marv Levy's** Alouettes in 1974 and 1977 and with **Hugh Campbell's** Eskimos in 1980. Yochum was a four-time All-CFL and was the CFL's 1976 Lineman of the Year.

YOCHUM

BILL YOEST played for Pittsburgh's North Catholic High School Falcons and at North Carolina State from 1970-73. He was a 1973 consensus All-American for coach **Al Michaels'** Wolfpack.

JOHN YONKONDY coached at mighty Swoyersville High School as the unsinkable Sailors were one of the most feared schools in Pennsylvania with a 56-3-4 record in the Luzerne County Conference from 1924-48 and 40-1-2 record in the Wyoming Valley Conference from 1949-56. Yonkondy developed four pros in **Lou** and **Walt Michaels**, **John Paluck** and **Chuck Sieminski**.

GEORGE YOUNG played for Wilkes-Barre's James Coughlin High School and at Georgia for **Wally Butts'** Bulldogs. He was an eight year veteran at defensive end with Cleveland 1946-53 as **Paul Brown's** Browns appeared in eight straight title games. Young earned five rings when the Browns won four straight AAFC titles from 1946-49 and beat LA in the NFL title game in 1950.

JOHN YOVICSIN was an end for the Steelton High School Steamroller under **Nelson Hoffman** and at Gettysburg College from 1937-39 for **Henry "Hen" Breen**. He was an Eagle in 1944. Yovicsin was head coach at Gettysburg College from 1952-56 and had a 32-11-0 record. He was head coach at Harvard from 1957-70 and had a 78-42-5 record as his Crimson shared two Ivy League titles in 1966 and 1968. His over-all collegiate record in 19 years was 110-51-5.

JOE YUKICA was an end for the Midland High School Leopards under coach **Jim Myers** and at Penn State from 1950-52 for **Rip Engle**. He was coach of State College High School in 1954 and the **Don Caum**-led Central Dauphin High School Rams in Colonial Park, Pennsylvania from 1955-59. Yukica was head coach of New Hampshire University in 1966-67 and went 7-9-2, Boston College from 1968-77 and went 68-37-0, Dartmouth from 1978-86 and went 36-47-4 with the 1978 Ivy League championship. His over-all college record was 111-93-6.

MITCH ZALNASKY from Tyre was an end at Pitt 1963-65 for **John Michelosen**. The 1963 Panthers went 9-1 for the #3 ranking in the nation. He was a Winnipeg Blue Bomber in 1966-68.

CHARLIE ZAPIEC was an end for Philadelphia's LaSalle High School Explorers under **John "Tex" Flannery**. He was a linebacker at Penn State from 1969-71 for **Joe Paterno** and was a 1971 All-American. Zapiec played in Canada for Montreal from 1973-78 as **Marv Levy's** Alouettes appeared in four Grey Cups and beat Edmonton in 1974. He was four-time All-CFL.

ZARNAS

GUST ZARNAS was a single-wing quarterback for the Har-Brack Union High School Tigers in Brackenridge, Pennsylvania under **Dick Williams**. He was a guard at Ohio State from 1935-37 and was a 1937 All-American for **Francis Schmidt's** Buckeyes. Zarnas was with the Chicago Bears in 1938 and Green Bay in 1939 as **Curley Lambeau's** Packers defeated New York for the NFL championship. He went in the College Football Hall of Fame in 1975.

RAY ZELLERS rushed for 1,344 yards and 11 TD's in 1990 for Pittsburgh's David Oliver High School Bears under coach **Joe Zeglowitsch**. He played at Notre Dame from 1991-94 for **Lou Holtz**. Zellers was the second round draft choice of New Orleans and was with the Saints 1995-98 and Washington 2000.

WALT ZIRINSKY scored 99 points in 1937 for the Northampton High School Konkrete Kids under **Woody Ludwig**. He was a star fullback at Lafayette from 1939-41 for **Edward "Hook" Mylin**. After World War II, he played for the Cleveland Rams who won the 1945 NFL crown for **Adam Walsh**.

LOU ZIVKOVICH from Rankin was a tackle at New Mexico State 1958-60 for **Warren Woodson's** high-octane Aggies' offense. He played in Canada from 1961-64 with Calgary, Edmonton and Winnipeg.

SCOTT ZOLAK quarterbacked the Ringgold High School Rams in Monongahela, Pennsylvania under **Bill Connors**. He played at Maryland from 1987-90 for **Joe Krivak's** Terrapins and was a 1990 All-American honorable mention. Zolak was with New England from 1991-98 and was a back-up QB as **Bill Parcells'** Patriots lost Super Bowl XXXI in 1997 to Green Bay. He has been with the NY Jets since 1999.

VIC ZUCCO from Renton was a fullback for the Plum High School Mustangs and at Michigan State 1954-56 for **Duffy Daugherty's** nationally ranked Spartans. He spent four years with Chicago 1957-60.

ABOUT THE AUTHOR

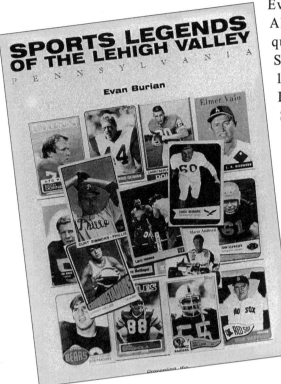

Evan Burian was born in 1946 in Allentown, Pennsylvania. He was a quarterback for the Emmaus High School Green Hornets from 1961 to 1963 under coaches William "Luke" Lobb and then Al Neff. A 1963 All-State honorable mention QB, Burian went to West Texas State University, which has been renamed West Texas A & M University, on a football scholarship and graduated in 1968. On the state level, Burian was associated with the Philadelphia Eagles' farm club, the Pottstown Firebirds of the Atlantic Coast Football League before he became part owner and General Manager of the Allentown Jets of the Eastern Basketball Association. On the national level, Burian was in the front office of both the Kentucky Colonels in the American Basketball Association and the Houston Astros of Major League Baseball. The Emmaus native was also associated with Houston's college football classic, the Bluebonnet Bowl. On his creative side, this is Burian's fourth book about sports history in Pennsylvania. His other three critically acclaimed books include *Sports Legends of the Lehigh Valley*, plus *Coach Birney Crum and Allentown High*, and the *History of Emmaus High School Football*. Burian also researched, wrote and narrated the historical gridiron series, *It Happened in Football*, which was broadcast in Houston, Texas in 1991.